Allegorical Play in the Old French Motet

The Sacred and the Profane
in Thirteenth-Century Polyphony

Figurae:

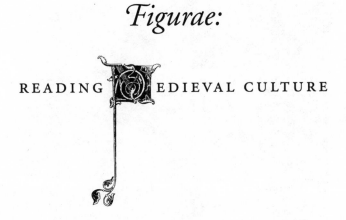

READING MEDIEVAL CULTURE

The motet *S'Amours eüst point de poer* (531a/600) / *Au renouveler du joli tans* (531b/601) / *ECCE JAM* (M61) in the thirteenth-century Montpellier codex. Montpellier, Bibl. Interuniv., Section Médecine, MS H196, fol. 270r.

Allegorical Play in the Old French Motet

The Sacred and the Profane in Thirteenth-Century Polyphony

Sylvia Huot

Stanford University Press, Stanford, California, 1997

Stanford University Press

Stanford, California

© 1997 by the Board of Trustees of the

Leland Stanford Junior University

Printed in the United States of America

CIP data appear at the end of the book

Stanford University Press publications are
distributed exclusively by Stanford University Press
within the United States, Canada, Mexico, and
Central America; they are distributed exclusively
by Cambridge University Press throughout
the rest of the world.

Acknowledgments

It is a pleasure to thank the many friends and colleagues who have contributed to this project. Margaret Switten and Meg Bent both read complete drafts at various stages of writing and made many helpful suggestions. Others who offered ideas, information, and general insights include Wulf Arlt, Rebecca Baltzer, Kevin Brownlee, Mark Everist, Dolores Pesce, Susan Rankin, and Nancy Regalado. Thanks also go to my husband, Leo Krumpholz, for the many acts, both large and small, that fostered the completion of this study.

This project has been funded by Graduate School Summer Research Stipends from Northern Illinois University and by a grant from the George A. and Eliza Gardner Howard Foundation, which I gratefully acknowledge. Research for this study was conducted at various libraries and would not have been possible without the helpful cooperation of librarians and staff at the Newberry Library, Chicago; Founders Memorial Library, Northern Illinois University; the Bibliothèque Nationale, Paris; the Institut de Recherche et d'Histoire des Textes, Paris; and the Bibliothèque Interuniversitaire, Section Médecine, Montpellier.

Chapter 1 contains material that first appeared in my essay "Transformations of Lyric Voice in the Songs, Motets, and Plays of Adam de la Halle," *Romanic Review* 78.2 (1987): 148–64. Copyright by the Trustees of Columbia University in the City of New York. This material is reprinted by permission from the *Romanic Review*. Chapter 3 contains material first published in my essay "Languages of Love: Vernacular Motets on the Tenor FLOS FILIUS EJUS," in *Conjunctures: Medieval Studies in Honor of Douglas Kelly*, ed. Keith Busby and Norris J. Lacy (Amsterdam: Rodopi, 1994), pp. 169–80. This material is used with the permission of Editions Rodopi B.V.

Contents

Note to the Reader

Motet texts and tenors are identified throughout by the numbers assigned to them in Ludwig's *Repertorium*. The letters preceding tenor identification numbers indicate whether the tenor's source is in the chant used for the Mass (M) or the Office (O) or in a setting of the *Benedicamus Domino* (BD). Trouvère songs are identified by the number assigned to them in Spanke's revision of Raynaud's general catalog. Texts are quoted from a variety of editions, given in the notes. Unless stated otherwise, italics in motet quotations are the editor's and indicate a refrain. Chant texts of the Office are quoted from the *Corpus Antiphonalium Officii*, abbreviated in the notes as *CAO*. The graduals and alleluias of the Mass that served as sources for motet tenors are quoted from the list in Tischler, *The Style and Evolution of the Earliest Motets*. Biblical quotations are taken from the Vulgate text. All translations, unless indicated otherwise, are mine.

Allegorical Play in the Old French Motet

The Sacred and the Profane
in Thirteenth-Century Polyphony

Introduction

The Vernacular Motet and Its Dual Heritage

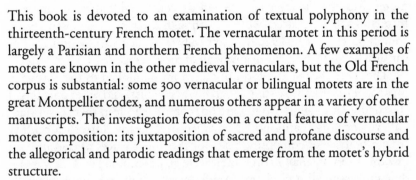

This book is devoted to an examination of textual polyphony in the thirteenth-century French motet. The vernacular motet in this period is largely a Parisian and northern French phenomenon. A few examples of motets are known in the other medieval vernaculars, but the Old French corpus is substantial: some 300 vernacular or bilingual motets are in the great Montpellier codex, and numerous others appear in a variety of other manuscripts. The investigation focuses on a central feature of vernacular motet composition: its juxtaposition of sacred and profane discourse and the allegorical and parodic readings that emerge from the motet's hybrid structure.

Motets were of course a musical art form, intended for oral performance. It is highly unlikely that people in the thirteenth century encountered them through reading a book, with the possible exception of composers studying the repertoire or singers learning new pieces.[1] Indeed, the standard layout of motets in medieval manuscripts, with texted voices in parallel columns or on facing pages and the tenor across the bottom of a column or the page (see frontispiece), does not facilitate the coordination of parts: only in performance do the different parts of the motet come together, so that the piece can be appreciated as a whole. Motets are, however, intricate poetico-musical works, composed within a learned milieu, transmitted through a written tradition, and susceptible of detailed textual analysis. In the following study, the word *reading* refers to the understanding or interpretation of any text, including one destined for performance. Though not strictly appropriate to musical genres, *reading* in its modern usage carries implications of critical analysis that are lacking from *hearing, listening,* or *singing*. The reading in question might be that of a composer, that of a musician who participated in the performance of the motet, or that of an audience member who heard it: my use of the term includes visual and aural reception as well as meditation on the piece.

A motet consists of two or more parts, sung simultaneously. The cantus firmus or tenor, normally the lowest voice, typically is a melismatic passage from the liturgy—a syllable, word, or phrase—sung in a slow rhythm.[2] This phrase can be repeated, sometimes with rhythmic variation, as needed to accommodate the length of the upper voice(s). The tenor is accompanied by an upper voice, known as the motetus or duplum; additional voices, if any, are referred to as the triplum and the quadruplum, respectively. Each upper voice carries its own text.[3] A three-part motet—that is, one with two texted voices—is known as a double motet. Motet texts are characterized by considerable diversity in verse form and subject matter. Moreover, though the texts juxtaposed within a given motet may be lexically, metrically, and thematically similar, they can also be quite different in any or all of these respects.

The motet began as a form of sacred music, linked to the corpus of organa, or polyphonic settings of graduals, alleluias, and other portions of the chant. Although its origins are not completely clear, there is substantial evidence that Latin motets emerged in the early thirteenth century from a practice of composing texts for the upper voices of clausulae, or excerpts from organa.[4] Latin motets were also composed with new melodies unrelated to liturgical organa and clausulae, but such pieces generally employed tenors consisting of melismatic phrases from the chant—most often, the same tenors that figure in motets based on clausulae. Vernacular motets also came into being during the early thirteenth century—by midcentury, the French motet was a well-established form—and the two repertoires are closely related. They are linked in part through the occurrence, relatively infrequent, of bilingual motets: those combining at least one French and at least one Latin text among the upper voices. Even more important is the phenomenon of contrafactum, or the composition of new text for a preexisting melody—either an individual motet part or an entire multivoice composition.[5] Although many contrafactual texts were composed in the same language as their model, one can also find numerous examples of French and Latin motet texts composed on the same melodies. The latter process worked in both directions: a French motet could serve as model for a new Latin composition just as a Latin motet could for a French one. In addition, although some French motets employ vernacular refrains or rondeaux as tenors, the vast majority use Latin tenors. Thus, even a secular French motet maintains explicit ties to the liturgical origins of the genre.[6]

At the same time, the vernacular motet is closely linked to the varied corpus of vernacular lyric. The motet emerged during an important period in the history of Old French lyric. The composition of narratives with lyric insertions began in the early thirteenth century; by midcentury the compilation of chansonniers was under way.[7] With the exception of the rondeau motet, of which only a few examples are known, motet texts bear no formal resemblance to other lyric forms.[8] They are not strophic, nor do they follow set patterns of versification: lines vary in length, and rhymes repeat seemingly at random. But motet texts are tied to the vernacular lyric corpus through their use of refrains, including many of those that appear in rondeaux, in strophic songs employing refrains, or as lyric insertions in narrative works.[9] More important, motets feature the stock figures and situations, language, and poetic stances—what one might term the poetic registers—associated with the various corpora or genres of Old French lyric.[10] Many motet texts draw on the *chanson courtoise*. There are also pastourelle motets, featuring such figures as Robin, Marion, and Emmelot, and *reverdie* motets, in which the lyric persona expresses his amorous joy in harmony with the flowering of the countryside and the songs of birds. Some motets present quasi-narrative vignettes with such figures as Fair Aelis, Isabeaus, Eglentine, and Aie, known from the repertoire of rondeaux and *chansons de toile*; others present a *chanson de mal mariée*. And although the French motet corpus is dominated by secular themes, it does include a few devotional texts, most of them in praise of the Virgin.

There has been surprisingly little work on motet texts, although that situation has begun to change in the past few years.[11] What has been done shows that they are intricately constructed and that they reflect many of the same interests as other literary genres of the period.[12] Given the special status of the motet as polyphonic poetry, studies have often focused on those with at least two texted voices and have emphasized the relationship between the texts in a given piece. This approach has been fruitful: scholars have shown that motets draw on a wide range of vernacular lyric languages. Some employ two or three texts of the same lyric register, offering different perspectives on a central motif or reinforcing the standard treatment of a given theme; others combine generically diverse texts in innovative ways. The intertextual and polyphonic dynamics of the motet need to be examined on a much larger scale, and the field of inquiry must include a consideration of the tenor, largely neglected in literary discussions of vernacular motets despite its clear importance to the motet's musical structure.[13] In Latin sacred motets the tenor is crucial to textual dynamics: the texted voices expand on the tenor's liturgical origins, often incorporating words or phrases from the chant or from its biblical source; they may comment on the feast in question or develop an appropriate doctrinal point.[14] The few vernacular motets that employ vernacular tenors exhibit a similarly close relationship between tenor and upper voices. The function of the Latin tenor in vernacular motets is usually much less obvious; indeed, in some cases the tenor is used as a musical basis for the piece without seeming to figure at all in its literary dynamics. Closer examination, however, often reveals the tenor's crucial role in the poetic economy of the motet: it underpins the texts as well as the melodies of the upper voices.

The simplest form of textual linkage between the tenor and the upper voices is the incorporation of words from the tenor—in French translation, of course—into the other texts, often at the beginning or the end of the piece. Thus one might find that the word *flor* (flower) or *florie* (flowery) figured prominently in a motet using the tenor FLOS FILIUS EJUS (THE FLOWER [IS] HER SON [O16]), or that the word *vrai* (true) or *verité* (truth) appeared in one built on the tenor VERITATEM (TRUTH [M37]).[15] More complicated patterns of intertextual play are also common. The motet might exploit either the liturgical or the biblical context of the tenor or simply its literal meaning as a decontextualized Latin phrase. There may be a transposition of the sacred model into the language and format of vernacular lyric, possibly with a suggestion of an allegorical relationship, or possibly with parodic overtones. This allegorical or parodic movement may be worked out through a narrative recasting of the sacred event or a translation of its central thematic into a different set of terms. Given the preference for amorous themes in motet texts, such correspondences often turn on the identity of Christ as Lover and Bridegroom of the Church or on the movement between the Blessed Virgin as object of adoration and bride of God, and the lady who is the object of erotic desire. There is ample precedent for the allegorization of erotic love poetry in the Song of Songs and the exegetical and literary traditions that it inspired; this and other analogues for the motet are discussed in the following chapters.

Most vernacular motets of the thirteenth century are anonymous, both musically and textually.[16] This phenomenon may be related to another aspect of motet composition—namely, the practice of creating new motets out of preexisting elements. Contrafacta are widespread, showing that the author of a motet's texts was not necessarily the composer of its musical setting. In addition, it seems to have been fairly common to compose additional parts for known motets: many pieces are transmitted in versions with varying numbers of voices, sometimes even within the same manuscript. Thus, a motet could be the work of a single poet-composer, but it could also be the work of as many as three or four people, each responsible for the text and/or the music of one or more of its voices. The accretion of voices and the recombination of parts, in varying arrangements and with varying contrafactual texts, are analogous to the narrative continuation and interpolation so characteristic of medieval romance. By adding or removing voices from a motet, or by composing a new text for one or more of its parts, poets and composers could alter the character of a given composition, bringing out latent meanings, foregrounding and expanding on certain features and obscuring others. I will examine selected examples of motet "families," showing how the addition, subtraction, or substitution of texts results in the generation of related but often quite different pieces.

The vernacular motet in the thirteenth century can be associated with such clerical and intellectual centers as Paris and Arras. Among the few vernacular motets of known authorship, for example, are those attributed to the celebrated Artesian trouvère Adam de la Halle. The use of motets as entertainment for the educated—probably the clerical—classes is confirmed by the late-thirteenth-century theorist Johannes de Grocheio: "Et solet in eorum festis decantari ad eorum decorationem, quemadmodum cantilena, quae dicitur rotundellus, in festis vulgarium laicorum" (And [the motet] is customarily performed at the festivities [of the literati], just as the song called "rondeau" is at the festivities of the laity).[17] In Paris, a community of clerics with the requisite skills for the composition and performance of motets was the Masters of the Organum. The documentary evidence indicates that these men, trained in liturgical polyphony, routinely supplemented their meager incomes by performing in secular settings. One such setting was the infamous carols—which preachers constantly vilified as lascivious and even demonic gatherings, but which were nonetheless immensely popular—frequented by university students as well as townspeople. As Christopher Page has argued, the combined liturgical and freelance activities of the Masters of the Organum would ensure that such men were intimately familiar with the clausulae that furnished the melodies for so many motets and with the vernacular songs that inspired their texts; they would also have had the compositional skills needed for the creation of new motets.[18] And the community of university students, as well as members of the cathedral clergy, would be a likely audience for the resulting hybrid compositions.[19]

We can gather a better idea of the motet milieu from references in literary sources. Although one searches in vain for detailed accounts of motet performance, general descriptions of festivities often allude to them. In the *Dit de la panthère d'amours* (ca. 1290–1328), for example, the God of Love holds court in the forest with sumptuous musical entertainment. There is dancing, the *sons poitevins* without which no festive occasion was complete, and a variety of musical instruments; and singers perform *chançonetes*, *motès*, and *conduis*.[20] The same list of song types appears in the unorthodox vision of Heaven conjured up by Nature's priest Genius in Jean de Meun's continuation of the *Roman de la Rose*, where those who engage in procreative sexual activity are assured of a blissful afterlife in a flowery meadow, caroling and singing "motez, conduiz et chançonnetes."[21] These accounts are idealized images of the carols and other recreations of young clerics and students, as well as townspeople and courtiers. In both cases the association of song and dance with a bucolic setting—field or forest—and with the pursuit of love reflects elements normally found in descriptions of the carol, whether aristocratic, clerical, or bourgeois. The theologian Henri de Malines, for example, relates that as a student in Paris (ca. 1266–70) he attended carols and other dances held in wooded areas (*in virgultis*).[22] The rondeaux and the refrains associated with the carol typically allude to idyllic rustic settings. Similar allusions appear in numerous motet texts, often through the incorporation of preexisting refrains or formulaic expressions.[23] One can assume that the carols and other musical revelries frequented by students and *clercs* in Paris and Arras provided an important venue for the vernacular motet. Particularly well suited to the carol—though there is no actual evidence for their use in this or any other setting—are certain forms strongly associated with Picardy and Artois: the rondeau motet and the "miniature" motets that consist of a single refrain accompanied by a tenor.

Other allusions to motets confirm their association with a clerkly milieu. A song cataloging the cultural advantages of Arras states that God, feeling out of sorts and in need of entertainment, came to that fine city:

> On voit les honors d'Arras si estendre.
> Je vi l'autre jor le ciel lassus fendre,
> Dex voloit d'Arras les motès aprendre. (vv. 4–6) [24]

The honors afforded to Arras keep growing. The other day I saw the sky above split open: God wanted to learn the motets of Arras.

The ensuing narrative of God's Artesian holiday places the motet in a context that includes love songs—"Ghilebers canta de se dame ciere" (Gilbert sang of his beloved lady [v. 20])—as well as more bawdy entertainment—"Il fist le paon, se braie avala" (He strutted like a peacock, he dropped his pants [v. 25])—and even intellectual disputation:

> Compaignons manda por estudiier:
> Pouchins li ainsnés, ki bien set raisnier
> De compleusion, d'astrenomiier,
> Je vi k'il fist Diu le couleur cangier,
> Car encontre lui ne se seut aidier. (vv. 10–14)

He sent for study companions: Poucins the elder, who is skilled in disputation of natural complexions and astronomy. I saw that he made God change color, for he [God] couldn't hold his own against him.

This is precisely the milieu of the vernacular motet, combining higher education, musical training, familiarity with vernacular love lyric, and a somewhat irreverent sense of humor.

If motets graced the festive dances of young students and *clercs* and provided a form of entertainment worthy of God himself, however, they also appeared in a somewhat less edifying setting, the student tavern. An amusing scene in the *Roman de Renart* depicts a drunken rendition of what might be motets by Renart and his two companions in pilgrimage, Belin and the archpriest Bernard:

> Tant but Belin que il s'envoise;
> lors a conmencié a chanter,
> et l'arceprestre a orgener,
> et dant Renart chante a fauset. [25]

Belin drank so much that he feels merry; then he began to sing, and the arch-priest to do the organum, and Lord Renart sings [a triplum] in falsetto.

Within the motet repertoire some texts point strongly to such scenes of Goliardic revelry. The following motetus, for example, is transmitted with various accompanying texts in three manuscripts:

> A la cheminee
> el froit mois de genvier
> voil la char salee,
> les chapons gras manger,
> dame bien paree,
> chanter et renvoisier.
> C'est ce qui m'agree:
> bon vin a remuer,
> cler feu sans fumee,
> les dés et le tablier
> sans tencier.[26]

By the fire, in the cold month of January, I want salt meat and plump capons to eat, a well-dressed lady, song and merriment. That's what I like: good wine to drink, a bright fire without smoke, dice and a gaming table without quarreling.

Scenes of drunken revelry also figure in motets such as *Entre Jehan et Philippet* (862) / *Nus hom ne puet desiervir les biens* (863) / *Chose Tassin* and Adam de la Halle's *Entre Adan et Hanikel* (725) / *Chief bien seantz* (726) / *APTATUR* (O46); and motets such as *Entre Copin et Bourgeois* (866) / *Je me cuidoie tenir* (867) / *Bele Ysabelos m'a mort* allude to the merry life to be led in Paris. One must assume that the motet, a blend of High Style courtly lyric, Low Style popular lyric, and sacred music, was at home in various settings, some more decorous than others.

It is sometimes suggested—though the evidence is tenuous—that vernacular or bilingual motets were performed during church services, at least on special occasions. Some controversy surrounds this question, and it is certainly improbable, to say the least, that secular love songs—which is what most vernacular motets are—ever had an officially sanctioned role in the liturgy, however much they might lend themselves to ingenious allegorical readings.[27] From the repeated complaints and condemnations that issued from high ecclesiastical offices, however, one can only conclude that secular, irreverent, and overly ornamental songs of some sort were part of the celebration of saints' days and other feasts, with certain holidays—for example, the feasts of Saint Stephen and Holy

Innocents—being characterized by particularly rowdy behavior.[28] A tantalizing hint of a bilingual motet in an ecclesiastical context occurs in what is known as the Tournai Mass, which concludes with the motet *Cum venerint* (631) / *Se grasse* (630) / ITE MISSA EST (M88b).[29] The triplum is a reminder to the wealthy that they must give alms to those who come begging; the motetus recasts the exhortation to merciful generosity as an elegant courtly lament for unrequited love. Anne Walters Robertson has suggested that this piece might be associated with a paraliturgical Annunciation drama.[30] Perhaps, then, there were occasions when vernacular motet texts were used in religious celebrations.

This initial overview of the vernacular motet has three fundamental points. First, it is a learned genre, musically and intellectually demanding. Given the close ties between the Latin and the French repertoires, it seems inescapable that vernacular motets were cultivated in the same clerical milieu as the Latin ones, performed—if not exclusively—for a sophisticated audience of fellow clerics and members of the university and at ecclesiastical and aristocratic courts.[31] The elite quality of the motet is often cited, usually with reference to Grocheio's famous statement in *De musica* (ca. 1300): "Cantus autem iste non debet coram vulgaribus propinari eo quod eius subtilitatem non advertunt nec in eius auditu delectantur sed coram litteratis et illis qui subtilitates artium sunt quaerentes"[32] (For this music should not be performed before the unlettered, who would not understand its subtlety or take pleasure in hearing it, but rather before the educated and those who cultivate the subtleties of the arts). This does not necessarily mean, of course, that motets never were performed for and by the *vulgaribus*, a term by which Grocheio designates the uneducated and presumably undiscerning laity. Indeed, if Grocheio troubled to make the point, it may be because motets were being performed in contexts that he disapproved of. Clearly, he considered motets to be special. The difficulties of interpreting vernacular and bilingual motets, which often employ liturgical tenors in inventive and comical ways, suggest that, at least initially, these pieces were composed by and for educated people familiar with chant and biblical exegesis, and sensitive to a variety of poetic and rhetorical strategies.

Second, the Latin motet troped the chant and expounded doctrine, but vernacular ones drew on the extremely varied corpus of vernacular lyric. Some explored the basic paradigm of a given genre, such as the pastourelle, by combining different versions of it or developing its dramatic potential, just as Latin ones expanded on the narrative context or doctrinal background of the chant texts. Others set up an opposition between lyric genres, contrasting the *chanson courtoise* with the pastourelle, for example, or the *chanson de mal mariée*.[33] And the presence of the Latin tenor allowed constant experimentation with the allegorical or parodic troping of the sacred text in the language of secular lyric, a process that itself entailed a reevaluation of lyric discourse. Originating in the early period of chansonnier compilation and the first use of lyric poetry in a narrative framework, the vernacular motet reflects that same impulse to study the vernacular corpus, to experiment with both the codification and the transformation of its generic paradigms. Its analytic, intellectualized approach to vernacular lyric can be compared to the careful arrangement of texts according to genre in a compilation like trouvère chansonnier *a* (Vat. Reg. 1490), which was divided into *chansons courtoises* (arranged by author), pastourelles, motets and rondeaux, *chansons pieuses*, and jeux-partis. A text like Jean Renart's *Roman de la Rose* or Gerbert de Montreuil's *Roman de la Violette* reveals a similar interest in orchestrating vernacular lyric genres by means of a wide variety of lyric types, each chosen to correspond to the narrative moment at which it is inserted.[34]

But if the motet draws on the rich repertoire of vernacular lyric, it does so in service of a new aesthetic. The shape of the motet text is determined by the musical structure of the polyphonic setting rather than by the metrical structure of the stanza. Formally, the vernacular motet is linked to the Latin motet corpus; in terms of content and generic register, it is rooted in vernacular lyric. This separation of poetic form and content is typical of the literary innovations of thirteenth-century French poets. In the *Roman de la Rose*, the *Roman de la Poire*, and the corpus of *dits amoureux*, lyric elements—such as first-person discourse and the introspective focus on love psychology—are divorced from the song's stanzaic structure, treated in other formats, and combined with a variety of narrative and expository settings. The corpus of Old French motets represents a parallel development: remaining within the domain of lyricism and musical performance, it offers ongoing experimentation with the range of vernacular lyric genres and the potential meanings in their creative juxtaposition. The growth of a written tradition of vernacular lyric and the generic transformations accompanying this process are essential background to the rise of the vernacular motet.[35]

Third, the vernacular motet is a playful and frequently humorous genre, often characterized by what Page has called "a tone of festive lightness."[36] This intellectual playfulness is reflected in its innovative expansions on vernacular lyric and its mixing of languages and traditions. Although they have received less critical acclaim in the modern period, many Old French motets exhibit the comic wit, *joie de vivre*, and erudition that we associate with the Carmina Burana. The interactions of the texted voices with one another and with the tenor are often complicated. A single piece may encompass a multifaceted dialogue between the texts of the upper voices; between each text, individually, and the Latin tenor; and between the tenor and the upper voices collectively. In addition, there are at least two outside contexts: the scriptural and ritual sources of the tenor, and the vernacular lyric corpus. The unexpected parallels and contrasts that emerge from this confluence of literary languages provide both humor and a new understanding of the texts involved.

The dialogue and mutual commentary of chant texts and secular lyric, the free play of contrasting elements within the motet corpus, lead to an intricate fusing of literary codes. An attempt to reconcile the competing voices of a motet, to resolve the relationship between its component parts into either allegorical correspondence or parodic difference, can be difficult. An image of lovers or an amorous refrain, for example, might represent dangers of the flesh, which prayer can overcome, or it might function as a metaphor for spiritual yearning and the love of God, in the manner of the Song of Songs. Allegory and parody are in fact closely related techniques: they juxtapose two different literary or iconographic codes that share certain motifs. Both the allegorical and the parodic text rely on the reader's recognition of a relationship between overt and covert patterns of signification: between the "foregrounded" language and imagery the text presents and the "background" text or context that prompts a reevaluation of the textual surface. Allegory, however, requires a leap of faith, a bridging of the gap between the two registers; parody highlights the difference between them. Whereas allegory operates according to a principle of figurative correspondence, parody employs ironic distancing.

In spite of this straightforward distinction, medieval texts—including motets—often defy classification. Such texts are best understood as instances of allegory used for parodic purposes. Many an Old French motet features the allegorical technique of recasting a moment from sacred history or a passage from Scripture in the language and imagery of secular literature; the tenor even provides the key to decoding the allegory by suggesting a liturgical or scriptural referent. Yet the vernacular motet also displays the two characteristics that Kathryn Gravdal has identified with transgressive, or literary, parody: "First, it is oppositional, in that it introduces an opposing diction, character, stylistic tendency, or social space in a literary genre to which they do not belong. Second, it is combinational, in that it juxtaposes registers, characters, or scenes from different genres, placing them side by side." [37] The vernacular motet introduces the language of such genres as the pastourelle, the *chanson courtoise*, and the *chanson de toile* into what was originally a devotional genre with liturgical ties; it juxtaposes the tenor, drawn from sacred chant—and sometimes one or two devotional texts in French or Latin as well—with a secular text or texts. In its use of contrafacta, it may even combine the melody of a sacred motet or clausula with newly composed secular words. As will become clear, the vernacular motet is often susceptible of simultaneous allegorical and parodic readings; motet composers play with the very boundary between allegory and parody, testing the limits of figurative correspondence. In this respect the motet exemplifies the form of intertextuality that Paul Zumthor has termed *conjonction de discours*: a construct in which two or more literary codes are deployed so that neither dominates, and thus either may serve as the interpretive key to the text. [38]

It is important to bear in mind, as both Page and Gravdal stress, that parodic use of a canonical text or genre is not necessarily irreverent. The same point is made by Linda Hutcheon, who defines parody as a hybrid form involving a dialogue between forms of coded discourse. [39] Although the difference between parodic foreground and parodied background is treated ironically, the parodied text is not necessarily the target of the irony, nor is the implied critical judgment necessarily derisive: in Hutcheon's words, parody is "imitation with critical ironic distance, whose irony can cut both ways . . . and the range of pragmatic ethos is from scornful ridicule to reverential homage" (p. 37). This insight is essential for an understanding of medieval parodies of liturgical and scriptural texts. The Bacchic Mass, for example, is not a blasphemous effort to profane the sacred ritual or to equate it with drunkenness. Although certainly playful and highly amusing for those to whom the texts and rites of the Mass were virtually second nature, the parody aims at clerics who are so devoted to drink that they have in effect made it their God: they, and not the Mass, are mocked. [40] Mikhail Bakhtin's analysis of medieval parody, with some nuancing, provides a useful context for the study of the motet. [41] He explains parody as a literary and linguistic hybrid, as a transposition "of sacred texts or of scholarly wisdom . . . into the key of gay laughter, into the positive material bodily sphere" (*Rabelais and His World*, p. 83). Equally important is his insight that the seeming revolt against authority embodied both in parodic texts and in carnival's mocking rituals serves ultimately to reinforce cultural norms: the very transgression of the law simultaneously posits its higher authority. As Bakhtin shows, the *parodia sacra* is fundamentally dialogic; to read it as simply irreverent reduces it to a polemical monologue conducted by one literary form at the expense of another.

It is the dialogic quality of parody that I wish to stress, a dialogue that goes in both directions and reflects an unresolved tension between an authoritative, canonical text or genre and one with lesser or different authority. This tension may derive from a variety of factors, and in the Old French motet, it is essentially twofold, entailing the contrast of Latin and vernacular as well as sacred and profane discourse. The fusion of chant and vernacular lyric in the fabric of the motet results in a new genre, a new art form, that requires us to revise our reading of both elements. Secular text and sacred tenor comment upon and transform each other as they become component parts of the same hybrid system. The vibrancy and immediacy of the vernacular text reinvigorate the solemn music of the chant; the sacred associations of the tenor illuminate the texts of the upper voices, revealing or creating a potential allegorical meaning that would not otherwise be discerned. At the same time, the devotional tone of the tenor highlights the frivolity or pretentiousness of the upper voices; they in turn may appropriate the tenor entirely, investing it with a new, purely secular meaning. Although one side may dominate, the polyphonic character of the motet precludes its reduction to a single voice or meaning. The vernacular motet exemplifies the ludic, experimental quality of intertextuality stressed by Laurent Jenny in his discussion of the avant-garde: the generation of a new literary language through the creative appropriation of the old.[42] It is also fundamentally medieval, a lyric version of the well-known topos of *translatio studii*—the reverent assimilation and radical transformation of Latin imperial and ecclesiastical culture into that of the vernacular.

The motet is hardly the only medieval literary genre to explore the interaction of sacred and profane discourses. Such issues are central to much of the literature of what is commonly known as courtly love.[43] The shared language and imagery—one might use the term *iconography*—of spiritual and erotic love have been well documented: the erotic and nuptial imagery of mystical discourse, the language of adoration, patient suffering, and humility fundamental to courtly lyric and romance. The moral and spiritual transformation caused by the onset of love is sometimes portrayed in terms suggesting religious conversion.[44] Both hagiography and courtly literature may posit a love that exists outside of or in opposition to marriage, a higher value transcending societal norms and regulations—the virgin martyr on the one hand, Tristan and Iseult or Lancelot and Guinevere on the other. The crossover of language allows the construction of potent metaphors, capable of expressing complex psychological states. And much medieval humor turns on deliberate "misreadings" that confuse devotional and erotic registers. The most obvious locus of such wordplay is the fabliau, but the phenomenon is by no means limited to that genre. In Gui de Mori's reworking of the *Roman de la Rose*, the deluded Lover cites 1 John 3:14 in defense of his erotic pursuits: "Qui non diligit, manet in morte" (Whoever does not love, remains in a state of death).[45] Gérard de Liège cites vernacular refrains in his Latin writings, using them as illustrations of spiritual love; he also adapts the model of the five stages of love to describe the soul's love of God.[46] Medieval writers used either type of love as a metaphor for the other, and this crossover of language could have didactic as well as comic purposes.

Courtly love and spiritual love also share rhetorical strategies. Robert Glendinning, for example, has examined the use of oxymora in erotic and devotional discourse.[47] In both cases the oxymoron is employed in the exploration of the unknowable and in the effort to express the deep paradoxes that characterize erotic and spiritual devotion. Both discourses also share the technique of allegory, which in secular texts often explicitly derives from theological or moralistic prototypes. The use of personification allegory in the *Roman de la Rose* and its tradition imitates and transforms the Latin tradition exemplified in such texts as the *Psychomachia* and the *Anticlaudianus*.[48] A somewhat different use of erotic allegory appears in the famous *Minnegrotte* episode of Gottfried von Straßburg's *Tristan und Isolde*. Gottfried's elaborate description and exegesis of the lovers' chamber, modeled on conventional allegories of the Church, implicitly elevates their love to the status of a religion. His parody of Christian allegorical discourse invites meditation on the nature of love and on the ramifications of positing erotic desire as the interpretive key to a system of literary figures.[49]

Some vernacular texts, in fact, confront directly the claims of churchmen that secular poetry and music imperil the soul. The notion that carolers and fornicators are bound for Hell is answered in an amusing passage in the early-thirteenth-century parodic text *Aucassin et Nicolette*.

Warned that his devotion to Nicolette is endangering his soul, Aucassin declares that he would rather not go to Heaven:

Il i vont ci viel prestre et cil viel clop et cil manke qui tote jor et tote nuit cropent devant ces autex et en ces viés croutes, et cil a ces viés capes ereses et a ces viés tatereles vestues, qui sont nu et decauc et estrumelé, qui moeurent de faim et de soi et de froit et de mesaises. . . . Mais en infer voil jou aler, car en infer vont li bel clerc, et li bel cevalier qui sont mort as tornois et as rices gueres, et li buen sergant et li franc home: aveuc ciax voil jou aler. Et s'i vont les beles dames cortoises que eles ont deus amis ou trois avoc leur barons, et s'i va li ors et li argens et li vairs et li gris, et si i vont herpeor et jogleor et li roi del siecle.[50]

Those old priests go there, and those old cripples and amputees who crouch day and night in front of altars and in old crypts, and those who wear ragged old capes and tatters, naked and barefoot and exposed, who are dying of hunger and thirst and cold and disease. . . . But I want to go to Hell, for handsome *clercs* go to Hell, and handsome knights who died in tournaments and in rich wars, and good soldiers and noblemen: I want to go with them. And courteous beautiful ladies go there, who have two or three sweethearts in addition to their husbands, and also gold and silver and vair and gray furs, and harpists and *jongleurs* and worldly kings go there.

Aucassin's devotion to earthly love and its attendant festivities and fineries results in an inversion of the conventional value system. Christians are taught to aspire to a spiritual afterlife characterized by joyous celebration, love, and sumptuous plenitude; for Aucassin, it is Hell, not Heaven, that fits this description. The absurdity of his preference for damnation would have been apparent to any medieval audience, and it is part of the complex parody of the *chantefable*. Still, the humor is double-edged, mocking not only courtly lovers' self-absorption and delusion but also preachers' hyperbole, which sometimes does impart a positively joyless character to Christian piety.

Another possible approach to the conflict of spiritual salvation and earthly love—each with its attendant poetry and music—is to bridge the gap, either by positing a vision of Heaven that obviates any such conflict or by redefining the significance of love poetry. The first alternative is exemplified in high comic fashion in the discourse of Genius in Jean de Meun's *Rose*. Genius collapses the distinction of which Aucassin complained: in his sermon, Heaven is a place where lovers frolic in flowery meadows, singing motets, caroling, and otherwise enjoying themselves. No longer need the young man devoted to worldly pleasures and human love aspire to an eternity in Hell: Heaven itself is the locus for the eternal enjoyment of such pastimes.[51] The second alternative appears in the *Court de Paradis*, in which Heaven is again the setting for caroling and amorous pursuits. Here, however, the carol and the vernacular refrains sung by its participants have become expressions of love for Christ.[52]

Each of the three stances outlined above is represented within the motet repertoire. Aucassin's comically defiant vision of Heaven as a dull and cheerless place can be correlated with motets in which the juxtaposition of secular lyric and sacred tenor highlights their dissonance, forcing an ironic reading of either the texted voices or the tenor. Genius's view, that eros and its musical celebration are to be equated with spiritual fulfillment, is paralleled in motets where the texted voices create a secular recasting of spiritual themes into which the tenor is appropriated. In such a composition, for example, the tenor IN SECULUM (FOREVER [MI3]) — from the Easter gradual *Hec dies. Confitemini Domino*, which refers to everlasting divine mercy — might in its new context be a comment on undying love or on the erotic "mercy" that an amorous lady affords her lover. In still other motets the tenor might dominate, determining a spiritual reading of the upper voices; such pieces can be compared to the appropriation of secular refrains in the *Court de Paradis*. In practice these distinctions are not necessarily a means of categorizing motets, since a given piece can easily have more than one reading. But the point remains that motet composers constantly play with the tension between sacred and profane love and song and with various ways to highlight or resolve this tension. And the very allowance of multiple readings, the questioning of the nature of love and the relationship between erotic and spiritual devotion, itself characterizes much medieval literature. One could apply to the motet Eugène Vinaver's judgment on the *Lancelot-Graal*: it "presupposes in the reader the ability to savor a contrast without seeking to reconcile the two sides, the readiness to contemplate two boldly juxtaposed ideals."[53]

In part because the polyvalent language and iconography of love were dangerous in their potential misreadings, the Church regularly condemned secular music and literature. Page cites evidence that the carol may have been a kind of "popular liturgy": the dances, held in churchyards or other sacred places, celebrated religious holidays, particularly the feast days of locally important saints.[54] The moralizations by churchmen often represent the carol as a parodic liturgy of sexual license, which diverts the public from the real liturgy. In a sermon preached in 1272, for example, Daniel of Paris rebuked his audience for caroling on Christmas,

dismissing the claim—evidently one he expected his listeners to know—
that such songs imitate the angelic celebrations at Christ's birth.[55] Other
polemicists were more explicit in their characterization of the carol as an
unholy liturgy: "Item in chorea habet diabolus sacerdotem canantem et
clericum respondentem et quasi omnes horas fecit cantari per vicos et
plateas; et sicut sacerdos mutat vestimenta quando debet celebrare, si isti
quando debent choreas ducere . . . et loco officii Dei faciunt officium
diaboli"[56] (In a carol the devil has a priest who sings and a cleric who
responds, and causes nearly all the Hours to be sung in the streets and
public places; and just as the priest changes his garments when he has
to celebrate the Mass, so do these when they have to lead carols . . .
and in place of the Office of God they perform the Office of the devil).
Throughout the preachings against the carol is an obsessive concern with
its character as a locus of unbridled sexuality, threatening chastity and
marriage alike. In the songs of the carol, erotic imagery is not a metaphor for spiritual yearning or mystical union; marriage is criticized not
from the perspective of celibacy, but because it conflicts with adulterous
pleasures.

In the polemics of twelfth- and thirteenth-century preachers, then,
the dangers of secular lyric are its very similarities to sacred music: the
responsory format of the carol, its function as communal celebration, its
discourse of love and desire.[57] Highlighting these structural similarities
enabled preachers to define secular lyric, and in particular the carol, as an
anti-liturgy, whose heretical or demonic character was then established
by its licentious tone. Of course, even the most strident condemnations
of the carol did little to curb its popularity, and within the university
community some chose to defend secular music and dance, including the
carol, as a legitimate form of recreation.[58] The opposition or concordance
of sacred and secular poetry and music was one of the central issues in
late medieval culture, and where some sought to strengthen the distinction, others worked to dissolve it. This polemic is an important part of
the background against which the vernacular motet arose, and must have
contributed to the clerical and university communities' appreciation of
the genre.[59]

The motet, in sum, is not an isolated phenomenon. It participates
fully in the cultural world of thirteenth-century France, which also saw a
proliferation of erotic allegories and pious contrafacta, of parodic rework-
ings of sacred texts and their rhetorical strategies, and of appropriations
of secular songs and motifs into a devotional context, as well as the

flourishing literature of courtly love, with its endless explorations of interpretive dilemmas and conflicting codes. But the motet is particularly well suited to cultivating a playful dialectic of sacred and profane discourses. Rather than presenting different literary languages and registers sequentially, or evoking one within the framework of another, the motet affords a simultaneous rendition of different musical and literary texts, each preserving its own integrity and its own intertextual associations. The polyphonic structure of the motet makes it unique among medieval literary genres. As such it allows a focused exploration of the meeting and interaction of sacred and profane traditions, and of the allegorical and parodic treatments of their interplay.

The study that follows explores in detail the ways that motets are constructed around points of contact between sacred and secular discourse. It begins with two chapters providing background for the analysis of the motet. The first examines the polytextual structure of the motet and identifies various techniques used in the creation of textual polyphony; it also addresses ways in which the motet draws on, and transforms, the vernacular lyric corpus. The second chapter examines the interaction of erotic and devotional language and imagery in a variety of texts and genres, and establishes a dual context for the reading of motets: that of sacred parody and that of spiritual allegory. The next three chapters offer close readings of selected motets, organized according to the liturgical associations of the tenor and the particular correlation of spiritual and secular motifs by which the motet operates. Chapter 3 examines the figure of the amorous maiden, primarily through motets with Marian tenors; Chapter 4 treats the themes of absence, separation, and reunion, primarily through motets with tenors associated with the Passion, Ascension, and Pentecost. Chapter 5, focused largely on motets with tenors taken from the Easter liturgy, considers the persona of the male lover and the ways he can be identified with Christ as a figure of suffering. In each case, motets are analyzed according to the interpretive techniques set up in the first two chapters. Insofar as possible for a given motet, that is, we will look at the dialogic relationship between its multiple voices — including the tenor — from two fundamental perspectives: the moral and spiritual allegorization of erotic discourse on the one hand, and the parodic eroticization of sacred discourse on the other.

Chapter I

Varieties of Textual Polyphony
Intertextual Dialogue in the Vernacular Motet

Primo accipe tenorem alicuius antiphone vel responsorii vel
alterius cantus de antiphonario et debent verba concordare cum
materia de qua vis facere motetum.

First select a tenor from any antiphon or responsory or other
melody in the antiphonary, and the words should correspond to
the material that you want the motet to treat.

—Egidius de Murino

The motet, constructed of independent texts that are performed simultaneously, affords an opportunity for intertextual play that is unparalleled
in other literary forms. It is often in the relationship of the motet's two,
three, or four voices that the real artistry of the piece resides, as well as its
affective power for humor or pathos. In this respect, there is considerable
variety within the corpus of French and bilingual motets. In some cases
the individual voices are closely related, perhaps even sharing refrains or
lines of text, and virtually paraphrase one another. In others, however,
a contrast or dialogue between the texts may take various forms; further
complicating this intertextual dialogue is the interaction of the texted
voices and the tenor, with its liturgical associations.

The question naturally arises as to how well an audience understood
the words of a motet during a performance. No doubt it was often impossible to understand all the words, especially in a three- or four-part
motet and in a single hearing. On the other hand, many motets have just
two parts, of which only the motetus is texted. It would not be particularly difficult to understand the words of a single text being sung to the
accompaniment of untexted vocalization. The tenor melodies, especially
those derived from such major feasts as Easter, Pentecost, Assumption,

and Christmas, would be familiar to anyone with some knowledge of the liturgy. Certainly the clerical audience, with which these pieces are strongly associated, would have understood the tenors and might have also recognized contrafacta among the upper voices. And although a three- or four-part motet would present a considerable challenge to the listener, one could likely learn its words after repeated performances. Ardis Butterfield has argued that the interaction of motet texts during performance is crucial in the generation of new, often humorous, meanings.[1] Finally, even though not all members of the audience could follow the textual twists and turns of motets, a certain inner circle did: the composers and performers themselves. One must consider that performers constituted an important "audience," especially for motets with multiple upper voices, and that such pieces may have been performed as often for the singers' private enjoyment as for the entertainment of a larger group.

The juxtaposition of contrasting perspectives within the motet takes a variety of forms. One finds examples of a male voice combined with a female voice; of a declaration of love and an antifeminist polemic; of the courtly world juxtaposed with that of the pastourelle. An amorous text might accompany one offering political diatribe or social commentary, or it might be used with a hagiographic poem or hymn to the Virgin. In all cases, the polytextuality of the motet allows considerable play with the range of Old French lyric. The basic paradigm of amorous desire can be examined from a variety of perspectives and expressed through the language and imagery of different lyric genres. The lady, for example, may be loved for her beauty, admired for her purity, enjoyed for her uninhibited sexuality, or condemned for her resistance to masculine desire; she may speak in her own voice, expressing distaste for her husband, loyalty to her beloved, or regret for an absent lover; she may be nun, shepherdess, courtly maiden, or wife. The polyphonic structure of the motet requires us to read contextually. Depending on the other text or texts with which it is joined, a love lament or tale of seduction might be a spiritual allegory, a religious parody, a serious or humorous illustration of societal woes, or part of a larger dramatization of the effects of love. In this chapter, I survey some of the ways the multiple voices of a motet might interact with one another. Only after forming a basic understanding of the dynamics of the motet as a genre can we proceed to an in-depth consideration of how specific tenors are troped, redefined, or parodied in individual motets and motet families.

Male and Female Voices

One option that motet composers had for creating tension, dialogue, or contrast between the texts of motetus and triplum was to assign a male voice to one and a female voice to the other. At its simplest, this technique results in man and woman respectively stating their mutual love and desire. In *Dieus, de chanter maintenant* (176) / *Chant d'oisiaus et fuelle et flor* (177) / *IN SECULUM* (M13), for example, the male persona of the triplum and the female persona of the motetus formulate parallel declarations of love:

Tr	M
Dieus, de chanter maintenant	Chant d'oisiaus et fuelle et flor
por quoi m'est talent pris,	et tans joli
qu'au cuer ai un duel, dont sui peris,	mi font ramembrer d'amors,
se cele qui j'aim ne me soit confortans?	si que je ne pens aillors
Et quant je remir et pens	qu'a vos, amis.
a sa simplece	Tant avés, ce m'est avis,
et son semblant,	biauté et valour et pris,
son cler vis,	que vostre serai tou dis
ses ieuz dous regardans,	sans nule mesproison.
il n'est mal, qui me blece;	*Qui donrai je mes amors,*
por ce l'amera	*douz amis, s'a vos non?*
mes cuers, a son comant l'avra.	Ja vers vos ne faussera
Or me doinst Dieus, que m'amor bien	mes cuers, qui a vos s'otroie.
emploie,	*Por bien amer avrai joie,*
cele part vois, car tart m'est que la voie.	*ou ja nule l'avra.*

T: IN SECULUM[2]

Tr: God, why am I seized with desire to sing now, when I have a pain in my heart from which I will perish if she whom I love does not comfort me? And when I reflect and think about her sincerity and her appearance, her bright face, her sweet gazing eyes, there is no pain that can hurt me; therefore my heart will love her, she will have it at her command. Now God grant that I use my love well, *I am going that way, for I am eager to see her.*

M: Birdsong and leaf and flower and the pleasant season cause me to remember love, such that I can think of nothing but you, friend. It seems to me that you have so much beauty and valor and worth, that I do no wrong if I am yours always. *To whom will I give my love, sweet friend, if not to you?* Never will my heart, which is pledged to you, betray you. *I will have joy from loving well, or no woman will have it.*

T: FOREVER

Both of the texted voices open with the motif of song—the lover's and the birds'—and develop in tandem. Initially, the man expresses the pain he experiences if his lady does not return his feelings (Tr, vv. 1–4). Such fears, however, are simultaneously put to rest with the lady's declaration of love, a free offering of the "comfort" for which the man hoped (M, vv. 1–5). In the middle part of the piece, each lover meditates on the beauty and worthiness of the other, leading again to a mutual declaration of love and a double pledging of hearts. The two statements of desire culminate in the refrains with which each text closes, pointing to a joyous rendezvous in the not-so-distant future. The result is somewhat similar to that created in numerous romances and *dits* in which men and women sing rondeaux and refrains back and forth in scenes of public festivity and flirtation, or in a text such as the *Roman de la Poire* where lover and lady communicate through allegorical personifications singing refrains. The tenor, from the Easter gradual *Hec dies. Confitemini Domino*, alludes to the lyric season of springtime, which is also invoked in the opening words of the motetus. Recontextualized by the amorous discourse of the motet, its reference to eternal mercy—"quoniam in seculum misericordia ejus" (for his/her mercy is forever)—also underscores the undying love and amorous "mercy" shared by the lovers.

The relationship between the two texted voices is enriched by a consideration of the ways the motet draws on the informing matrix of trouvère lyric. In the opening lines the two voices combine to form the standard *début printanier*,[3] and the subsequent divergence of male and female voices represents an expansion of the typical trouvère monologue. As an example of the classic trouvère chanson, we can examine *La douce voiz du louseignol sauvage* by the Châtelain de Couci:

> La douce voiz du louseignol sauvage
> Qu'oi nuit et jour cointoier et tentir
> M'adoucist si le cuer et rassouage
> Qu'or ai talent que chant pour esbaudir;
> Bien doi chanter puis qu'il vient a plaisir
> Cele qui j'ai fait de cuer lige homage;
> Si doi avoir grant joie en mon corage,
> S'ele me veut a son oez retenir. (vv. 1–8)[4]

The sweet voice of the wild nightingale that I hear chirping and singing night and day so sweetens and soothes my heart that now I have the urge to sing for joy; I should well sing since it pleases her to whom I have pledged my heart in homage; thus I should have great joy in my heart, if she chooses to retain my services.

This stanza sets up love and birdsong—itself a manifestation of love as a natural force, since the nightingale is the quintessential bird of love— as twin sources of inspiration for the trouvère's song, designed to bring pleasure to the lady and to inform her of her lover's feelings. Subsequent stanzas develop the lover's declarations of fidelity as well as his confusion in the lady's presence, presumably because of his strong passion and his fears of rejection. Here, for example, is the second stanza:

> Onques vers li n'eu faus cuer ne volage,
> Si m'en devroit pour tant mieuz avenir,
> Ainz l'aim et serf et aour par usage,
> Mais ne li os mon pensé descouvrir,
> Quar sa biautez me fait tant esbahir
> Que je ne sai devant li nul language;
> Nis reguarder n'os son simple visage,
> Tant en redout mes ieuz a departir. (vv. 9–16)

Never has my heart been false or changeable toward her, and so it should go all the better for me; thus I love and serve and adore her unwaveringly, but I don't dare reveal my sentiments to her because her beauty so bedazzles me that I lose the faculty of language in her presence; I don't even dare meet her clear gaze, so much do I fear not being able to turn my eyes away.

In closing, the lyric persona sends his song directly to the lady: "Chançon, va t'en pour faire mon message / La u je n'os trestourner ne guenchir" (Song, go to bear my message there where I dare not wander or stray [vv. 33–34]). There is thus some suggestion of communication between lover and lady; but this communication remains oblique. Essentially, the chanson presents a closed circle within the consciousness of the lyric persona. Incapable of addressing the lady directly, unable even to approach her, he can realize his love only in the form of song, and the song becomes itself a statement of his inability to do anything other than sing.

In large part, the triplum *Dieus, de chanter maintenant* expresses, in concise form, the same motifs as the chanson: the urge to sing, the lover's fears, his fixation on the lady, her beauty and goodness, and his unswerving dedication to love. The refrain at the end of the triplum, however, adds a note of optimism the chanson lacks. This particular lover, setting off to visit the lady, evidently is less inhibited than the trouvère. This alone imparts a presence to the lady in question. She is not merely to be adored from afar and celebrated anonymously in song: she can actually be approached. But the most important difference is the emergence of the lady's own voice in the motetus. In the opening lines, triplum and motetus share motifs of song, memory, and love—all standard elements in the first stanza of a chanson, here broken into constituent parts. It is only a few lines into the piece that the gender difference between the voices becomes explicit, with the triplum's reference to "cele qui j'aim" (she whom I love [Tr, v. 4]) and the address to "vos, amis" (you, friend [M, v. 5]) in the motetus. It is as though lover and lady simultaneously grow out of the initial tight configuration of lyric motifs, each voice answering to the desire of the other. The motet cannot be termed a dialogue, since the two voices do not respond to each other; indeed, the male voice speaks about the lady in the third person rather than addressing her directly. But the mere presence of the female voice alters our perception of the male persona and his articulation of desire. Unlike the *chanson courtoise*, the motet allows the enunciations of male and female desire to develop in parallel, leading to the closing implications of amorous contact and consummation.

In other motets the implied intrigue is less idyllic, with the male and female personae respectively expressing grief or frustration at the obstacles that make love more difficult, though never impossible. In the case of the man, the primary obstacle is usually rejection by the lady, although it may also include the interference of slanderers, spies, and guardians. The woman often complains of the restrictions placed on her by her mother, her husband, or other guardians; she may also hesitate for fear of betrayal. Nonetheless, male and female personae alike invariably declare their unshaken commitment to love. Motets of this type thus address the motif of love's joys and travails from the masculine and the feminine perspective, combining texts that draw on different generic repertoires: *chanson courtoise, chanson de mal mariée, chanson à danser*. The technique of juxtaposing different lyric types can also be observed in some romances with lyric insertions, where action arises from the implicit intergeneric dialogue. This orchestration of the different lyric genres and their respective visions of love and of male and female desire operates, for example, in Jean Renart's *Roman de la rose ou de Guillaume de Dole*, where assorted lyric insertions of all kinds embellish and comment upon the story and upon one another.[5]

A motet, needless to say, is more focused than a romance; the generically diverse texts that it conjoins serve to illuminate some particular theme or motif. Contrasting views of the amorous ideal, for example, are at the center of *Nus ne set les biens d'amors* (286) / *Ja Dieus ne me doinst corage* (287) / PORTARE (M34a):

| | |
| Tr | M |

Nus ne set les biens d'amors,
s'il n'en a senti dolours;
mout en vient honors
et valor et courtoisie,
car c'est trop grant signourie
d'amer par amours.
Car j'ai bele amie,
pleisant et jolie,
s'en sui plus fins amourous.
En non Diu, que que nus die,
je les sent, les maus d'amors;
si les servirai toz jors.

Ja Dieus ne me doinst corage
d'amer mon mari,
tant com je aie ami,
tel com je l'ai choisi,
preu et vaillant et joli,
deduisant, cortois et sage.
Mes li miens maris s'errage
de savoir son grant damage;
si veut savoir, qui
j'ai doné de m'amor gaige.
Je li respondi:
"Fi, vilains au fol visage!
Vous ne sarés hui,
qui amiete je sui."

T: PORTARE[6]

Tr: No one knows the pleasures of love if he has not felt the pains; from that come much honor and valor and courtesy, for it is a greatly noble thing to be in love. For I have a beautiful sweetheart, pleasant and pretty, thus I am a finer lover. *In the name of God, whatever anyone says, I feel them, the pains of love; I will always serve them.*

M: *May God never move my heart to love my husband, as long as I have a sweetheart,* such as I have chosen, worthy and valiant and handsome, merry, courteous and wise. But my husband is crazy to know his great shame; he wants to know to whom I have pledged my love. I answered him: *"Fie, foolish-looking churl! You won't know today whose sweetheart I am."*

T: TO CARRY

In the triplum a male persona praises the value of love, source of all virtue. He expresses joy at having a *bele amie* (Tr, v. 7) and vows to serve love forever. The motetus is the song of a *mal mariée*: boasting of her lover and his many fine qualities, she mocks her husband and taunts him with a refusal to disclose the lover's identity. The combination of two generic types results in a humorous collision of high and low registers. In the language of the *chanson courtoise,* centered as it is on the male lover, the lady is an abstract figure, silent embodiment of the singer's desires or source of his pain. In the *chanson de mal mariée,* however, the lady emerges as a flesh-and-blood character. She is an active participant in a network of relationships including both her lover and her husband, and she has a quick tongue and a lively temper.

The lofty claims for love's nobility made in the triplum are undercut by the fabliau-like picture of adultery and marital squabbling in the motetus: this, the motet suggests, is the price at which the "honor and courtesy" of love are purchased. The lover's internal meditation on his lady's beauty and goodness, his acceptance of love's sorrows, and his vow of eternal service are grounded in the trouvère model of love as an ideal independent of contact with the lady and of societal approval or disapproval. The closed system of the triplum explodes when the motetus redefines love as adultery. The interplay of contrasting and conflicting discourses in the motet can be compared to that of the *Roman du Castelain de Couci*, which embeds the twelfth-century trouvère's abstract and idealized songs in a narrative of adultery, intrigue, and vengeance.[7] The motet crystallizes in a few lines essential aspects of the elaborate dynamic worked out in the romance.

Implicit in the preceding example is a contrast between male and female experiences of love: the amorous man is largely free of all constraints other than those the lady herself imposes, whereas the married woman must reckon with her husband's interference. The fears of man and woman—rejection by the lady; punishment from society or betrayal by a false lover—are more explicitly the focus of other motets. The contrasts are played out neatly in *A une ajornee* (154) / *Doce dame, en qui dangier* (155) / *IN SECULUM* (M13):

Tr	M
A une ajornee	Doce dame, en qui dangier
s'est Margot levee;	sui sanz changer,
paree est de ses atours,	por vostre amor anoncier
chapel a de flors,	vous pri, que n'aiés pas chiere
bel et coloree.	la gent mal parliere,
Pour deduire seule en va;	qui sert de trichier.
un damoisel encontra,	Mes s'aucuns voz veut proier
qui pleint a celee	de servir de tel mestier,
d'amors les dolors	dites li sans esparnier
et chante tous les jours:	au comencier:
"*Se Diu pleist, tele m'amera,*	"*Fuiés, losenger!*
que j'aim par amours."	*Mes cuers vous het.*
	Ja vilains m'amor n'avra,
	ja n'i bet!"

T: IN SECULUM[8]

Tr: At daybreak Margot rose; she is decked out in her finery, she has a wreath of flowers, pretty and colorful. She goes off alone to amuse herself; she met a boy who secretly laments the pains of love and sings every day: *"If it please God, she whom I love will love me."*

M: Sweet lady, in whose power I am unchangingly, I beg you, to keep your love, not to esteem slanderous people who serve to deceive. But if anyone wants to beseech you to serve in that way, tell him at once without sparing him: *"Away, flatterer! My heart hates you. No unworthy man will have my love, nor should he aspire to it!"*

T: FOREVER

The triplum explores contrasting images of the lady while presenting the voice of male desire. Drawing on the register of the rondeau, the text focuses on the eroticized figure of Margot. Dressed for pleasure, she encounters a lovelorn *damoisel*. The boy's lament and forlorn hope figure the masculine fear of feminine rejection; Margot, clearly from a lyric repertoire in which feminine desire is a powerful force, offers a corrective to the unresponsive lady of the *chanson courtoise* and a reassuring promise of reciprocity in love.

In the motetus, the three-part construct is reversed: here, two images of the male lover are contrasted in a text that gives a voice to the lady. The first-person persona addresses the lady and declares his love and submission to her will; he then warns her not to be swayed by the claims of false lovers. The triplum closes with the lovelorn boy's song; the motetus, with a song that the male persona recommends to his lady as a means of dismissing those who are unworthy. And just as Margot offered a corrective to the distant courtly lady, so the protagonist of the motetus presents himself—a loyal, sincere lover—in opposition to the duplicitous and self-interested flatterers who make love a dangerous pastime for women. By placing this refrain in the mouth of his lady, the persona of the motetus recasts her potential rejection of love as a discriminating rejection of false lovers, thereby creating the possibility that she will accept him. Indeed, distinguishing himself from such unworthy figures, the lyric persona portrays himself as the answer to woman's desire for a trustworthy, noble lover—just as the beautiful and fun-loving Margot appears on the scene at the right moment to fulfill the boy's hopes for love. In spite of its brevity, the motet offers a complex picture of male and female personae and of the vicissitudes of love, as figured in the various conventional stereotypes of vernacular lyric.

In another motet from the Montpellier codex, *Joie et solas ne m'i vaut* (684) / *Jonete sui, brune et clere et plesant* (685) / EJUS (O16), masculine and feminine perspectives on the joys and travails of love are coordinated around a particular motif, the woman's decision to embrace love.[9] The triplum presents the lament of a male persona: he bemoans the absence of mercy in the lady he loves, declaring that he will die if she fails to take pity on him. In the motetus, a young girl explores her conflicting emotions with regard to love. Lacking experience—"onques d'amors ne sai rien" (I have never known anything of love [M, v. 2])—she now feels moved to love, but with some trepidation. On the one hand, she recognizes the danger of betrayal:

> Car trop me dout et me crieng,
> que fause Amor ne me viegne au devant,
> qui du tout me tiegne en son lien. (M, vv. 5–7)

For I greatly worry and fear that false love may overcome me, and capture me completely.

On the other hand, she is tormented, lamenting: "li doz tans passe / et je ne faz rien" (the sweet time is passing and I'm not doing anything [M, vv. 13–14]). The latter sentiment clearly prevails, for the motetus ends with the declaration that "li tans vient, qu'amer covient" (the time has come when I must love [M, v. 17]). Throwing caution to the winds, the girl commits herself to amorous adventure. Her decision is an enactment of precisely the conversion that the male persona of the triplum hopes for in his own lady:

> Et se pitié, que plus vaut que reison,
> ne l'en semont,
> trop mesprendroit. (Tr, vv. 12–14)

And if pity, which is worth more than reason, does not induce her [to love], it will be a great wrong.

Both voices thus acknowledge that the woman's decision to love involves a victory of emotion over reason. In the triplum, which examines love from the male perspective, this feminine conversion is the triumph of pity; in the motetus, which presents the female perspective, the conversion is brought about by a desire (*grant talans*, M, v. 3) strong enough to overpower the girl's entirely reasonable fears. In this way the motet unites opposing views of a woman's role in love: as a participant motivated by her own desire to seek a lover, or as one who reacts to the desires of a suitor and responds with pity for his amorous torment. The contrast is similar to that in *Nus ne set les biens d'amors | Ja Dieus ne me doinst corage | PORTARE*. In both cases, moreover, the tenor derives from the liturgy of

Assumption: the responsory *Stirps Jesse. Virgo* (O16) and the alleluia *Dulcis virgo* (M34a), respectively. The tenor with its Marian associations thus subtly suggests a spiritual resolution in the figure of Mary, who is both exalted and humble, source of love and mercy.

Our next example of conjoined male and female personae—*L'autre jour* (200) / *Au tens pascour* (201) / *IN SECULUM* (M13) (Musical Example 1) —offers a more integrated scenario.[10] In its *mise-en-scène* of the pastoral world, it bears comparison to Adam de la Halle's *Jeu de Robin et Marion.* Adam uses the stock figures of the lyric pastourelle in a loosely structured drama, which involves scenes or episodes corresponding to types of the pastourelle: a knight attempts to seduce, and later to abduct, Marion; Robin and Marion enjoy a picnic; a group of shepherds and shepherdesses gathers to sing, dance, and play games. Throughout the play, the characters sing songs and refrains that are appropriate to their status and to the role in which they are defined; in all, it is as though several different pastourelle poems had been woven together. Like the drama, though condensed, the motet allows the expression of more than one voice and the presentation of more than one scenario. The triplum presents the encounter between the lyric persona and an unnamed shepherdess, much like the beginning of *Robin et Marion*: the shepherdess is alone and singing of love (Tr, vv. 5–6); Marion opens the play by singing the rondeau *Robins m'aime, Robins m'a.*[11] And just as the knight asks Marion for her love and is told that she prefers Robin, so the shepherdess proclaims an unwillingness to betray her lover: "j'aim Robin sans fausseté, m'amor li ai donnee, / plus l'aim que riens nee" (I love Robin without falseness, I have given him my love, I love him more than anything alive [Tr, vv. 14–15]).

The motetus describes a musical contest among five shepherds who play dance tunes on various musical instruments; the best appears to be Robin, who executes a lively *estampie* in honor of his beloved (M, vv. 13–17). The two texted voices are thus symmetrically linked through references to the pastoral couple. The triplum focuses on the shepherdess, who briefly alludes to Robin as her lover; the motetus focuses on Robin and his companions, with only one allusion to Robin's *amie*—presumably the shepherdess of the triplum. Underscoring the symmetry is the correlation of the two voices in their musical setting: the shepherdess's declaration of love for Robin (Tr, vv. 13ff.) and Robin's performance in her honor (M, vv. 13ff.) begin simultaneously at the midpoint of the piece, with the start of the second cursus of the tenor. The phrases "plus l'aim que riens nee" (Tr, v. 15) and "pour l'amour de s'amie" (M, v. 17),

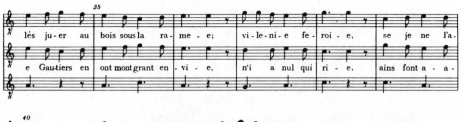

Tr: The other day in the morning, at dawn, in a valley, I came upon a shepherdess and gazed at her. She was alone, singing of love; and I said, "*Simple and gentle one, if it agreed with you I would gladly be your sweetheart.*" She answers wisely, "Sir, leave me be, go back to your land. I love Robin truly, I have given him my love, I love him more than any living thing; he went off to sport in the woods, beneath the branches; I would do a vile thing if I didn't love him, for he loves me without trickery. I have no wish to leave him for you."

M: At Eastertide, all the shepherds of the region gathered at the bottom of a valley. In the meadow Hebert led the dance with pipe and tabor; Robin didn't like it when he saw him; he takes up the challenge to do a better *estampie*. Then he grabbed his drone, took his hood, hoisted up his tunic, and did a merry *estampie* for the love of his sweetheart. Rogier, Guiot, and Gautier are greatly envious, none of them laugh it off, but they all make the wager that before evening, his pipe will be overcome.

T: FOREVER

Musical Example 1. From Gordon Athol Anderson, ed., *Compositions of the Bamberg Manuscript: Bamberg, Staatsbibliothek, Lit. 115 (olim Ed.IV.6)*, Corpus Mensurabilis Musicae, 75. © 1977 by American Institute of Musicology / Hänssler-Verlag, D73762 Neuhausen-Stuttgart. All rights reserved. International copyright secured. Legally protected. Duplications are not allowed.

explicitly invoking love, are sung simultaneously. Furthering the structural cohesion around Robin and his lover is the note of triumph each achieves. The shepherdess scorns her would-be suitor, declaring that to love him would be "vilenie" (Tr, v. 17), and Robin's performance draws a reaction of envious admiration. Together the two voices create a scenario comparable to *Robin et Marion*: the triplum corresponds to the recurring subplot of Marion and the knight, and the motetus corresponds to the games and festivities in the group scenes. Instead of sequential intercuts, as in the play, the motet's two episodes are simultaneous: Robin and his unnamed lover appear in parallel vignettes, each alluding to the other. The shepherdess's rejection of her would-be suitor and her protestations of love for Robin underlie his musical performance, executed out of love for her; this inspired performance itself justifies the girl's determination to remain true to her shepherd lover.

Private and Public Spaces

In the preceding example—*L'autre jour* / *Au tens pascour* / IN SECULUM—the contrasting focus on male and female personae corresponds to a different kind of opposition as well: Robin's dual identity as lover and as rustic performer. In the triplum, he is the boyfriend of the shepherdess; in the motetus, he interacts with his companions in musical competition. In both, however, his amorous relations with the shepherdess are significant in his relationships with the masculine world: in the triplum he is the rival of the would-be suitor and potential protector of the shepherdess; in the motetus love inspires his *estampie*. Robin's private identity as lover thus informs his public identity. This pattern of contrasting the public and private, or amorous and communal, facets of the lyric persona obtains in a number of motets and assumes various forms. An "external" portrait of the lover as third-person member of a social community may be contrasted with an "internal" record of his amorous sentiments, voiced in the first person, or with a portrait of the lady, the inspiration for his participation in the community of singers, lovers, and revelers. The motet as a whole may thus build up a composite portrait of the lyric persona in different contexts, or it may develop an analogy between the experience of the lover and that of society at large.

A motet by the Artesian trouvère Adam de la Halle, *Entre Adan et Hanikel* (725) / *Chief bien seantz* (726) / APTATUR (O46), juxtaposes a detailed portrait of the lady in the motetus with a lively description of four youths—among them "Adan," an obvious counterpart of the author himself—singing and dancing:

Tr	M
Entre Adan et Hanikel,	Chief bien seantz,
Hancart et Gautelot	ondes et fremians,
a grant esbanoi, qui ot	plains frons reluisans et parans,
lor revel.	regars atraihans,
Quant il hoquetent,	vairs, humilians,
plus tost clapetent	catillans et frians,
que frestel	nés par mesure au viaire afferans,
li damoisel,	bouchete rians,
mais qu'il aient avant baisié	vermellete, a dens blans,
Saint Tortuel.	gorge bien naissans,
Et si chantent tout sans livre,	col reploians,
viés et nouvel;	piz durs et poignans,
Gautelos fait l'ivre	boutine soulevant,
si proprement et si bel,	maniere avenans
qu'il samble a son musel,	et plus li remanans,
qu'il doie traire a sa fin.	ont fait tant d'enchant,
Et quant il font le moulin	que pris est Adans.
ensamble tout quatre	
et au plastre batre	
en hoquetant,	
sont si deduisant,	
si gay, si joiant	
et si riant	
cil quatre enfant	
que nule gent tant.	
T: APTATUR[12]	

Tr: Anyone who hears the revelry of Adam and Hanikel, Hancart and Gautelot has great delight. When these boys sing hockets they clap faster than a piper can play, as long as they've first kissed Saint Tortuel [that is, had a drink]. And they sing everything without a book, old and new. Gautelot plays the drunk so exactly and so well that he seems ready to drop from revelry. And when all four together play the windmill and strike the floor, singing hockets, they are so delightful, so merry, so joyous and so full of laughter, these four youths, that no one else can equal it.

M: Handsome head, waves and curves, broad forehead shining and lovely, attractive gaze, fair, humble, averted and voluptuous, nose well proportioned to the face, laughing little mouth, red with white teeth, full throat, supple neck, hard and prominent breasts, rounded stomach, pleasant manner, plus all the rest, have caused such enchantment that Adam is captivated.

T: IT IS FITTING

The two texted voices present the two sides of Adam's lyric persona, public performer and lover, here shown as mutually dependent. Adam's name is the second word of the triplum and the final word of the motetus. Within this frame, his identity pervades the piece through rhyme and alliteration. The motetus is constructed entirely on the rhyme -ans, culminating in *Adans*: the lady's portrait rhymes with her lover's name. This pattern suggests a complementary relationship between lover and lady subtly reminiscent of Narcissus, a quintessential lyric figure: the lady is Adam's mirror, reflection of his desire and psychic backdrop of his public performance. It is from her that he draws his identity as trouvère—lover, singer, poet—and he in turn recreates her as the object of his love and the central image of his songs.

Adam's presence is intensified at the beginning and end of the triplum through repetition of the sounds of his name. The four dancers are named in the first two lines, and the names of the middle two bear a phonetic relationship to his: *Han*ikel and *Han*cart. Following the list of names, *Adan* is echoed again: "*a grant* esb*an*oi" (has great delight [Tr, v. 3]). The rhyme with *Adan* is stressed in the musical setting, with "Han[cart]" and "esban[oi]" paralleling the syllable -ans in the motetus. The rhyme returns in full force at the end of the triplum, where the last six lines rhyme in -ant. The first recurrence of this rhyme (Tr, v. 20) follows immediately upon the rhyme -ant in the motetus (M, v. 13); the remainder (Tr, vv. 21–22, 24–25) coincide, in performance, with the motetus rhymes (M, vv. 14–17).[13] Contrasting with this pervasive phonetic presence is Gautelot, the fourth dancer, whose name is constructed on entirely different sounds and who assumes center stage as drunken reveler during the middle of the motet (Tr, vv. 13–16). The interplay between *Adan* and the rhythmical -ans/-ant rhymes at beginning and end, and Gautelot in the middle, suggests the movements of dance, as one performer circles another. This verbal play stresses Adam's identity as performer, perceived in relation to other performers; his presence as poetic subject, stamped into the phonetic texture of the piece, serves to unify the voices.

The trouvère's dual identity as lover and performer is here evoked with some complexity. In the private dimension, Adam is enraptured by the silent spectacle of the lady, source of *enchant* (M, v. 16). This enchantment infuses him and is expressed again as *chant* (Tr, v. 11) in the active, musical spectacle of song and dance. In this way the inspiration of the private love experience is recreated in the public arena, and so reaches the community at large: "a grant esbanoi, qui ot / lor revel" (anyone who hears their revelry has great delight (Tr, vv. 3–4)]. The trouvère participates in three contexts of widening scope: private love (Adam, his lady); group performance (Adam and his three male companions); and communal celebration (represented by the implied spectators). Performance is the medium that conjoins the most private and the most public contexts. Finally, the audience for whom the motet is performed is an extension of the audience in the text, just as Adam de la Halle, author and member of the extratextual world, is the counterpart of the textual Adan. Performance serves as well to mediate between the actual community of Arras and its idealized poetic image.

Given this reading of the motet, the tenor word *APTATUR* (IT IS FITTING) is a fine commentary on the piece. Even here, *Adan* is subtly evoked in the vowels of the first two syllables. And the word itself sums up the series of relationships built into the piece: the conjoining of lover to lady, private self to public persona, performer to audience, and motetus to triplum indeed expresses a world in which all parts harmonize and nothing is out of place.

A similar effect is created in the anonymous three-part motet *Entre Copin et Bourgeois* (866) / *Je me cuidoie tenir* (867) / *Bele Ysabelos m'a mort*.[14] The triplum presents a group of Parisian students, indicating that "i a tel, qui a bele amie" (there is one among them who has a beautiful girlfriend [Tr, v. 5]) who has caused him to miss "mainte leçon" (many a lesson [Tr, v. 8]); she is identified as "la bele Ysabelot" (Tr, v. 10). The motetus is a first-person declaration of love; no names are given, but under the circumstances it makes sense to see the motetus as the amorous monologue of the student whose life is described in the triplum. The motetus in fact relates to the triplum in much the same way that a lyric insertion or monologue relates to its frame narrative: the third-person lover, described in the triplum from the outside, here acquires a voice and expresses his internal feelings. In the triplum we are told of his fixation on Fair Isabel: "il ne puet penser s'a li non" (he can think only of her [Tr, v. 13]). This amorous obsession is borne out in the motetus: describing his love, the persona declares, "ne ja remuer / n'en quier mon cuer de cest pensé" (nor do I ever want to make my heart turn from this thought

[M, vv. 8–9]). The tenor, finally, is fully texted: rather than deriving from the chant, as most tenors do, this one is a French virelai delineating the beauty and hard-heartedness of the girl named in the triplum, Fair Isabel. The three voices together create a portrait of the amorous student and his *bele amie*, in the public context of Parisian life and in the private context of amorous desire.

Although most thirteenth-century French and bilingual motets employ either devotional or amorous themes, some incorporate political themes. In a few instances texts treating political issues or social commentary may be combined with texts on the usual theme of love; a unifying motif, such as faith or betrayal, is often developed in both voices. In this way the relationship between the individual and society at large develops somewhat differently: instead of contrasting public and private visions of the lyric persona, these pieces posit the private crises of the lyric protagonist as an illustration—whether serious or ironic—of the general state of society. For example, the motet *Quant vient en mai qu'erbe va verdoiant* (382) / *Ne sai que je die* (380) / *IOHANNE* (M29) contrasts a scene of amorous betrayal in the triplum—a weeping shepherdess reveals that Robin has abandoned her for another, and she vows to woo him back with gifts—with a diatribe in the motetus against the corruption of society, now governed by villainy, pride, felony, hypocrisy, and avarice. The tenor participates in the overall thematics, deriving from an alleluia commemorating a saint—John the Baptist—whose martyrdom was the direct result of moral degeneracy in the royal court. Without its triplum, as it appears in three manuscripts, the motet is a stern warning against the disastrous results of political and social decay.[15] The inclusion of the triplum does not change the moral tone, but it does add a lighthearted note: drawing on the pastourelle register, the triplum provides comic relief. Robin's treatment of his former lover may indeed exemplify the social vices lamented in the motetus, but it is also typical of shepherds' antics in the pastourelle. In effect, the pastoral world provides a stage on which the political and amorous woes of aristocratic society can be played out in less threatening form.

Adam de la Halle's motet *Aucun se sont loé d'amours* (834) / *A Dieu quemant amouretes* (835) / *SUPER TE* (Musical Example 2),[16] on the other hand, offers a more serious treatment of the same construct; it can be seen as the inverse of his motet *Entre Adan* / *Chief bien seantz* / *APTATUR*. Whereas that piece portrayed a world in harmony—the trouvère and his lady, and the trouvère and his community—this one presents the breakdown of the

Music and texts by Adam de la Halle

SUPER TE ORTA EST[1]

(continued on next page)

(translation and caption follow on bottom of facing page)

love relationship and the dissolution of the community. The motetus is a *motet enté*, constructed on the refrain

> A Dieu quemant amouretes
> Car je m'en vois
> Souspirant en terre estrange

I commend my little sweethearts to God, for I am going away, sighing, into a foreign land.

This refrain is also the basis for one of Adam's rondeaux, about the experience of departure and the singer's regrets for the lovely ladies.[17] But whereas refrain and rondeau alike treat only the sentiments of the lyric *je*, the motet shifts the focus to the singer's community: by means of the line "hors du douz païs d'Artois" (out of the sweet land of Artois [M, v. 4]), we pass from the departing subject to Arras itself, locus of departure. Indeed, we learn now that it is not merely the *je* who must leave Arras, but the very flower of Artesian society (M, v. 13). In the closing line, completion of the motetus and of the refrain with which it opened, *souspirant* no longer modifies exclusively the *je* of the opening lines, but the many who are leaving the now fragmented community.

Tr: Some have praised love, but I more than anyone should place blame, for at no time have I ever found loyalty there. At first I expected to win a sweetheart by behaving loyally, but I could be at that for a long time, for the better I loved, the more pain I had to endure. Never did she whom I loved deign to show me a sign in which I might take comfort nor hope for mercy. She made every effort to reject me, she gave me much to think of before I could forget her. Now I know without a doubt that a loyal man who wishes to love is lost, nor should anyone get involved in it, so I believe, except one who intends to act with deceit.

M: *I commend my little sweethearts to God, for I am going away,* grieving for the sweet little ones, out of the sweet land of Artois; which is changed and afflicted, because the bourgeois have been so hard pressed that there functions neither justice nor law. Great coins have blinded counts and kings, justices and prelates, so many times, that the flower of knighthood, mistreated by Arras, is leaving friends, homes, and belongings and fleeing, two here, three there, *sighing, into foreign lands.*

T: IS RISEN UPON THEE

Musical Example 2. From Hans Tischler, ed., *Motets of the Montpellier Codex.* Recent Researches in the Music of the Middle Ages and Early Renaissance, 2–8 (Madison: A-R Editions, Inc., 1978–85).

The details of this communal breakdown are not specified; Adam tells us simply that justice is no longer respected, and that

> Gros tournois
> ont avuglé contes et rois
> justices et prelas (M, vv. 10–12)

Great coins have blinded counts and kings, judges and prelates.

It is generally assumed that this statement alludes to the fiscal scandal of 1269, which entailed currency devaluation and the exile of a number of bourgeois from Arras.[18] This somber picture of political decay, responsible for the dissolution of Arras and thus for the speaker's separation from his *amouretes*, contrasts with the fanciful use of the language of feudal power in the rondeau, where the singer says that he would gladly make all ladies queens—using the more lyrical diminutive *roïnetes*—were he king (vv. 7–8). From the imagined kingship of the lyric *je*, around whose presence the lyric world of love coheres, we have moved to the real figures—count, king, prelate—around whom the political community coheres. In the rondeau, the displacement of this central figure, and the consequent collapse of his world, are suggested in a lighthearted fashion. In the motet, this displacement and dissolution have already taken place: the *je* is no longer the central focus of the lyric construct; the king no longer serves to unify the community. It is true that, as in *Entre Adan / Chief bien seantz / APTATUR*, the experience of the lyric persona is exemplary of the community at large. There, however, the experience was one of fascination, inspiration, joy. Here, it is one of alienation and departure, and so cannot serve as the basis for communal spirit.

If the *je* has been displaced from the motetus, he nonetheless assumes center stage in the triplum. Here the lyric protagonist's tale of despair in love is framed by general statements, placing his experience in a larger context of loss and betrayal and once again giving him exemplary status. In the opening lines, the singer distinguishes himself from those who have a favorable experience of love: "Aucun se sont loé d'amours, / mes je m'en doi plus que nus blasmer" (Some have praised love, but I more than anyone should place blame [Tr, vv. 1–2]). And after detailing his inability to win over his lady through loyal service, he generalizes his experience: "loiaus homs est perdus, qui veut amer" (a loyal man who wishes to love is lost [Tr, v. 17]). The triplum thus recasts the social crisis in the motetus as a crisis of love.

An association of lady and community—source of private and public alienation, respectively—is suggested by the double application of the word *douce* in the motetus: the singer laments his departure from the *doucetes* (M, v. 3) and the *douz païs d'Artois* (M, v. 4). Heightening this association is the juxtaposition of M, v. 4 and Tr, v. 6 in the musical setting: *païs d'Artois* is sung against *amie par loiaument* and represents the same progression of vowels. This stresses the dual nature of loss in the motet as a whole: loss of the lady, of loyalty to love; loss of the homeland, of loyalty to social ideals. The theme of loyalty betrayed ties the voices together. As the motet draws to a close, the statement that "loiaus homs est perdus, qui veut amer" (a loyal man who wishes to love is lost) not only reflects on the experience in the triplum but also comments on the lines immediately following in the motetus: "et fuient, ça deus, ça trois, / *souspirant en terre estrange*" (and they flee, two here, three there, *sighing, into foreign lands* [M, vv. 16–17]).

Finally, the simultaneous violation of social and amorous codes is expressed by the voices at the midpoint of the motet. The triplum reads "Ne m'i vot moustrer / samblant" (She did not deign to show me a [favorable] sign [Tr, vv. 10–11]), juxtaposed with "lois. Gros tournois" (law. Great coins [M, vv. 9–10]) in the motetus. The lady's semblance, once the source of inspiration and joy, no longer offers her lover any hope or comfort; laws that once ensured the coherence of society, and its currency, the medium of social exchange, have ceased to operate. Because of the distribution of rests in the musical setting, alternating between the two voices, the worthless currency—emblem of social and economic collapse—is embedded in the statement of amorous loss: Ne m'i vot moustrer / Gros tournois / samblant. The implied analogy between economic and amorous values is, indeed, one that Villon will exploit a century and a half later in his satirical comparison of a woman past her prime with "cried-down money."[19] This construct at the heart of the piece reflects the framing and juxtaposing of public and private contexts that govern the structure of the motet as a whole.

Suspension and Fulfillment of Desire

We have seen motets that treat successful and unsuccessful love; in some cases, the quality of the love relationship was central to the thematic unity of the piece. Not all motets, however, derive their unity from the representation of amorous joy or disappointment; some are constructed on the opposition of success and failure. Highlighting the tension between the fulfillment and the frustration of desire, for example, is the juxtaposition of two differing accounts of seduction in *L'autre jour par un matinet* (628) / *Hier matinet* (629) / *ITE MISSA EST* (M88a):

Tr	M
L'autre jour par un matinet	Hier matinet
m'en aloie esbanoiant	trouvai sans son bercheret
et trouvai sans son bercheret	pastoure esgaree.
pastoure plaisant	A li vois ou prajolet,
grant joie faisant.	si l'ai acolee.
Lés li m'assis mout liement,	Arriere se traist
s'amour li quis doucement.	et dist: "J'aim mieus Robinet,
Ele dist: "Aymi!	qui m'a plus amee."
Sire, j'ai ami	Lors l'embrachai;
bel et joli a mon talent:	ele dist: "Fui de moi!"
Robin, pour qui refuser	Mes onc pour ce ne laissai.
voell toute autre gent.	Quant l'oi rigotee,
Car je le voi et bel et gent	s'amour mi pramet
et set bien muser,	et dist: "Sire, biau vallet,
que tous jours l'amerai,	plus vous aim que Robinet."
ne ja ne m'en partirai."	
T: ITE MISSA EST [20]	

Tr: The other day in the morning I went out to enjoy myself and found a pleasing shepherdess without her shepherd, making merry. Happily I sat down beside her, sweetly I asked for her love. She said: "Oh no! Sir, I have a boyfriend who is handsome and merry and to my liking: Robin, for whom I mean to refuse all others. For I see how handsome and worthy he is, and he plays the bagpipes well, so I will always love him, nor will I leave him."

M: Yesterday morning I found a shepherdess wandering without her shepherd. I went to her in the meadow and embraced her. She pulled away and said: "I prefer little Robin, who loves me more." Then I kissed her; she said: "Get away from me!" But I didn't give up just for that. When I had sported with her, she promised me her love and said: "Sir, handsome gentleman, I like you better than little Robin."

T: GO, THE MASS IS [ended]

Triplum and motetus present a successful and an unsuccessful seduction. In effect, the motetus gives the more complete story. The triplum ends with the shepherdess's protestations of love for Robin, developed at some length (Tr, vv. 8–16). In the motetus, the declaration of love occupies a mere two lines: " 'J'aim mieus Robinet, / qui m'a plus amee' " ("I prefer little Robin, who loves me more" [M, vv. 7–8]). The male protagonist loses no time in pursuing his desires. After a terse " 'Fui de moi' " ("Get away from me" [M, v. 10]) from the shepherdess, he overpowers her, and her closing words indicate a complete change of heart.[21] If the two texts are seen as composite parts of the same story, the shepherdess's claims in the triplum that she loves Robin take on a comic air in view of her rapid capitulation in the motetus—provided, of course, that one accepts at face value the textual fantasy of her love for the knight who has overpowered her.

Another reading is also possible, however, one that privileges the triplum and tenor together against the motetus. The tenor is the formula for announcing that the Mass has ended and bidding the congregation to depart. Such a tenor is highly unusual. No other extant motet has this particular setting of the *Ite missa est*, although one motet does employ the phrase in a different musical setting: the bilingual *Cum venerint miseri degentes* (631) / *Se grasse n'est a mon maintien contraire* (630) / ITE MISSA EST (M88b), which appears in the Tournai Mass.[22] Here, both texted voices address the granting of mercy, charitable or erotic, to those who come seeking it. In the triplum the wealthy are instructed not to refuse beggars: having sought God's mercy in church, they should dispense charity to those supplicants who come to their own dwellings. And in the motetus a man complains that his lady turns him away without pity, ignoring his service. In its only two appearances as a tenor, then, *Ite missa est* is associated with the refusal and dismissal of a would-be lover: as the Mass is ended, so are his attempts at seduction. Moreover, the phrase also appears in the Old Provençal narrative poem *Flamenca*. There the protagonist utters it sorrowfully at the departure of his beloved, whose bath he has been watching through a peephole: the erotic "worship" comes to an end, and he must leave, his desires still unconsummated.[23]

In its various associations with vernacular love poetry, the phrase *Ite missa est* thus marks the obstruction of desire through the lady's refusal or her disappearance. As such it adds a humorous commentary to the uncertain narrative of *L'autre jour* / *Hier matinet* / ITE MISSA EST. As an echo of the shepherdess's attempted dismissal of the knight, the tenor suggests a definitive closure to the story that is consistent with the version presented in the triplum—despite his boasts, the knight is in fact sent away.[24] Again, the double vision in the motet represents two sides of the lyric paradigm: the fantasy of fulfilled desire plays out against the backdrop of frustration and rejection.

The above example belongs to a single register, the pastourelle. In other cases, however, the opposition of frustrated and fulfilled desire is expressed in the contrast between rustic and courtly love. To illustrate the ways this is developed, I offer two examples, one featuring a conflict between two male personae and the other turning on the relationship between the male persona and the lady he desires. In the first, a male persona expresses contradictory feelings about a shepherd who is evidently more successful in love. This particular motet exists in both three- and four-part versions, which I will discuss separately. Both versions have the same tenor and motetus; the triplum of the double motet is the quadruplum of the more expanded version, which itself has a different text as triplum. I begin with the double motet, *Par un matinet l'autrier* (658) / *Hé, bergiers! si grant envie* (657) / *EJUS* (O16):

Tr	M
Par un matinet l'autrier	Hé, bergiers! si grant envie
oï chanter un fol bergier,	j'ai de toi
s'en sui mout mus,	de ce que si bonne vie
qui se vantoit qu'il out geü tous nus	as envers moi,
entre les dous bras s'amie;	qu'onques loiautei ne foi
il se vantoit de folie,	trover n'i poi
car tes amours est vileinne;	la ou je l'ai deservie,
mais j'ains certes plus loiaument que	et toi, qui de rien servie
nus,	n'as amours, joïr t'an voi
car quant bele dame m'aimme,	et vanter t'oi
je ne demant plus.	*en l'aunoi: "Jui en l'aunoi*
	es bras m'amie."

T: EJUS[25]

Tr: The other day in the morning I heard a foolish shepherd singing—I was very upset by it—who boasted that he had lain entirely naked in the arms of his beloved. His boasting is folly, for such love is churlish; but I certainly love more loyally than anyone, *for when a beautiful lady loves me, I ask for nothing more.*

M: Hey, shepherd! I have such great envy of you, that you lead such a good life compared to me, I who can never find loyalty or faith there where I have deserved it; and you, who have not served love in any way, I see you take your pleasure and I hear you boast, *among the alders, "I lay in the alders in the arms of my beloved."*

T: HER

In the triplum, the lyric persona condemns the shepherd for boasting of his sexual exploits, stressing his coarseness and folly. The protagonist contrasts the shepherd's behavior with his own—he is capable of steadfastness and of accepting his lady's love without needing physical gratification. In the motetus, however, the lyric persona seems to have less faith in his lofty ideals, and he recognizes a certain advantage to the pastoral life. Although the lyric persona is contemptuous of the carefree shepherd, one can now see that the shepherd represents the actualization of the courtly lover's fantasies: if only he were not bound by the code of courtesy, he, too, would be able to display his sexual prowess. The courtly protagonist's only consolation, given his lady's disinterest, is to concentrate on his own social superiority, measured by his virtues of discretion and refinement. From the contrast between the two players, differently expressed in the two texted voices, there emerges a double message of class envy and class pride. And ultimately, the motet presents the conflict between two ideas of what it means to be a successful lover: adherence to courtly ideals, or sexual conquest.

The motet is transmitted in three parts in two sources, but in an additional two versions, there is a fourth part, *Hé sire, que voz vantés* (659), inserted between the two upper voices as a new triplum.[26] Without significantly altering the dynamics of the piece, the third texted voice expands the debate by allowing the shepherd to reply:

> Hé sire, que voz vantés,
> que vous avez
> deservie
> cortoisie et loiautez.
> Tel folie
> ne dites mie,
> qu'en vostre amie
> tel vilanie
> aiés trové;
> car reprové
> m'avés fausement,
> qu'onques amor nul jor
> ne servi loialment:
> *N'onques nul ne les senti,*
> *les maus d'amors,*
> *si com je sent.*

Hey, sir, you boast that you have deserved courtesy and loyalty. Don't speak such folly, saying that you found such baseness in your beloved. And you have reproved me falsely, saying that I never served love loyally: *No one has ever felt the pains of love as I do.*

The shepherd attempts to turn the tables on his adversary, who in *Par un matinet l'autrier*—now the quadruplum—accuses him of folly in boasting about his sexual conquest. In the triplum that figures in the four-part version, the shepherd asserts that aristocratic claims to refined love service constitute foolhardy boasting. The shepherd also refutes the claim, made in the motetus, that he had never served love (M, vv. 8–9), insisting on the force of his desire as proof. The inclusion of this text in the motet contributes to the ironic contrast between two amorous codes by filling in the shepherd's perspective: if active sexuality is the mark of a successful lover, then the knight's claims to have served love without actually realizing his desires are empty words and, indeed, admissions of failure.

The second example, *Encontre le tans* (496) / *Quant fuellent aubespin* (497) / *IN ODOREM* (M45), suggests a solution to this dilemma by allowing the lyric persona to participate in both worlds.[27] In the triplum, the persona describes the beauty of the woman he loves and laments that he has not as yet been successful. The text is a long conventional statement of courtly longing: the protagonist has given himself completely to the lady, he is hers forever, he will die if she continues to reject him. In the motetus, the protagonist describes his encounter with a shepherdess who attempts to run from him. Through force and persuasion, he has his way with her. Nothing specifically connects the male personae of the motetus and the triplum, but the texts can be seen as representing the two sides of a single poetic construct. The pastoral world is a place where the pining lover can satisfy his desires, for the code that he follows does not require him to accept at face value the refusal of a shepherdess. At the same time, his restraint with regard to the lady in the triplum and his steadfastness in the face of unrequited desire establish his credentials as a courtly lover. This function of the pastoral world—a means of fulfilling desires that are blocked in the courtly world—is explicit in some pastourelles that begin with the protagonist's statement that he went out riding to escape the pains of unrequited love, and proceed to his seduction or rape of a shepherdess. The motet accomplishes this same effect through juxtaposition of the different texts, allowing the delicious pain of unrequited courtly longing to form the backdrop against which the encounter with the shepherdess takes place.

On one level, our examples entertained medieval audiences as variations on the great lyric theme of love. A more careful reading, however, allows us to see the implied critique of the courtly lover.[28] In *L'autre jour* / *Hier matinet* / *ITE MISSA EST*, the implications of the knight's definitive rejection deflate the boasting tone of the motetus. In this light, one is tempted to believe that despite his rusticity, Robin probably does love the shepherdess sincerely—whereas the knight's fancy is momentary. Similarly, the protagonist's undignified behavior in the motetus *Quant fuellent aubespin* belies the grandiose lament in the triplum: this hardly seems a man likely to die of unrequited love, even though there are repeated allusions to his impending "death" (Tr, vv. 17–18, 41–42, 44–45). The shepherdess, though of a different social class, apparently shares the sentiments ascribed to the hard-hearted lady in the triplum: "ce que li dis, mout petit prise" (she little valued what I said to her [M, vv. 26–27]). In effect, the conquest fantasy in the motetus thinly veils the protagonist's desired course of action against the lady if she continues to resist him. One is reminded of the lyric persona's dilemma in the debate motet *Par un matinet / Hé, bergiers! si grant envie / EJUS.* Although he attempts to maintain a self-righteous and contemptuous disregard for the shepherd's casual sexuality, he cannot hide his wish for such freedom. It is precisely this conflict of social code and irrepressible desire that is portrayed in *Encontre le tans / Quant fuellent aubespin / IN ODOREM.* Here the courtly lover, beyond merely fantasizing about rustic sexual freedom, forthrightly takes advantage of what he perceives as a world untrammeled by the restricting codes of courtesy. Such behavior, posited as the underside of courtly adoration, imparts an ironic tone to the lover's hyperbolic protestations.

Sacred and Secular Love

In addition to the juxtaposition of different kinds of secular lyric, motets can also bring together sacred and secular texts. Devotional texts are the exception in the vernacular motet corpus, but there are motets—some of them bilingual—that combine a declaration of love with a devotional text, usually one in praise of the Virgin.[29] As is well known, there is considerable overlap between the language of Marian adoration and that of the courtly love lyric; it is not surprising that motet composers explored the levels of meaning inherent in this language by using it for two different purposes within the same piece. As we will see in many examples discussed below, it is not always easy to distinguish an explicit celebration of the Virgin, a love poem that can be read allegorically as referring to the Virgin or Ecclesia, and a poem of erotic desire. It is this very ambiguity that motet composers use. Although some motets combining sacred and secular texts are entirely in French, most bilingual motets also fall into this category, since most Latin motet texts are spiritual or moralizing in nature. Indeed, the widespread phenomenon of contrafacta, as well as the inherently additive nature of the motet, can result in motet families where assorted texts and contrafacta in French and Latin, some spiritual and some secular, exist in two-, three-, and four-part combinations that include French, Latin, and bilingual versions. In such families one can see the different ways that a given musical composition might be texted so as to serve in sacred celebration or secular festivity, appealing to a range of intellectual and aesthetic values.

A simple example of a motet that exists as a two-part devotional composition and as a three-part mixed version is *Aucuns vont souvent* (613) / *Amor, qui cor vulnerat* (614) / *KYRIE ELEYSON* (M86d). It is a three-part motet in two manuscripts, and a two-part motet—lacking the vernacular triplum—in two others.[30] The Latin motetus condemns erotic love:

> Amor, qui cor vulnerat
> humanum, quem generat
> carnalis affectio,
> numquam sine vicio
> vel raro potest esse,
> quoniam est necesse,
> ut quo plus diligitur
> res, que cito labitur
> et transit, eominus
> diligatur Dominus.

Love, which wounds the human heart, generated by carnal lust, can never or rarely be without sin, for it must needs be that the more a thing is loved that quickly decays and passes, the less will the Lord be loved.

The liturgical supplication for divine mercy in the tenor stresses again the importance of placing one's faith in God, as well as underscoring the need for divine assistance in doing so.

The vernacular triplum, however, is a defense of worldly love against those who, "par leur envie" (out of envy [Tr, v. 2]), deride it. True love for one's *amie* is the source of all courtesy, honor, and social comportment. The loyal lover is a veritable paragon of virtue:

> que ja en li n'iert assise vilanie
> ne couvoitise d'amasser d'argent.
>   . . .
> Et si n'a en li felonnie
> n'envie sus autre gent,

mes a chascun s'umelie
et parole courtoisement. (Tr, vv. 10–11, 14–17)

for never in him will there be found baseness or the desire to hoard money. . . .
And thus there is no wickedness in him, nor envy of others; rather, he is humble
before all and speaks courteously.

The inclusion of this text transforms a didactic motet into something
more complex. The praise of worldly love in the triplum might illustrate
the blindness condemned in the motetus: the deluded lover, fancying
himself morally improved by that which dooms him, can only hope to be
saved by the divine mercy sought in the tenor. Conversely, the triplum
might be a refutation of the stern moral tone in the motetus: those who
condemn love speak only from envy and are unable to appreciate its value.
In this secularized reading, the tenor's request for mercy might even be
directed against preachers who give lovers a difficult time. Choosing one
text as dominant in the motet thus entails an ironic reading of the other.
In its three-part format, the motet presents a debate about the nature
of love, which recalls the thirteenth century's greatest vernacular poem,
the *Roman de la Rose*. There, too, arbitration of the various characters'
conflicting views is left to the reader.

This motet also allows a third reading, in which the texts are parallel
condemnations of sinful or deceitful love. The motetus does leave open
some possibility for an acceptable form of carnal love, in the qualifying
words, "numquam sine vicio / *vel raro* potest esse" (can never *or rarely*
be without sin [M, vv. 4–5; emphasis added]). The triplum consistently
qualifies the love that it defends — *loiaument* (loyally [Tr, v. 4]), *sans bois-
die* (without deceit [v. 8]), and *vraiement* (truly [v. 9]). And in closing
it alludes to false lovers who fail to measure up to the code of honor:
"et sachiés, qu'il n'aime mie, / ains ment, s'il se demaine autrement" (and
know that he does not love, but lies, if he behaves otherwise [Tr, vv.
20–21]). One could thus see the motet as a two-sided critique of false,
self-interested love: the triplum condemns such sentiments because they
do not conform to the code of courtly values, and the motetus shows
their conflict with spiritual obligations. False love disrupts the social community and alienates the soul from God. True love finds expression both
in the love of God and — as the motetus barely acknowledges, but the
triplum develops at length — in an honorable human love. Such a con-
tinuum is hardly foreign to medieval belief, according to which divine
love was the basis of friendship and of conjugal love. In this reading, the
tenor's plea for divine mercy and assistance applies equally to both texts,

for they address the necessity of moral conversion and adherence to love in its true, salvific form.

The combination of secular texts with Marian or hagiographic texts creates similar effects of ironic or parodic opposition as well as allegorical correspondence. I illustrate this phenomenon with a single example, the motet *De la virge Katerine chantera* (536) / *Quant froidure trait a fin* (535) / *Agmina milicie celestis* (532) / *AGMINA* (M65).[31] The tenor is from an alleluia used for the feast of Saint Catherine, and the piece derives from the three-part conductus motet *Agmina milicie celestis* (532) / *AGMINA* (M65) in honor of Saint Catherine and attributed to Chancellor Philip of Paris (d. 1236). It is in this form that it appears in most manuscripts. A vernacular, secular version of the conductus, in which the only texted voice is the triplum *Quant froidure trait a fin* (535), has also survived. The Bamberg manuscript contains a Latin double motet with a newly composed triplum also in honor of Saint Catherine: *Agmina militie cadentia* (533) / *Agmina milicie celestis* (532) / *AGMINA* (M65). The two conductus motets and the Latin double motet are internally consistent: two are constructed entirely of Latin devotional texts, and one features a single text, in French, that treats erotic love.

The bilingual version of the motet appears only in the La Clayette manuscript, which is the sole manuscript source for bilingual four-part compositions. Here, two texts devoted to Saint Catherine, one in Latin and one in French, frame the vernacular triplum with its celebration of amorous desire. The explicit eroticization of the female body situates the triplum clearly in the secular realm: the male protagonist praises the beautiful face and breasts of the lady he loves, and he claims to be in danger of dying from the force of his desire. In fact, he attributes his predicament to the effects of the potion "dont Tristrans morut ja" (which killed Tristan [Tr, v. 30]). This might be a parody of the Eucharistic wine: a drink that leads to fatal passion rather than spiritual renewal. In any case the love celebrated in the triplum has little in common with *caritas*, nor is *cele por qui je chant* (she for whom I sing [Tr, v. 9]) likely to lead her admirer to nobler forms of love. The motet revolves around the juxtaposition of two very different kinds of love for two very different maidens. The triplum's closing statement of dependence on the lady—"Je ne sai combien vivrai / Fors tant sanz plus com li plera" (I know not how much longer I will live unless it pleases her to let me [vv. 31–32])—parodies the closing reference in the motetus to Catherine as intercessor: "Oleum hec gracie / Dat et precum suffragia" (she grants the soothing balm of grace and the privilege of her intercession [vv. 31–32]).

Depending on one's perspective and the context in which it was performed, such a motet might be a moralizing piece, in which the frivolity of carnal passion is condemned through its juxtaposition with the adoration of a saintly maiden; or it might be a humorous piece, in which the lyric topos of expressing in song one's love for a beautiful, noble maiden is developed in two directions at once, dramatizing the bivalence of amorous discourse. The quadruplum—one of only two surviving vernacular motet texts with hagiographic themes[32]—comments on its protagonist's pious faith with a refrain, "A mon cuer le demandez, ne mie a moi" (ask it of my heart, not of me [v. 22]), that is equally at home in secular love poetry. The appropriation of secular terminology for devotional purposes is apparent in the account of Chancellor Philip's composition of the conductus *Agmina milicie / AGMINA*, origin of this motet: the narrator asks Saint Catherine to remember Philip, "Car molt te tenoit a s'amie" (For he strongly clung to you as his friend/sweetheart).[33] Although the word *amie* does simply mean "friend," in courtly lyric and romance it is the standard term for the beloved lady for whom the knight performs his exploits or of whom the trouvère sings. Just as the knight or trouvère expects some reward for his love, so Catherine is expected to reward Philip's devotion by remembering him in her prayers of intercession.

It is likely that *Agmina milicie* is itself a contrafactum of the secular lyric text *L'altrier cuidai aber druda* (537), a strophic song using the same melody.[34] In this poem, a version of the story recounted in the pseudo-Ovidian *De vetula*, the lyric persona declares that he has lost all interest in love, since the trauma of finding himself in bed with a hideous old woman instead of the beautiful maiden he expected. Poetic language itself is degraded by the grotesque old woman: the conventional description of enticing physical features becomes a catalog of horrors, and expressions of eternal love are replaced by curses and declarations of undying hatred. The secular model for Philip's hagiographic motetus thus describes how the substitution of one female body for another changes erotic desire into revulsion. This degeneration is reversed in Philip's pious contrafactum, in which religious adoration replaces the erotic encounter. Instead of blocking erotic desire through physical loathing, the male subject can sublimate his desire into a spiritual love. Where the old woman represents a grotesque perversion of sexuality, Catherine transcends sexuality entirely: virginal of body, pure of spirit, she dwells now in the presence of the Heavenly Bridegroom.

The bilingual motet, with its two additional texts by two different poets, more explicitly demonstrates the possibilities for movement between erotic and spiritual love. The Latin devotional language of the motetus is vernacularized in the two upper voices; the triplum transposes it into the erotic register; and in the quadruplum this eroticized vernacular language of love is reappropriated for devotional purposes. The motet plays with the ambiguities of poetic language and its power to establish semantic fields wherein words, phrases, and entire sentiments—it is my heart that guides me; my life depends on the good graces of the lady I adore—can be invested with different meanings and given completely different moral valences.

The Profusion of Voices

In this final section, we will examine two motets that exploit a polyphonic structure in a unique manner. In each example, the three texted voices have identical beginnings, diverging into separate texts only partway into the piece. Although in each piece the three upper voices have different musical settings, the passage from textual unison to textual polyphony would nonetheless stand out in performance. The result is to stress both the opening word or words—whose simultaneous enunciation by all three voices gives them a clarity rarely encountered in four-part motets—as well as the phenomenon of polytextuality, which is striking in its contrast to the monotextuality of the opening section. In the first example, *Viderunt. Por peu ne sui* (7) / *Viderunt. Por peu li cuers* (6) / *Viderunt. Par pou le cuer* (5b) / VIDERUNT OMNES (M1), the word shared by the three texted voices appears in the tenor as well, and repeated words and phrases also link the upper voices:

> Q: *Viderunt.*
>   Por peu ne sui departis
>   de cele, dont n'avrai congié.
> Tr: *Viderunt.*
>   Por peu li cuers ne me parti,
>   qu'ele me dit douner congié.
> M: *Viderunt.*
>   *Par pou le cuer ne me parti,*
>   *quant a la bele pris congié.*
> T: VIDERUNT OMNES[35]

Q: *They saw.* I nearly parted from her, from whom I will never take leave.
Tr: *They saw.* My heart nearly parted from me, for she bid me leave.
M: *They saw. My heart nearly parted from me when I took leave of the fair one.*
T: THEY ALL SAW

This peculiar motet, unique in its incorporation of the tenor incipit into all three upper voices, presents a dense verbal texture. The first line of the triplum is the same as that of the motetus; the first line of the quadruplum ends in the same two syllables as in the other two voices; and all three voices close on the same word. These parallels are maintained in the musical setting, facilitating comprehension of the key words and phrases. The Latin tenor derives from a Christmas gradual announcing the birth of Christ as an event revealed to all humanity: "they all saw" God's appearance on earth. In the motet, however, this experience of universal witness is both secularized and trivialized—what everyone saw is nothing more spectacular than the lover's histrionic departure from his lady—to create a lighthearted, humorous little piece. The movement between mono- and polytextuality is central to the artistry of this motet. The moments of unison, contrasting with those of divergence, help to stress its thematics of amorous leave-taking and of the indiscretion that allowed all to see the lovers' farewell. In addition, the quotation of the tenor in the upper voices suggests a link between the motet texts and the gradual that is the tenor's source. The universal joy at the arrival of Christ is thus contrasted with the personal sorrow of the singer departing from his lady—itself quite possibly the occasion for a universal amusement rather different in nature from the rejoicing inspired by the Incarnation.[36] The effect, again, is one of humor, a gentle mocking of the lover who takes his emotions a little too seriously.

A more interesting exploitation of polytextuality appears in the motet *Trois serors sor rive mer . . . La jonete* (343a) / *Trois serors sor rive mer . . . La moiene* (343b) / *Trois serors sor rive mer . . . L'aisnee* (343c) / PERLUSTRA-VIT (M25):

> Q: Trois serors sor rive mer
> chantent cler.
> La jonete
> fu brunete,
> de brun ami s'ahati:
> "Je sui brune, s'avrai brun ami."
> Tr: Trois serors sor rive mer
> chantent cler.
> La moiene a apelé
> Robin, son ami:
> "Prise m'avés el bois ramé,
> reportés m'i!"
> M: Trois serors sor rive mer

chantent cler.
L'aisnee dist a:
"On doit bien bele dame amer,
et s'amour garder,
cil qui l'a."
T: PERLUSTRAVIT[37]

Q: Three sisters at the seashore are singing brightly. The youngest was a brunette, she hoped for a brown-haired lover: "I am brown-haired, so I will
have a brown-haired lover."

Tr: Three sisters at the seashore are singing brightly. The middle one called
Robin, her lover: "You captured me in the leafy wood, now take me
back there!"

M: Three sisters at the seashore are singing brightly. The oldest said: "One
should certainly love a fair lady, and he who has her love should keep it."

T: HAS FILLED/HALLOWED

In certain anthologies this motet has been treated as a strophic composition, leading to confusion about its structure that has hampered critical
analysis. David Kuhn, for example, has insightfully described the songs
of the three sisters as corresponding to three stages of engagement with
love. The youngest, not yet involved, sings of her hopes for a lover; the
middle one bridges past and future by recalling her sexual initiation while
anticipating future encounters; and the oldest draws on her presumably
greater experience to offer a bit of wisdom about the etiquette of love.[38]
Kuhn's analysis is flawed, however, by his mistaken impression that the
opening lines of each voice— "Trois serors sor rive mer / chantent cler"—
are a refrain recurring at the beginning of each strophe. Since the three
"strophes" are in fact sung simultaneously, the words in question are not
a recurring refrain but a common text, occurring at the beginning of the
piece and sung in parallel musical settings, that ties the three upper voices
together. Only with the third line do the voices diverge, giving the love
songs of the three sisters.

The overall structure of the motet creates a dramatic effect—the three
characters are first identified and placed in a landscape, then allowed to
break into their respective songs. But a full appreciation of the piece is
only possible with a consideration of its tenor, which derives from the
first alleluia of the Mass for Pentecost: "Alleluia. Spiritus sanctus procedens a throno apostolorum pectora invisibile hodie perlustravit potentia"
(Alleluia. The Holy Spirit proceeding from the throne has today filled
and hallowed the hearts of the apostles with invisible power [M25]). The

motet, in fact, is an amusing and lighthearted transposition of the Pente-costal scene into the language and imagery of vernacular lyric. The group of girls awaiting their respective lovers parodies the group of disciples awaiting the return of their "Bridegroom," and the songs the girls sing mimic the outpouring of speech at the descent of the Spirit. The structure of the piece, passing from unison to the divergence of voices, recreates the effect of the linguistic diversity of Pentecost, where the disciples' single language gave way to a mixture of languages. And this compositional technique, as I have said, is so unusual that anyone familiar with the corpus of vernacular motets could not fail to be struck by its novel sound. A recognition that the tenor refers precisely to the effects of the Holy Spirit on the gathered apostles is all that is needed for the humor and the artistry of the piece to become clear.

Chapter 2

Earthly and Heavenly Revelry

The Sacred and the Profane in Vernacular Lyric

Legimus quod de omni verbo occioso reddituri sumus Deo rationem
in die iudicii. Et ideo debemus errantes corrigere, errores reprimere,
prava in bonum exponere, vanitatem ad veritatem reducere. Ergo
videamus que sit Bele Aalis.

We read that we will be obliged to give account to God of all idle
words in the Day of Judgment. Therefore we must correct those
in error, curb transgressions, expound lewd things into good,
and lead vanity back to truth. Therefore, let us see about Fair Aelis.

— "Fair Aelis" sermon

The relationship between sacred and profane discourse in medieval writings is complex. Most obviously, profane elements figure in sacred texts as negative examples, illustrating temptation and sin in a fallen world. But textual citations or imagery from secular literature may also be appropriated by a devotional text and invested with new significance, either through allegorical glossing or through citation in a context that imposes moral or spiritual meaning. The latter technique is illustrated in pious *contrafacta* of secular lyrics, some of which retain significant portions of the original text, and in the use of secular songs and refrains in devotional texts. Conversely, citations of sacred text are sometimes incorporated into secular compositions, where they may acquire an unexpected and often humorous new meaning.

In this chapter, I outline a context for examining the allegorical and parodic features of the motet. This is not an exhaustive survey of allegory and parody in medieval literature; I focus on specific forms of vernacular lyric, such as the rondeau, the refrain, the pastourelle, and the *chanson pieuse*, with attention to the use of amorous discourse in both erotic and devotional contexts. The detailed analysis of individual motets and a

closer consideration of how they are to be read are set forth in the following three chapters. It is my intent here to present several possible lines of
approach and to define what is important in the reading of the vernacular
or bilingual motet.

Allegory and Parody: Juggling the Codes

Let us begin our examination of the moral and spiritual dimension of
vernacular lyric with a consideration of medieval readings of Bele Aelis,
a stock figure of the rondeau. Beautiful, amorous, and inclined to song,
Fair Aelis appears in numerous pieces; her behavior generally involves
rising early, getting dressed up in her finery, and going outside to gather
flowers or meet her lover.[1] Several songs featuring Fair Aelis are among
those sung by the flirtatious courtiers of Jean Renart's *Roman de la Rose*,
of which the following is typical:

> Main se leva bele Aeliz,
> Mignotement la voi venir,
> Bien se para, miex se vesti,
> En mai.
> Dormez, jalous, et ge m'envoiserai. (ed. Lecoy, vv. 318–22)

Fair Aelis rose early, I see her come gaily, she was well groomed, better dressed,
in May. Sleep, jealous one, and I will have fun.

In Renart's romance, the songs of Fair Aelis, along with those involving
other stock figures such as Robin and Marion, Bele Aie, and Bele Doe,
are sung not by professional minstrels but by the members of the court;
they provide both entertainment and the occasion for flirtatious interaction between knights and ladies. The untroubled expressions of love,
desire, and joy in the rondeaux contrast with the more rarefied yearning of the courtly chansons sung by the emperor and his minstrel; but
there is no hint of devotional overtones in any of these songs. Indeed,
in describing the festivities at the imperial court, the narrator comments
coyly: "Il ne pensent pas a lor ames" (They aren't thinking of their souls
[v. 224]).

A completely different way of combining the "Fair Aelis" material
with an expanded discourse on love appears in a song by Baude de la
Kakerie, each stanza of which opens with a line evidently deriving from
some anterior rondeau or *chanson de toile*.[2] These lines are as follows:

> Main se leva la bien faite Aelis
> . . .

Bel se para et plus bel se vesti

. . .

Si prist de l'aigue en un dore bacin

. . .

Lava sa bouche et ses oex et son vis

. . .

Si s'en entra la bele en un gardin (vv. 1, 15, 27, 43, 59)

Fair Aelis rose early. . . . She was well groomed and more beautifully dressed. . . . She took water from a gilded basin . . . washed her mouth and her eyes and her face. . . . Then the fair one went into a garden.

The remainder of each stanza consists of elaborate declarations of love and praise of the virtues of loving, frequently citing the authority of the nightingale. There is no suggestion of spiritual allegory here either, with the possible exception of this curious development in the fourth stanza:

buer fu cil nes ki est loiaus amis:
li rousegnols l'en pramet paradis.
de ce sui lies et joians

. . .

vos ki d'amors vives,
paradis vos atent;
se diu plaist, jou i serai mis,
car jamais plus loiaus amis
ne vivra.
cascuns dit c'amours l'ocist,
mais je sui ki garira. (vv. 44–46, 52–58)

Fortunate is the one who is a loyal lover: the nightingale promises him paradise. I am happy and joyful about that. . . . You who live on love, paradise awaits you; God willing, I will be placed there, for no more loyal lover will ever live. Everyone says that love is killing him, but I'm the type who will persevere.

The nightingale's promise of Heaven to those who love is an interesting forerunner of Genius's promise in Jean de Meun's continuation of the *Roman de la Rose*; and surely the nightingale's promise is also ironic, a parody of the theme of love in devotional literature. It is true that the Song of Songs provides a precedent—amply exploited, moreover, in countless medieval poems, sermons, and other writings—for the spiritual interpretation of erotic desire. The biblical poem includes the motifs of the maiden rising from her bed, the pains of love, the garden, and the finery the beloved wears. These motifs were all subject to repeated and prolonged allegorization by medieval exegetes. And the nightingale, which supposedly sings ecstatically as it dies, consumed by love, was itself allegorized as a figure for Christ or for the soul overcome with longing for Christ and grief at his Passion.[3] But the context of Baude's poem — a tissue of popular refrains and standard formulations concerning the pains and joys of love, elaborated as background for the narrative of Fair Aelis — strongly points to earthly rather than spiritual love. Although the possibility for allegorical exegesis is never entirely absent, a spiritual reading of this poem would be virtually a parodic act in and of itself — at best, an intellectual game. The nightingale's extravagant promise invites meditation on the various possible readings, *in bono* or *in malo*, that the lyric *matière* might allow, but does not turn the poem into religious allegory.

Nonetheless, figurative readings of popular lyric were not impossible in the thirteenth century; though few, examples do survive of both the moral or tropological and the allegorical exposition of such texts. *Moralités seur ces .vi. vers* addresses the following lines:

> C'est la jus c'on dit es pres,
> Jeu et bal i sont criés.
> Emmelos i veut aler,
> A sa mere en aquiert grés.
> —Par dieu, fille, vous n'irés,
> Trop y a de bachelers au bal.[4]

It is down there in the meadows, games and dancing are announced. Emmelot wants to go, she asks permission from her mother. —By God, daughter, you'll not go, there are too many young men at the dance.

In the exposition, the meadows are the world; its flowers soon wilt and fade, as do worldly wealth, beauty, and power. The dances are worldly vanities; the bachelors who frequent them are the vices of pride, vainglory, gluttony, lust, greed, wrath, and hatred. Emmelot, drawn to worldly temptations, is the flesh; the mother who strives to protect her is the soul. Thus the moralizer makes a simple dance song into a lesson on the sins of the flesh, the ephemeral nature of worldly pleasure, and the need for eternal spiritual vigilance.

Allegorical exposition of the vernacular rondeau can be found in a different genre, the sermon. Medieval preachers, whether in an effort to make Church dogma accessible to those not versed in theology or as a literary exercise, occasionally drew on vernacular literature; and the various uses of this material reflect its lack of fixed meaning or universally understood allegorical significance. The vernacular secular text was available for appropriation according to the whim of the individual sermonizer. For the thirteenth-century Dominican Jacques de Vitry, for example, Fair Aelis is clearly a figure of worldly desire and frivolity: "Hujusmodi autem mulieres quando ad publicum exire vel etiam ire debent, magnam diei partem in apparatu suo consummunt. *Quant Aeliz fu levee*, et *quant ele fu lavee*, et *la messe fu chantee*, et *deable l'en ont emportee*"[5] (And in this way women, when they have to go out in public or elsewhere, spend a great part of the day preening themselves. *When Aelis had gotten up*, and *when she had washed*, and *the mass had been sung*, and *devils carried her away*). This view of Aelis corresponds to the comment made by Jean Renart's narrator: singing about her is not conducive to thinking of one's soul. The sermon, of course, uses Aelis to appeal to the congregation's everyday concerns; its overall purpose is moral instruction. Renart's romance, in contrast, is a secular tale in which the scenes of courtly flirtation, though they illustrate a certain frivolity on the part of the young and unmarried emperor, are certainly not employed in a context of stern moral reprimand. Both texts, however, imply a reading of Fair Aelis that is devoid of spiritual allegory.

In another sermon, also in Latin, we find a different treatment of Fair Aelis: one that outlines an allegorical reading such as hinted at, albeit humorously, in Baude de la Kakerie's song. The sermon in question is an exposition of the following verses:

> Belle Aalliz mainz s'en leva,
> Vesti son cors et para.
> En un vergier s'en entra,
> Cinc floreste i trova,
> Un chapelet fet en a,
> De rose florie.
> Por Dé, trahet vos en la,
> Qui n'amez mie.[6]

One would normally understand "Belle Aalliz" as the subject of the first six verbs, resulting in the translation: "Fair Aelis rose in the morning, got dressed and put on her finery. She went into an orchard, found five little flowers there, made a wreath from them, of blooming roses. For God's sake, move aside, you who do not love." The gloss elaborated in the sermon, however, sees Fair Aelis as the subject of the first three verbs. She is the *Sponsa* in the Song of Songs, identified with the Blessed Virgin: beautiful, sanctified even before "rising" at her birth, adorned for the Bridegroom. The subject of the next three verbs is the Holy Spirit, who entered the *virgultum* (orchard)—that is, the Blessed Virgin—when she conceived the Son of God. The Holy Spirit found five virtues—hope, faith, charity, humility, and virginity—and made from these the crown with which she became "queen of queens." The final sentence refers to heretics, Jews, Saracens, and hypocritical Christians, whose insufficient or misdirected love causes their banishment from the presence of God.

The allegorical reading is possible for the same reason the ironic one is—namely, the shared iconography of the sacred and the profane: the beautiful maiden dressed up to meet her lover; the existence of a code of love, adherence to which defines a social or spiritual elite; the enclosed garden and the carefully chosen flowers. If interpreted literally, Fair Aelis's behavior illustrates the sins of the flesh and the preoccupations of the world; allegorically, it becomes an illustration of spiritual conversion and sacred mysteries. One might well argue, of course, that the allegorical reading necessitates a certain violence to the poem's syntax: the introduction of a new subject for the verbs of vv. 3–5 hardly seems justified by anything in the text. The sermon is an example of what Rosemond Tuve has termed "imposed allegory."[7] Imposed or not, however, it is a thirteenth-century reading and demonstrates that the process of exegesis at times became a literary game from which no text was exempt. It was not entirely foreign to thirteenth-century intellectuals to seek out or provide the spiritual *surplus de sens* in a vernacular dance song. Indeed, such readings must have amused those trained in the arts of rhetoric and exegesis. As Michel Zink has pointed out in his analysis of the "Belle Aalliz" sermon, the fact that the text is in Latin indicates that it is not intended for the laity, but that it is a sort of clerical game—a joke for the educated preacher who exists at the crossroads of two languages and two cultures.[8]

Another example illustrates the extent to which the allegorical impulse could operate in the reading of the simplest and most conventional lyrics. In one manuscript, the "Belle Aalliz" sermon is followed by a second sermon, also in Latin, that explicates a vernacular lyric:

> Sur la rive de la mer
> Fontenelle i sordoit cler,
> La pucele i veaut aler;
> Violete ai trovee;
> Je doig bien conjei d'amer,
> Dame maul marié.[9]

On the bank of the sea a fountain flows clear; the maiden wishes to go there; I found a violet; I give leave to love, unhappily married woman.

The explication draws on standard Christological and Marian topoi. The bank of the sea is Mary, as an ingenious series of analogies explains: the shore is battered by the waves just as Mary is assailed by heretics and Jews; the sight of shore fills sailors with joy just as the Virgin brings joy to the hearts of sinners adrift on the seas of life; and so on. The fountain that flows on this shore must then be Christ, born of the Virgin and frequently represented with fountain imagery. And the maiden who wishes to approach the fountain and finds there a violet is none other than Mary Magdalene, who encountered Christ on Easter morning and for whom he was like a violet found in early spring or used for brewing tea: a harbinger of better days and an agent of healing. Magdalene is also the "dame maul marié," insofar as her soul is corrupted by the flesh to which it is wed; her salvation is the love of Christ.

It must be admitted that we are again in the presence of Tuve's "imposed allegory." None of these simple and highly conventional vernacular lyrics would be mistaken for a *chanson pieuse* if we encountered it in a more typical context—a collection of rondeaux, for example, or as a lyric insertion in a tale of courtly festivities such as Renart's *Roman de la Rose* or Jacques Bretel's *Tournois de Chauvency*. And it would be wrong to conclude on the basis of a moralizing poem and a couple of sermons that the medieval audience ordinarily gave much thought to the figurative meanings of rondeaux: such songs were for dance and entertainment. Yet through a playful application of exegesis they can become not only moral lessons but allegories for the Blessed Virgin, the Incarnation, or the encounter of Christ and the Magdalene. As will be seen below, the possibility of a moral or allegorical reading of rondeaux and pastourelles often colors the use of such material in motets. Like the vernacular or bilingual sermon, the vernacular motet is rooted in two different linguistic and cultural traditions, allowing for fruitful and sometimes surprising interactions.

The transposition of vernacular lyric into the spiritual register is somewhat different in the pious contrafacta of secular songs, many of which require few changes to transform the grief, desire, or pleasure associated with worldly love into that occasioned by the contemplation of the Passion, the adoration of Christ or the Virgin, and the bliss of spiritual union with God. The contrafactum differs from the allegorical exegesis of a song, because it acknowledges that only after changes can the song be understood as having a spiritual message. The contrafactum incorporates into the song itself the framework necessary to determine the pious significance of the poetic language. In one *chanson pieuse*, for example, the Bele Aelis material is reworked so that the spiritual nature of the love is explicit:

> La beguine main s'est levee,
> De vesture bien paree,
> Au moustier s'en est alee,
> Jhesu Crist va regretant.
> Ave Maria j'aim tant![10]

The beguine rose in the morning, all dressed up; she went to church, lamenting for Jesus Christ. Hail Mary, how I love!

In this stanza, a tropological reading of Bele Aelis transfers her amorous sentiments to the love of God, and her entry into the garden becomes the act of attending Mass. Rather than relying on the interpretive powers of reader or listener to make these associations, however, the author of the contrafactum makes them for us, replacing the key terms in the song with their counterparts in the devotional register.

The nature of the contrafactum process is illustrated quite clearly in a well-known song by Gautier de Coinci, which begins:

> Hui matin a l'ajornee
> Toute m'enbleüre
> Chevauchai par une pree.
> Par bone aventure
> Une flourete ai trovee
> Gente de faiture.
> En la fleur qui tant m'agree
> Tournai luez ma cure.
> Adont fis
> Vers dusqu'a sis
> De la fleur de paradis.
> Chascun lo
> Qu'il l'aint et lot.
> O! o!
> N'i a tel dorenlot!
> Pour voir, tot a un mot,
> Sache qui m'ot
> Mar voit, mar ot
> Qui lait Marie pour Marot. (vv. 1–19) [11]

This morning at daybreak, ambling along, I rode through a meadow. As luck would have it I found a little flower, beautifully made. At that I turned my attention to the flower that pleased me so; then I composed six verses about the flower of Heaven. I advise everyone to love and praise her. O! O! there is no tra-la-la like this. Truly, in a word, he who hears me should know: woe that he sees her, woe unto him, who leaves Mary for Marian.

The choice outlined in the song is clear: Marion (Marot, Mariete), the conventional shepherdess whose amorous escapades figure prominently in the pastourelle corpus, or Marie, Mother of God. As Gautier's piece demonstrates, with its use of popular refrains, one can sing virtually the same song of love and praise to either Marion or Marie; the important thing is to identify the object of one's adoring song:

> Qui que chant de Marïete,
> Je chant de Marie.
> Chascun an li doi par dete
> Une raverdie. (vv. 20–23)

Whoever may sing of Mariete, I sing of Marie; every year I owe her the debt of a *reverdie*.

Gautier links his transformation of a vernacular lyric genre with the psalmist's *canticum novum*, calling for abandonment of *viez pastourelles* and *vielles notes* in favor of *chançons noveles* (vv. 35, 36, 37). The closing stanzas elaborate praise of the Virgin and a prayer for salvation.

A motet text preserves what may have been Gautier's model for the first stanza of his song:

> Hyer matin a l'enjornee,
> toute m'ambleure,
> chevauchai aval la pree
> querant aventure.
> Une pucele ai trovee,
> gente de faiture,
> mais de tant me desagree,
> que de moi n'ot cure.
> Douz ot ris
> et simple vis,
> vers les ieuz et bien assis;
> seule estoit
> et si notoit:
> "O, o, o, o, o, o
> dorenlot,"
> si chantot.
> Mout li avenoit,

O, o, o, o,
et a chascun mot
souvent regretot
sa compaignete Marot.[12]

Yesterday morning at daybreak, ambling along, I rode through the fields seeking adventure. I found a maiden, beautifully formed, but displeasing in that she didn't care for me. She had a sweet laugh and simple face, well-placed gray eyes; she was alone, and was singing: "O, o, o, o, o, o, tra-la-la," she sang. It became her well, O, o, o, o, *and at each word she often regretted her little friend Marian.*

In this conventional pastourelle scenario, the male protagonist encounters an attractive, singing maiden while out riding. Gautier preserves the pastoral setting, but the pieces diverge when his protagonist finds not a maiden but a flower, which inspires contemplation of the heavenly maiden and metaphorical flower, Mary. The sexual tensions of the pastourelle are transposed into the longing of the inherently unworthy soul that hopes, through the intervention of the Virgin, to be purified and admitted into Heaven.

Gautier's contrafactum technique involves some of the same processes as the sermons. The turning point of the contrafactum is the *florete*, which functions as literal flower and as metaphor for the Virgin. In medieval poetry the flower can be a figure for an earthly maiden, and the impulse to pluck the flower and enjoy its beauty is often an erotically charged motif. Gautier is careful, however, to ensure that the meaning of his poem is clear. The movement from earthly to celestial, literal to figurative, is encompassed in the protagonist's meditative experience of the flower. He is aware first of its beauty, then of his attraction to it, such that it absorbs his attention; in a flash of inspiration he produces his song of love for the Virgin. Gautier does not attempt to allegorize the *pucele* of the pastourelle or the protagonist's desire for her; she is replaced by the heavenly *pucele*, just as the ordinary flower the protagonist finds is replaced in his thoughts by the *flor de paradis*. The relationship between text and contrafactum remains parodic: Marion cannot be a figure for Mary, since the love she inspires is the complete opposite of the Virgin's. For Gautier, what redeems the pastourelle is not an act of creative reading, but the creation of a new framework that redirects the meaning of its poetic language.

Even more than in the simple composition of contrafacta, the contextual redefinition of vernacular love lyric is evident in the use of songs and refrains as lyric insertions in devotional texts and, conversely, in the incorporation of devotional language or scriptural citations into secular lyric. Here, too, one sees clearly the polyvalence of the language of love. Let us examine these techniques more closely.

Rewriting the Sacred Text: Scriptural Parody

It was a common technique in vernacular devotional poetry to use Latin prayers and hymns as the foundation for a new composition that glossed or expanded upon the original text. Each word or phrase of the Pater noster or the Ave Maria, for example, might be the incipit of successive stanzas in a vernacular poem.[13] In this way the familiar words of the prayer determine the structure of the French poem, which in turn opens up and explicates the Latin original. The same technique is also used in parodic pieces, in which the fragmented devotional text becomes the point of departure for less edifying discourse. Although many such parodies revolve around the themes of clerical corruption, greed, or the pleasures of drink, there is one, the *Patrenostre d'amours*, in which a plea for love is constructed on the Our Father.[14] In some parts of the poem the declarations of love and the descriptions of the lady's beauty seem to have little or no relation to the text of the prayer that accompanies them, but there are other passages in which the theme of love is more closely adapted to the Latin text. The plea for forgiveness—"Et dimitte nobis debita nostra"—becomes a plea for the lady's mercy, for example, while the request for deliverance from evil—"Libera nos a malo"—is redefined as the wish to be freed from the pains of unrequited love. Submission to the will of the Lord is similarly recast as submission to the lady:

> *Fiat.* Certes veraiement
> Seroit fete delivrement
> Vostre requeste, douce suer,
> Se vous m'amiiez de bon cuer.
> Commandez ce que vous plera
> Et maintenant fet vous sera.
> Jel di por voir, ma douce amie,
> Sachiez de voir, je n'en ment mie.
> *Voluntas tua.* S'est enclose
> M'amor en vous. (vv. 29–38)

Be done. Certainly, truly, may your request be promptly fulfilled, sweet sister, if you love me with a good heart. Command what you wish and now it will be done for you. I say it truly, my sweet friend, know in truth, I am not lying. *Thy will.* Thus my love is enclosed in you.

Although the *Patrenostre d'amours* is not of the highest literary quality, it is representative of a pervasive delight in combining languages and literary codes. Two texts run parallel, the Latin prayer and the vernacular love poem that expands on and redefines the Latin phrases. In this respect the parodic Pater noster, Credo, or Ave Maria is like a motet in which a Latin tenor—usually only one or two words—accompanies a longer text in French, which in many cases expands on, recasts, or parodies the text from which the tenor is derived.[15]

There is, indeed, ample evidence that irreverent readings of biblical or liturgical passages circulated within the clerical community. Humorous distortions abound in Latin parodies, such as the *Gospel according to the Mark of Silver* or the Bacchic Mass.[16] In the *Merry Gospel according to Lucius*, for example, the Master instructs his disciples to commit adultery freely—"Maledicta enim arbor que non facit fructum" (For cursed is the tree that does not bear fruit)—and to drink heartily, "quia non in solo pane vivit homo" (for man does not live by bread alone).[17] The rhetorician Boncompagno da Signa (ca. 1170–ca. 1240) took delight in revealing the potential erotic meaning of numerous biblical passages, as in this excerpt from the *Rhetorica novissima*: "Quidam qui cognoverat monialem dixit: 'Non violavi thorum divinum, sed quia me in sua factura Dominus delectavit, cornu eius studui exaltare.' Item posset monialis dicere amatori: 'Virga tua et baculus tuus, ipsa me consolata sunt' "[18] (A certain man who had had carnal knowledge of a nun said: "I did not defile the divine bed, but since the Lord had favored me in his works, I wished to raise his horn." Moreover, a nun could say to her lover: "Thy rod and thy staff, they comfort me").

Needless to say, the humorous use of the Bible did not always sit well with moralists. During the quarrel over the *Roman de la Rose*, for example, Jean Gerson refuted Pierre Col's claim that the Bible provides a precedent for referring to female genitalia as sacred. In so doing, he alluded obliquely to a scabrous interpretation of a passage in the Gospel of Luke: "Omne masculinum adaperiens vulvam, sanctum Domino vocabitur" (Every male who opens the womb will be called sacred to the Lord [Luke 2:23]). Gerson hastens to specify the correct interpretation: "Quid, oro, sanctum Domino vocabitur? Si siles, respondeo: primogenitus" (What, I pray, will be called sacred to the Lord? If you are silent, I will answer: the firstborn).[19] Although Gerson does not identify the misreading that might have led to Col's claim, it is hardly difficult to imagine the use to which less pious *clercs* might put such a line. And Jacques de Vitry issued a stern warning in a sermon that told of a monk who, attempting to seduce a nun, closed a love letter with a passage from the Song of Songs: "Tota pulchra es, amica mea, et macula non est in te" (You are completely beautiful, my beloved, and there is no flaw in you [Song 4:7]). As he was concluding the letter, he suddenly choked to death, and his fate was taken as divine judgment by all who witnessed it: "ideo fuerat suffocatus, quod verbum spiritualis amoris carnali et immundo amori coaptauerat" (he had suffocated because he mingled the text of spiritual love with that of carnal and unclean love).[20]

Such warnings notwithstanding, the creative appropriation of biblical and liturgical language is a feature of much medieval Latin love poetry. A well-known example is *Si linguis angelicis loquar et humanis,* a poem that has received radically different readings in the modern period.[21] All critics agree that the poem treats of secular love and that it incorporates biblical language to do so. For example, the opening stanza, with its statement that speaking with the tongues of angels and of humans could not express the persona's experience in love, alludes to the famous passage in 1 Corinthians: "Si linguis hominum loquar, et angelorum, charitatem autem non habeam, factus sum velut aes sonans" (If I speak with human tongues and angelic as well, but do not have love, I am a noisy gong [1 Cor. 13:1]). The type of love Paul envisioned is hardly that celebrated in *Si linguis angelicis*—unless one allows an allegorical reading, but nothing in the text authorizes such a move. Robertson thus sees the allusion as ironic, a signal that the persona of this poem celebrating lust and seduction is indeed a noisy gong resounding in uncharitable self-importance. The opposing view, outlined by Dronke, is that the biblical language imparts a nobility to the experience of human love. Similar allusions recur throughout the poem, raising the same question of interpretation. The initial address to the maiden employs highly charged language:

> Ave, formosissima gemma preciosa!
> ave decus virginum, virgo gloriosa!
> ave lumen luminum, ave mundi rosa,
> Blanziflor et Helena, Venus generosa! (8:1–4)[22]

Hail, most beautiful precious jewel! Hail, ornament of virgins, glorious virgin! Hail, light of lights, hail, rose of the world, Blanchefleur and Helen, generous Venus!

The first three lines are indistinguishable from a conventional hymn to the Virgin. Yet the final line, identifying the maiden with a romance heroine and two pagan figures, undercuts the Marian imagery: the dazzling virgin is an earthly maiden and an object of human sexual desire. As he develops his plea for love, the male persona voices his lament in extravagant terms that recall the suffering Christ: he has borne the burden of all lovers' suffering ("Omnium amantium pondera portavi" [19:4]), he has been crucified—"per te cruciatus" (22:2)—for love of the girl standing before him. He expresses his hopes for recovery, should she grant him her favors, in language that recalls the antiphons "Justus ut palma florebit, sicut cedrus Libani multiplicabitur" (The just man will flower like the palm, like the cedar of Lebanon he will be multiplied [M52]), used for the Common of a Martyr, and "Justus germinabit sicut lilium et florebit in eternum" (The just man will sprout like the lily and flower in eternity [M53]), used for the Common of a Confessor: "Quod quidem si feceris, in te gloriabor, / tamquam cedrus Libani florens exaltabor" (For if you do [accept me], I will be glorified in you, I will be exalted, flowering, like the cedar of Lebanon [23:1–2]).

The martyr of love, "confessing" his sentiments as though he were describing a mystical vision, here transforms himself into a saint in the service of the blessed, if earthly, virgin he loves. It is true that the biblical language reflects the lover's grandiose view of his experience. A sympathetic reader, willing to suspend serious moral judgment—as many medieval readers surely were—might find that the rich allusiveness contributes to the poem's compelling representation of erotic desire. Nonetheless, the parodic qualities of the piece are unmistakable: it is ultimately a humorous portrayal of love's excesses and not a spiritualization of eros.

It is not difficult to find points of contact between such a poem and the motet repertoire. We have seen motets that combine secular love poems with Marian tenors or those identified with martyrs. In addition, several vernacular motets employ tenors derived from the antiphon *Justus germinabit*. An exemplary case is *Le premier jor de mai* (521) / *Par un matin me levai* (522) / *Je ne puis plus durer sans voz* (523) / *JUSTUS GERMINABIT SICUT LILIUM ET FLORE[BIT]* (M53).[23] This complex piece combines in its three texted voices the identification of love as inspiration for poetic composition; a narrative in which the male persona enters an orchard, asks a maiden for love, and is refused; and a plea for love addressed to the lady.[24] Each of the three texted voices creates a different context for the amorous persona's address to his lady. In the quadruplum, he addresses a general audience, elaborating both on the inspirational force of love and on his sorrow. He speaks of the lady only in the third person, even as he announces his intention to address her directly through song:

> Le premier jor de mai
> acordai
> cest quadruble renvoisié,
> car en cest tans
> sunt amant
> cointe et lié.
>
> . . .
>
> S'ele n'a de moi merci,
> ja n'avrai mes
> nul jour mon cuer joli!
> Por ce li pri
> et salu par cest nouviau chant ici:
> "Que se lui pleiz, a ami,
> qu'aucun confort aie prochein de li." (Q, vv. 1–6, 13–19)

This first day of May I composed this merry quadruplum, for in this season lovers are gallant and gay. . . . If she does not have mercy on me, my heart will never be merry! Therefore I implore her and greet her by this new song here: "That if I please her as a lover, I may have some comfort in her presence."

The triplum recasts the lover's request in the form of a pastourelle:

> Si trovai, seant en un vergier,
> tose chantant de cuer gai
> et legier.
>
> . . .
>
> Si la saluai
> et li dis bonement:
> "Bele au cors gent,
> de moi voz fas present." (Tr, vv. 4–6, 11–14)

Thus I found, seated in an orchard, a girl singing with a gay and carefree heart. . . . Thus I greeted her and spoke well to her: "Fair one of noble bearing, I give myself to you."

The motetus consists of a plea for mercy addressed to the lady:

> *Je ne puis plus durer sans voz,*
> *fins cuers savoreus et douz,*
> se n'avés merci de moi.
> Por voz sui en grant effroi
> et ai esté longuement. (M, vv. 1–5)

I cannot endure any longer without you, fine sweet delectable heart, if you do not have mercy on me. For you I am in great distress, and I have been for a long time.

The lyric persona's desires are not granted in any of the three texts. The girl of the triplum rebuffs him, and the other two texts make no provision for the female voice; they are simply articulations of masculine desire.

This motet contains many of the same elements as *Si linguis angelicis*, and the use of the antiphon *Justus germinabit* is similar in both cases. Taken at face value, the tenor is a statement of flowering and reproduction which, as background to the motet's tripartite statement of sexual desire, hints at a successful, procreative outcome to the lover's efforts. A consideration of the tenor's biblical and liturgical context, however, suggests an ironic undercutting of the lover's stance. The tenor, through its source antiphon, incorporates an image from Hosea.[25] Overall, the Book of Hosea encompasses a movement from divine retribution to mercy and redemption, employing erotic, nuptial, and botanical imagery. It opens with the account of the prophet's marriage to a prostitute, explained as an allegory for God's "marriage" to Israel—here characterized as sinful and faithless. The text then proceeds to a litany of the sins of Israel and a justification of divine retribution, concluding with a promise that divine mercy will allow a new "flowering" of God's people. The liturgical context—a celebration of confessor saints—reflects the fulfillment of that promise according to Christian exegesis: God's faithless bride, Synagoga, has been replaced by his new bride, Ecclesia. When read against the motet's declarations of desire and pleas for "mercy" in love, the biblical text invoked by the tenor suggests that the would-be seducer is a figure of moral and spiritual failings and contrasts the frivolity of amorous desire with the workings of divine love. Those who declare their love for God will prosper and grow; others will not.

Two distinct readings of the motet thus emerge. One valorizes erotic love as a source of poetic inspiration, an abiding passion to which the individual owes unquestioning loyalty, and a force that will ultimately lead to "germination" and "flowering"—be it psychic, poetic, procreative, or all three. The other reading condemns erotic love as fornication, the archetypal sin, and proposes in its place the spiritual flowering experienced by those who consecrate their lives to God. A sophisticated audience, cognizant of both readings, would be free to foreground the one they preferred: the piece might be a lightly self-ironizing celebration of love, a dramatization of the Fall sung against the backdrop of Redemption, or something in between. As so often, the motet highlights the interpretive process itself. By refusing to provide an explicit gloss, or to resolve clearly the conflict of registers by subordinating one to the other, it invites—indeed, forces—the audience to choose among the possible readings. Like the erudite love poems of the Carmina Burana, motets are highly crafted entertainment for an intellectual elite well versed in chant and popular lyric, and schooled in the arts of rhetoric and exegesis.

Contextualizing Love: The Lyric Insertion and the Motet

As we have seen, the motet, like the romance or the *dit* with lyric insertions, provided a framework in which the amorous discourse of vernacular lyric could be juxtaposed with textual material from a different genre or register. The practice of lyric insertion, which achieved great popularity in the thirteenth century, often entails interpretive revision, since the lyric text interacts with its new context. For a fuller comparison of the techniques of lyric insertion and motet composition, I turn now to three examples of lyric insertions in a devotional context: the Latin treatises of Gérard de Liège and two vernacular poems, the *Cantiques Salemon* and the *Court de Paradis*. These texts are fascinating examples of the phenomenon of "imposed allegory" as applied to popular lyric.

The Song of Songs is the locus classicus of erotic love poetry subjected to serious moral/tropological and allegorical interpretation. The importance of the Song of Songs in medieval culture is too well known to require detailed exposition here, and far too extensive for comprehensive treatment in the present context.[26] Latin literature of the High Middle Ages—including devotional and secular poetry, sermons, and portions of the liturgy—reflects the popularity and importance of this much imitated text, which was also the subject of many commentaries. Medieval preachers and writers were not unaware of its potential dangers for the uninitiated. Jean Gerson, for example, argued that at one time the Song of Songs had been forbidden reading for anyone under the age of 30, "affin qu'ilz n'y entendissent quelconque malvaise charnalitey" (lest they interpret it as some evil carnality); Saint Bernard recommended that it not be read by the young or by those having recently embraced monastic life.[27] The author of an Old French adaptation of the Song of Songs cautioned that his text should be kept from children.[28] And in another treatise Gerson fulminated against the error of reading the Song of Songs literally: "Illud quoque parum catholice alegatum est dixisse quosdam Cantica canticorum ob laudem filie Pharaonis edita: nam qui dixit irreligiose mentitus est"[29] (Also, it is hardly a Catholic tenet to have alleged, as certain have, that the Song of Songs was composed as praise of the Pharaoh's daughter: for whoever said that was impiously lying).

The Song of Songs was sacred Scripture, morally and spiritually edifying; but perhaps more than other portions of the Bible, reading it correctly was crucial. The Song of Songs provides a potent language for the Incarnation, the Passion, the establishment of the Church, and the mystical union of the soul and God. It offers a canonical precedent for the allegorization of erotic and bodily discourse, and it is the basis for a host of theological and literary texts ranging from hymns and treatises on the Incarnation to the fanciful exegesis of Fair Aelis. The allusions to the dangers that attended its reading show that the medieval audience was susceptible to the text's florid eroticism, its passionate language and explicit images. The precedent of the Song of Songs made it possible to redeem virtually any text by imposing an allegorical reading; at the same time, it allowed the recasting of sacred history and theological doctrine in erotic and bodily imagery. As such it is essential in this examination of sacred and profane discourse, and the ways in which one can be equated with the other.

We have seen the spiritual exegesis of popular lyric in the "Fair Aelis" and "Violete" sermons; a somewhat different manner of appropriating vernacular lyric is in the treatise *Quinque incitamenta ad deum amandum ardenter* by the thirteenth-century Cistercian Gérard de Liège.[30] In this text, and to a lesser extent in his *Septem remedia contra amorem illicitum*, Gérard uses a plethora of vernacular refrains and songs in which he redefines amorous language as applying to love of God. I will focus on a single example, the song *Grevet m'ont li mal d'amours*, which has the distinction of also being a motet text. Gérard uses the song to illustrate the humility and obedience of the soul that submits itself to the love of God:

Certe inde, scilicet pro peccatis suis, ipsa anima mansuetior fit ad correctionem, inde patientior ad adversitatem et laborem, inde sagatior ad cautelam, inde ardentior ad amorem . . . et deuotior ac sollicitior. Et hec dicit Bernardus: Unde talis anima bene potest cantare quoddam carmen quod uulgo dicitur:

> Grevet m'ont li mal d'amours,
> Mius en vaurai,
> Car plus sages en serai,

Et de foliser allours
Me garderai.[31]

Certainly from that—that is, because of its sins—this soul is made more docile in correction, more patient in adversity and labor, wiser and more cautious, more ardent in love . . . and more devoted and more solicitous. And Bernard says this: Thus such a soul can well sing that song that is sung in the vernacular: The pains of love have wounded me, I will be better for it, for I will be wiser, and I will take care not to commit folly elsewhere.

Gérard is probably referring to Bernard's first sermon on the Song of Songs, an exposition of the title *Cantica canticorum*, in which he reminds his audience of God's aid in triumphing over the temptations and adversities of this world: "et in exitu vestro de lacu miseriae et de luto faecis, cantastis et ipsi Domino canticum novum, qui mirabilia fecit. . . . Est quippe nuptiale carmen, exprimens castos jucundosque complexus animorum"[32] (And in your exit from the pit of misery and from the mire of impurity, you will sing a new song to that Lord who has performed wonders. . . . Indeed it is a wedding song, expressing the chaste and joyous embraces of souls). Saint Bernard, in other words, identifies the Song of Songs as a hymn of love and thanksgiving to God. Gérard retains the idea of singing a love song to God, but substitutes a vernacular refrain for the biblical song.

An expanded version of the song Gérard cited appears as motetus of the piece *Grevé m'ont li mal d'amer* (385) / *JOHANNE* (M29).[33] Although the tenor, from an alleluia for the feast of Saint John the Baptist, contains no verbal parallels with the motetus, there is a certain humor in combining a song about the pains of love and an allusion to a martyr—especially one whose death is attributed to the power of carnal lust. The reference to the Baptist, through whose sacrament the followers of Christ are cleansed of Original Sin, is also intriguing in view of the song's claim that suffering the pains of love will improve one's character. For the same melody there exists a Latin text in honor of Mary, *Virgo mater salutis* (386) / *JOHANNE* (M29), which focuses on humankind's liberation from sin as a result of Christ's mercy. Thus the vernacular and the Latin versions treat the theme of moral improvement and redemption, albeit in entirely different ways. Both additionally use the figure of the wound; indeed, the Latin text might be seen as an antidote for the vernacular text, with Christ as the healer of the *mal d'amer* and the only real source of spiritual improvement:

> Culpe sanet vulnera,
> Impium
> Extingat incendium. (vv. 6–8)

May he heal the wounds of sin and extinguish the unholy flame.

One sees thus a range of reactions to the same popular love song. In the devotional treatise, its language is unquestionably allegorized: submitting to the love of God and patiently accepting adversity improves the soul. In the motet, the moral tone of the text is potentially ambiguous. As a statement in praise of erotic love and its delicious "pain," it contrasts with the tenor, but other readings are possible. The "pains of love" might refer to the cleansing power of spiritual love and the acceptance of adversity, or to the bodily pains of martyrdom suffered for love of God—brought on, in John the Baptist's case, by Herod's own lustful pangs. The Latin text with which the French motet is associated—as model or as contrafactum—exploits the central metaphor of the wound in this latter sense, as an image for sin.

The exploitation of a polyvalent language of love, shared by vernacular lyric and the Song of Songs, is striking in the *Cantiques Salemon*, an anonymous Old French adaptation of Song of Songs 1–3, with extensive commentary on the text as an expression of the mystical marriage of Christ and the human soul. The text, which is unedited, appears in a single manuscript dating from circa 1300.[34] Interspersed throughout the text are lyric insertions, many of which can be identified as contrafacta of trouvère songs. For example, the song *Li amoureus m'ont doucement requize* (R1640), a lament in a woman's voice for the loss of her beloved, attributed in one manuscript to the duchess of Lorraine, appears in slightly altered form as the soul's lament for the crucified Christ, incorporated into the expansion of Song 1:12. Given the conventional personification of the soul as feminine—based in part on the Song of Songs itself—the woman's lament for her absent beloved is a standard motif in the *chanson pieuse*; it is also a feature of the motet repertoire, and I will examine below examples of this type, addressing in more detail the question of whether they are to be read as allegory or as parody of the devotional archetype.

A related motif appearing in both the *chanson pieuse* and the motet repertoire is that of the woman's search for her beloved, illustrated by another song appearing in the *Cantiques Salemon*. The commentary on Song 2:3, "Sub umbra illius quem desideravi sedi et fructus eius dulcis guturi meo" (I sat in the shade of the one whom I desired and his fruit was sweet to my taste), explains the tree as an allegory for Christ and his teachings. The motif of tree and forest is then elaborated in a strophic *chanson de rencontre*, beginning:

> En un bos menu ramé
> Pour deduire aloie.
> Celui qui tant m'a amé
> Et que tant amoie
> Sa et la querroie,
> Et ne trouvai mie.
> Lors errai: Amis, aÿe!
> J'ai perdu ma jo[i]e
> Se dire l'osoie. (fol. 43v)

I went into a dense grove to enjoy myself. Hither and yon I sought the one that I loved so much and who has so loved me; I did not find him. I went astray: Beloved, alas! I have lost my joy, if I dared say it.

In the second stanza, the persona explains that *li foretiers* (the forest guard)—her beloved—intervened to guide her; the final stanza describes her arrival at a tree bearing the sweet fruit that she had desired. The subsequent gloss explains that the song refers to the soul's search for Christ.

Ironically, the very currency of the forest as a setting for erotic adventure allows its incorporation into the *Cantiques Salemon*. One need only think of the many pastourelles—both motet texts and strophic monophonic compositions—that describe the sexual escapades of Robin and Marion out in the woods, or the erotic encounter enjoyed there by the lyric protagonist himself. Indeed, a fascinating counterpart to *En un bos menu ramé* appears in the Old French translation with commentary of Ovid's *Ars amatoria*:

> Pucelle vins en ce bois,
> Et pucelle m'en revois.
> Le forestier qui le garde
> Male nuit en ait des mois![35]

I came into this forest a maiden, and I leave as a maiden. May the forester who guards it have months of bad nights!

The disappointed maiden whom the forester does not guide to her heart's desire thus contrasts with the contented one to whom the forester granted the fulfillment of her wishes. In both cases the erotic metaphor is transparent; but in the *Cantiques Salemon* the erotic significance of the imagery is immediately transposed into a spiritual register, just as the entire Song of Songs is. So total is the allegorization of eros that it applies even to the metaphoric imagery of love poetry.

This allegorical adaptation of lyric discourse is of fundamental importance for the vernacular motet. Indeed, a second "forest" song incorporated into the discussion of Song 2:3 exists in an expanded version as a motet text, and a shortened version appears in the *Court de Paradis*. Motet, *Cantiques*, and *Court de Paradis* are most likely independent compositions, yet they represent similar uses of the same textual material. The song as it appears in the *Cantiques Salemon* is as follows:

> Je gars le bos que nul ne port
> Flourette ne verdure.
> Et si gars la raimme
> Que nus n'emporte
> Pour nul deport
> Chapel de fleurs s'il n'aimme. (fol. 44v)

I guard the forest so that no one may carry off flower or greenery. And thus I guard the thicket, lest anyone who does not love carry off a garland of flowers for entertainment.

Given the erotic associations of the forest and its guard, and of the act of picking flowers, it is easy to read this song as referring to the guarding of sexual favors that are granted only to a worthy lover. Again, however, the context—in which sexual union itself is an image for mystical union with God—imposes an allegorical reading of the lyric metaphor. A similar use of the song appears in the *Court de Paradis*.[36] There, a refrain consisting of the first and last lines of the *Cantiques Salemon* piece is sung by the four Evangelists in the context of festivities in Heaven, to which only the souls of the saved are admitted. As in the *Cantiques Salemon*, the forest open only to those who love might be the Church, the love of God, or the state of spiritual salvation; but in either case song and refrain alike express a doctrine of admittance to a privileged space or state, determined by one's spiritual status and proper devotion to love.

The motet—*Je gars le bois que nus n'en porte flourete ne verdure* (114) / *ET CONFITEBOR* (M12)—incorporates an additional six lines into the middle of the piece, elaborating on the lyric persona's commitment to loyal love. In themselves, these lines do not affect the allegorical potential of the text. The tenor is from an alleluia used in the dedication of a church and for the feast of the Purification of the Virgin: "Alleluia. Adorabo ad templum sanctum tuum et confitebor nomini tui" (Alleluia. I will worship at your sacred temple and praise your name). The choice of tenor, in other words, is compatible with a reading of the closely guarded forest as the *hortus conclusus* of the Song of Songs; hence, the motet text is an allegorical expression of the entrance of the Holy Spirit into the Virgin or of the admittance of the Christian soul to the company of the saved. But unlike the other two texts, in which the devotional register dominates, the motet remains equivocal. The spiritual reading is possible; yet one could also imagine a secular reading in which the "sacred temple" in the alleluia takes on an erotic significance, and the one whose name is praised is not God but the earthly beloved. This use of the sacred image is not unique in Old French literature. Its most famous, and certainly its most audacious, appearance is in the closing passage of Jean de Meun's *Roman de la Rose*, where the act of sexual intercourse is described through an elaborate extended metaphor of entering a sanctuary and worshiping sacred relics. Since the motet, unlike the two lyric insertions, does not depend for its meaning on some larger narrative or expository frame, nothing determines absolutely whether the love it celebrates is erotic or spiritual. And since neither reading dominates, the tension between the overtly erotic motetus and the overtly devotional tenor remains in the foreground: instead of resolution through allegory, the motet exhibits the dissonance of parody.

I turn now to a fuller consideration of the *Court de Paradis*. This short thirteenth-century poem describes a carol held in Heaven; Christ, flanked by Mary Magdalene and the Virgin, presides over the festivities. All the souls of the saved participate, arriving in groups according to their status: Old Testament prophets, martyrs, confessors, virgins, and so on. As each group joins in the dance, its members sing an amorous refrain that corresponds, at least generally, to that group's identity and participation in divine love: the prophets' song is about hopeful waiting, for example, and the martyrs' is about the pains of love. The currency of the refrains as popular songs, associated with the carol and with the celebration of erotic love, is shown by their appearance elsewhere in a secular context. Two, for example, are lyric insertions in the Old French translation of Ovid's *Ars amatoria*.[37]

The idea of a Heavenly carol is not limited to this text. The vilification of the carol by preachers and moralists did not prevent its appropriation into the devotional register as a literary or iconographic image, just as the language of erotic love poetry was taken over and invested with spiritual significance. It is conventional to imagine Paradise as a locus of angelic singing and celebration, and this motif is sometimes expressed in terms of the familiar carol.[38] Nuptial imagery is standard in depictions of Christ and the community of the saved—authorized by such texts as the Song of Songs, the epithalamium psalm *Eructavit cor meum* (Vulgate Psalm 44), and the Gospel parables of the Wise and Foolish Virgins and the Guest without a Wedding Garment—and the notion of the mystical marriage leads naturally to that of the Heavenly wedding celebration, complete with song and dance. A vernacular adaptation of the psalm *Eructavit cor meum* was composed in the late twelfth century for the countess Marie de Champagne, probably by Adam de Perseigne, and transmitted in numerous thirteenth- and fourteenth-century manuscripts; it portrays the Heavenly marriage of God and the Virgin in terms taken directly from the language of courtly lyric and romance.[39] As Marc-René Jung has pointed out, the festivities recall those surrounding the coronation of Erec and Enide in Chrétien's romance.[40] Both the Old Testament prophets who foretold the Incarnation and the Church choirs who commemorate it are compared to court musicians, summoned by a king for his son's marriage or coronation:

> Jugleor font sonez noviaus,
> Chançons et notes et fabliaus,
> Que droiz est que chasuns s'atort
> Contre la joie de la cort.
> Dammedés qui est rois et sire
> Fist autresi de son empire. (vv. 31–36)

Jongleurs make new music, songs and tunes and fables, for it is right that everyone participate in the joy of the court. Lord God who is king and lord did the same with his empire.

The relationship of Christ and the Virgin is characterized as an example of *fine amor* (for example, vv. 1439, 1447), and they are portrayed as a loving couple: "Li rois d'un douz reguart l'esguarde / Qui tote l'esprant et avive" (With a fond regard the king beholds her who completely enflames and animates him [vv. 1326–27]). And the devout soul is promised similar pleasures when, after death, it joins the Bridegroom/King in the *chambre celee* (hidden chamber [v. 1562]):

> Iqui te porras aaisier
> Et d'acoler et de baisier.
> Cil te fera joie et solaz
> Qui en la croix tandi ses braz. (vv. 1571–74)

Here you will be able to disport yourself with hugs and kisses. He who opened his arms on the Cross will give you joy and solace.

Although the scene might be straight out of a courtly romance, the extensive commentary, which includes Marian, tropological, and allegorical readings, leaves no doubt about the moral and theological significance of the events described.

Thus although the *Court de Paradis* may seem strange to the modern eye, it is amusing but not unconventional by thirteenth-century standards.[41] In fact, it appears in two devotional anthologies: a collection of prayers and devotional treatises in French and Latin (Bibl. Nat. fr. 1802), and a manuscript devoted largely to the works of Gautier de Coinci, containing *chansons pieuses*, miracle stories, an extensive series of poems built on the Ave Maria, and the vernacular *Eructavit* (Bibl. Nat. fr. 25532).[42] Far from being seen as an irreverent work, it was treated as a variation on the pious contrafactum: an appropriation of popular refrains that transposes the language of love into a spiritual register.

The relevance of the *Court de Paradis* here is that six of the refrains sung in the poem also appear in motets, where the tenor provides a sacred context. The use of these refrains offers analogies to their appearance in motets, reminding us that a devotional reading of such pieces, while not the only interpretation, is by no means impossible. I have discussed the refrain *Je gart le bos / Que nus n'en port / Chapiau de flos s'il n'aimme* (I guard the forest so that no one will carry away a garland of flowers unless he loves [*Court de Paradis*, vv. 427–29]), for example, which also occurs in the *Cantiques Salemon* and a motet. The idea of the privileged space for those who love—whether that love is erotic or spiritual—is also invoked in the refrain *Tout cil qui sunt enamoraz / Viegnent dancier, li autre non* (All those who are amorous come and dance, and not the others [vv. 412–13]), sung by the Virgin as the carol begins. This refrain figures in the motet *Li jalous par tout sunt fustat* (467) / *Tuit cil qui sunt enamourat* (468) / PROPTER VERITATEM (M37), where two texts referring to a true lovers' dance, which excludes jealous people, are combined with a tenor from the Assumption gradual *Propter veritatem. Audi filia*. Once again, the juxtaposition of refrain and sacred celebration is the same in the motet and the *Court de Paradis*. I discuss the motet at greater length in Chapter 3; for the moment, we can note that the priorities of the motet and the *Court de Paradis* are reversed. In one case, the model of the sacred marriage of the Virgin and Christ underlies the secular celebration of love, and in the other a secular dance refrain is incorporated into the celebration of love in Heaven, led by the Virgin and her Bridegroom/Son.

The motif of Christ as Bridegroom of the Church similarly informs

the refrains by which the various groups of souls express their love. The re-
frain *Se j'ai amé folement, | Sage sui, si m'en repent* (If I have loved foolishly,
I am wise now and I repent [vv. 348–49]) is sung by the souls of widows
as they join the festivities. Its application is clear: as married women they
have experienced sexual love, but now they devote themselves to the love
of Christ. When used in motets, this refrain refers to the lyric persona's
regret that he "foolishly" loved anyone other than the lady to whom he
now devotes himself, or perhaps that he loved in a flighty or insincere
manner. It appears thus in the motet *Chascuns dist que je foloie* (149) | *Se
j'ai amé folement* (150) | IN SECULUM (M13). The basic paradigm, then, is a
conversion from false or imperfect love to a love that is true and absolute. The tenor IN SECULUM, from the Easter gradual *Hec dies. Confitemini
Domino*, celebrates God's mercy and the redemption of humanity; it is an
appropriate accompaniment for a song of repentance.[43] The movement
effected in the motet—the notions of conversion and of mercy and forgiveness become part of the world of erotic love—is reversed in the *Court
de Paradis*, where the conversion from false to true love has a spiritual
significance. Neither text implies a profanation of the Passion narrative or
of the Christian doctrine of redemption; in both, the difference between
the sacred model and its secular counterpart is the source of humor. But
as in the previous example, the sacred model dominates in the *Court de
Paradis*, investing the refrain with spiritual meaning. The motet offers
the possibility for a literalized, secular reading of the tenor through its
appropriation into a secular context.

In one instance a refrain is adapted slightly in order to highlight its
devotional application: *Touz li cuers me rit de joie | Quant Dieu voi* (My
whole heart laughs with joy when I see God [vv. 504–5]). Ordinarily the
refrain refers to the joy of seeing one's sweetheart; in the Old French *Art
d'amours*, for example, it is "Tout le cuer me rit de joye | Quant je la voy"
(My whole heart laughs with joy when I see her [p. 170]).[44] It is also in
the motet *Tant me fait a vos penser* (17) | *Tout li cuers me rit de joie* (18) |
OMNES (M1).[45] The motet is not about seeing God, but it is about seeing—
and not seeing—the beloved lady. In the motetus, the lyric persona first
says: "Tout li cuers me rit de joie | de vostre biauté veir" (My whole heart
laughs with the joy of seeing your beauty [vv. 1–2]). He then states his
regret at their separation and his fear about the relationship: "Por Diu, ne
m'oubliés mie, | se plus sovent ne vos voi" (For God's sake, don't forget
me if I don't see you more often [vv. 9–10]). Yet the leap from seeing the
lady to seeing God is not absent in the motet either. It is suggested by the

tenor, which derives from a gradual for the third Mass on Christmas Day: "Viderunt omnes fines terrae salutare Dei nostri; jubilate Deo, omnis terra. ℣ Notum fecit Dominus salutare suum: ante conspectum gentium revelavit justitiam suam" (All the ends of the earth have seen the salvation of our God: rejoice unto God, all the earth. ℣ The Lord has made known his salvation: he has revealed his justice in the sight of the Gentiles).

Thus the motet makes a small joke—albeit subtle, since no devotional text among the upper voices stresses the parallel—by contrasting the joy of seeing one's girlfriend and the sorrow of no longer seeing her, with the joy experienced by all the earth at the sight of its Redeemer and Bridegroom. The familiarity of the refrain would have allowed readers of the *Court de Paradis* to appreciate the same joke: sight of the beloved and sight of God are fused in the experience of the souls united with Christ in Heaven. Again, the difference between the *Court de Paradis* and the motet is one of reversed priorities: in one case the secular refrain appears in a spiritual context that invests it with new meaning, and in the other the sacred text is a hyperbolic formulation of the central motif in a secular love song. The *Court de Paradis* represents an allegorical—and witty—use of popular refrains; the motets offer a true parodic juxtaposition, which implies no disrespect for the religious doctrine at issue. In both cases, as in other examples cited above, the poet's artistry lies in juxtaposing sacred and secular texts that have a common motif; and the humor lies in the inevitable recognition of the dissonance in the artful *conjointure*.

Most interesting of all, with regard to the motet corpus, is the use in the *Court de Paradis* of two refrains to mark the arrival of female souls as they move toward Christ. First, *Renvoisïement / I vois a mon ami* (Gaily I go there to my beloved [vv. 335–36]) is sung by the chorus of virgins; about twenty lines later the souls of married women sing *Ensi doit dame aler / A son ami* (Thus should a lady go to her beloved [vv. 359–60]).[46] These two refrains also form a two-line motetus (435) sung to the tenor *HODIE*, which derives from an alleluia for Assumption: "Alleluia. Hodie Maria virgo caelos ascendit. Gaudete quia cum Christo regnat in eternum" (Alleluia. Today the Virgin Mary ascends to Heaven. Rejoice, for she reigns with Christ in eternity [M34]). This alleluia is the source of several tenors in vernacular motets that, as a group, make an interesting comparison to the *Court de Paradis*. One motet uses nearly the entire alleluia: *Cele m'a s'amour donnee* (433) / *ALLELUIA. HODIE MARIA VIRGO CELOS ASCENDIT. GAUDETE QUIA CUM CHRISTO REGNAT.* The others employ portions of the alleluia.[47] Some, constructed of refrains, are short—the following examples are quoted in their entirety:

> M: Mieus vueill sentir les maus d'amer
>   que faillir a amie. (434)
>   T: ALLELUIA

M: I would rather feel the pains of love than fail my beloved.
T: ALLELUIA

> M: Renvoisiement i vois a mon ami,
>   ensi doit on aler a son ami. (435)
>   T: HODIE

M: Gaily I go there, to my lover; thus should one go to her lover.
T: TODAY

> M: J'ai fait ami a mon chois
>   preus et sage et cortois;
>   si me tient por amie,
>   s'alongera ma vie. (436)
>   T: GAUDETE

M: I have chosen a lover, bold and wise and courteous; if he accepts me as his sweetheart, it will lengthen my life.
T: REJOICE[48]

In addition, seven Latin and five French motet texts survive for the tenor REGNAT. There is good reason to view the vernacular motets built on this family of tenors as a coherent group. First, aside from those composed on REGNAT, each of the pieces cited above is the unique example of a motet using that tenor. Second, of the nine vernacular motet texts employing these tenors, all but two—both using REGNAT—are transmitted in the Artesian manuscript N; some appear additionally in MS W_2 or in MS R, which collection of motets is closely related to that in MS N. The Latin motets correspond musically with clausulae, and one of the French texts not included in MS N is closely linked to the Latin corpus: the vernacular triplum of the bilingual motet Quant repaire la verdor (438) / Flos de spina rumpitur (437) / REGNAT is musically related to the triplum of the conductus motet Flos de spina rumpitur (437) / REGNAT, the tenor and motetus of which are constructed from clausulae. The vernacular motets transmitted in MS N, however, are all independent compositions, with no corresponding clausulae and no Latin contrafacta.

The evidence thus strongly suggests a specifically Artesian cultivation of this particular Assumption tenor in vernacular motets, and especially in motets employing amorous refrains.[49] Both male and female voices are represented within the corpus and are combined in *Cele m'a s'amour donee / ALLELUIA. HODIE . . . REGNAT*. If this corpus was performed together in sequence—and the texts are so short that one could easily include them all in a single performance—the result would be a dialogue between male and female lovers, sung to the backdrop of an alleluia for Assumption. The effect is virtually a parody of the Assumption liturgy, which draws heavily on the Song of Songs: the Mass and Divine Offices for Assumption, celebration of Mary's joyous reunion in Heaven with her Bridegroom/Son, ring with praises of the beloved's beauty, invitations to amorous trysts, and allusions to the fountains and flowering gardens where the lovers meet. Latin motets on the tenor *REGNAT*, focusing on Mary's identity as Queen of Heaven, served to embellish the liturgy.[50] The French motets composed on tenors from *Alleluia. Hodie* represent a vernacularization and secularization of this liturgical celebration of mystical love, substituting the language of courtly lyric for that of the biblical love poem.

The impulse to recast the drama of Assumption in the language of secular lyric is similar in one sense to the *Court de Paradis*, where celestial celebration of divine love is rewritten as a carol with secular refrains. In another sense, however, the motets are quite different from the *Court*. As we have seen, the latter poem consistently assimilates the secular refrain into its devotional framework, thereby fully investing it with spiritual significance. Though amusing, the *Court de Paradis* is not an ambiguous poem. The same cannot be said for the motets, in which it is seldom clear whether the tenor provides the context for a reading of the upper voices, or vice versa. This capacity to function simultaneously as allegory and as parody causes the motet to stand out against the literary background we have examined here.

Chapter 3

The Amorous Maiden

Est tocius mundi gaudium,
viri solacium

. . .

cordis elevacio,
omnis amaritatis consolacio.

She is the joy of all the world, the solace of man . . .
the heart's uplifting, the consolation for all bitterness.

—Anonymous verse

It is a commonplace that the language of devotion to the Blessed Virgin is so similar to that used to express love and devotion to ladies of this world that at times the two registers can scarcely be distinguished. The *pucele*—resplendent with beauty, summoned by her lover, unabashedly voicing her own desire—is common to devotional and secular literature, and so are the *dame*, whose suppliants pledge their love and beg her for mercy, and the *reine*, who presides over a festive dance or a wealthy court, whether worldly or heavenly.[1] These correspondences are exploited in the motets that combine texts linked to the vast repertoire of secular lyric—pastourelle, *grand chant courtois, chanson de toile,* or rondeau— with tenors drawn from the liturgy of the Virgin. In the large corpus of motets whose tenors derive from chant passages for such feasts as Assumption or the Nativity of the Virgin, some are naturally more complex than others. In some the associations of the tenor are central to the literary dynamics of the piece; in others the tenor has a purely musical function. In order to address these issues, I will first examine the liturgy from which the tenors derive, and then turn to selected examples of motets composed on Marian tenors from the responsory *Stirps Jesse. Virgo* (O16) and the gradual *Propter veritatem. Audi filia* (M37).

Liturgical Contexts: The Bride of Christ

The liturgy of the Virgin—her Nativity, Annunciation, Purification, and Assumption, as well as the closely related liturgy for the Common of Virgins—is rich in allegorical imagery drawn from such texts as the Song of Songs, the epithalamium *Eructavit cor meum* (Vulgate Psalm 44), and the hymn to Holy Wisdom in Ecclesiasticus 24.[2] The language of these rituals, suffused with a sublimated eroticism, abounds in lush imagery of flowering gardens, bubbling fountains, and aromatic spices, as in these antiphons for Assumption:

Tota pulchra es, amica mea, et macula non est in te; favus distillans labia tua, mel et lac sub lingua tua, odor unguentorum tuorum super omnia aromata; jam enim hiems transiit, imber abiit et recessit, flores apparuerunt, vineae florentes odorem dederunt, et vox turturis audita est in terra nostra: Surge, propera, amica mea; veni de Libano, veni, coronaberis.[3]

You are completely beautiful, my beloved, and there is no spot in you; your lips dripping honeycomb, honey and milk under your tongue, the fragrance of your unguents above all spices; now the winter is passed, the rain has departed and withdrawn, flowers have appeared, flowering vines have put forth their fragrance, and the voice of the turtledove is heard in our land: Arise, hasten, my beloved; come from Lebanon, come, you shall be crowned.

Fons hortorum, puteus aquarum viventium quae fluunt impetu de Libano.[4]

Fountain of the gardens, well of living waters which flow swiftly from Lebanon.

Sicut cinnamomum et balsamum aromatizans odorem dedisti, sancta Dei Genitrix.[5]

You gave off an odor, fragrant as cinnamon and balsam, holy Mother of God.

The mystical marriage of Christ and his Bride is celebrated in vivid language: "Quam pulchra es, amica mea, quam pulchra es, et decora! oculi tui columbarum, absque eo quod intrinsecus latet. ℣ Pulchra es, amica mea, suavis et decora sicut filia Jerusalem"[6] (How beautiful you are, my beloved, how beautiful you are, and lovely! Your eyes are doves' eyes, besides what is hidden within. ℣ You are beautiful, my beloved, sweet and lovely like a daughter of Jerusalem). The Bridegroom summons his beloved with expressions of ardent desire: "Veni, electa mea, et ponam te in thronum meum, quia concupivit Rex speciem tuam. ℣ Audi filia et vide, et inclina aurem tuam, quia concupivit Rex speciem tuam"[7] (Come, my chosen one, and I will place you on my throne, for the King has desired your beauty. ℣ Listen daughter and behold, and incline your ear, for the King has desired your beauty). The Bride, of course, is equally filled with desire; she sings of her love and of the gifts that her beloved has given her, as in these two responsories for the feast of Saint Agnes:

Dextram meam et collum meum cinxit lapidibus pretiosis, tradidit auribus meis inaestimabilis margaritas, et circumdedit me vernantibus atque coruscantibus gemmis. ℣ Induit me Dominus cyclade auro texta, et immensis monilibus ornavit me. Et circumdedit.[8]

He girded my right arm and my neck with precious stones, he placed price-less pearls in my ears, and clothed me in lush and sparkling gems. ℣ The Lord clothed me in a robe woven of gold, and ornamented me with lavish necklaces. And he clothed me.

Ipsi sum desponsata cui angeli serviunt, cujus pulchritudinem sol et luna miran-tur; ipsi soli servo fidem, ipsi me tota devotione committo. ℣ Jam corpus ejus corpori meo sociatum est, et sanguis ejus ornavit genas meas. Cujus pulchritudi-nem.[9]

I am betrothed to him whom the angels serve, whose beauty is admired by the sun and the moon; to him alone I owe faith, to him I commit myself in total devotion. ℣ Now his body is joined to my body, and his blood embellishes my cheeks. Whose beauty.

The controlling metaphor of the Blessed Virgin or virgin saint as the Bride of Christ thus permeates the liturgy, authorizing its use of nuptial imagery and its evocation of the amorous tryst. The allegorical reading of the Song of Songs, which reached new heights in the twelfth century, allows the incorporation of this poem's sensuous language directly into the liturgy.

Although many parts of the Bible contribute to the complete liturgy for the various feasts of the Blessed Virgin and the virgin saints, three biblical texts are particularly important for the motif of the mystical marriage: the Song of Songs, the parable of the Wise and Foolish Vir-gins (Matt. 25:1–13), and Vulgate Psalm 44. The Song of Songs brings to the liturgy its dramatic *mise-en-scène* of the Bride and Bridegroom who seek each other in gardens, through city streets, and out in the fields; its ecstatic vision of reunion is expressed in an almost kaleido-scopic rush of imagery. Because of the antiphonal structure of the Song of Songs—a dialogue between *Sponsa* and *Sponsus*, with choruses of youths and maidens—this text lends a special immediacy to the liturgical com-memoration, as though the sacred events were recurring in the present.[10]

The Bridegroom's statements as he watches for his approaching beloved are particularly useful as a dramatization of Christ's reception of the Virgin on the occasion of her Assumption: "Vidi speciosam sicut columbam, ascendentem desuper rivos aquarum, cujus inaestimabilis odor erat nimis in vestimentis ejus; et sicut dies verni circumdabant eam flores rosarum et lilia convallium. *V* Quae est ista quae ascendit per desertum sicut virgula fumi, ex aromatibus myrrhae et thuris? Et sicut dies verni"[11] (I saw a beautiful woman like a dove, ascending above the banks of the waters, whose inestimable odor was overpowering in her garments; and like a spring day she was surrounded by rose blossoms and lilies of the valley. *V* Who is this that ascends through the desert like a plume of smoke, from the fragrance of myrrh and incense? And like a spring day).

A slightly different perspective on the mystical marriage of the soul is given in the parable of the Wise and Foolish Virgins, which is prominent in the Office for the Common of Virgins. Rather than celebrating the Bride's arrival in Heaven and the expectant joy of the welcoming Bridegroom, this text stresses the need for vigilance on the part of the Bride, focusing on the dramatic moment of the Bridegroom's arrival: "Haec est virgo prudens, quae veniente sponso accepit oleum in vasis suis, et ornatis lampadibus introivit cum eo ad nuptias. *V* Media autem nocte clamor factus est: Ecce sponsus venit, exite obviam ei"[12] (This is the prudent virgin, who, when the bridegroom came, took the oil in her flasks, and with her lamps lit entered with him to the wedding feast. *V* But in the middle of the night there was a clamor: Behold, the bridegroom is coming, go out to greet him). And Psalm 44, *Eructavit cor meum*, contributes its account of a royal wedding, stressing the beauty and finery of the bride and her entourage, the desire of the king, and the festivities. Besides being sung on the feast of Assumption, this psalm figures in numerous antiphons, alleluias, and graduals for the various feasts of the Virgin and the virgin saints, some of which are cited above.

Besides that of the mystical marriage, other themes important to the Marian liturgy are Mary's inviolate virginity, her powers of intercession on behalf of her devotees, and her role in the Incarnation and the resulting redemption of humanity. The following alleluias for Assumption illustrate the interconnectedness of these ideas:

Post partum, virgo, inviolata permansisti: dei genitrix, intercede pro nobis.[13]

After giving birth, Virgin, you remained inviolate; mother of God, intercede for us.

Per te, dei genitrix, nobis est vita perdita data que de celo suscepisti prolem et mundo genuisti salvatorem.

The life that had been lost is given to us by you, mother of God, who received the progeny from Heaven and gave birth to the Savior of the world.

Ora pro nobis, pia virgo Maria, de qua Xpistus natus est nobis, ut peccatoribus sit misertus.[14]

Pray for us, pious virgin Mary, from whom Christ was born unto us, that he take mercy on sinners.

The invocations of amorous union, verdant landscapes, and festive celebrations are thus combined with prayers for divine mercy, allusions to the mystery of the Incarnation, and expressions of joy and gratitude for the redemption of humanity. The relevance of Marian worship for the individual participant is twofold. First, the worshiper can identify with Mary as Bride of Christ through a tropological reading: the Church collectively and each member individually are also brides of Christ and can look forward to eventual union in Heaven with the *Sponsus*. Second, this possibility of admittance to Heaven is contingent upon the remission of sins made possible by the Incarnation and realized in the extension of divine mercy to each individual—and in this process Mary as intermediary is essential. The individual virgin saints similarly are brides of Christ and act as intercessors for those who keep their cult alive.

The liturgy of the Virgin and the virgin saints was deeply familiar to the clerical composers of vernacular motets, many of which employ Marian tenors; the liturgy was, in fact, a principal medium for the transmission of the Marian interpretation of the Song of Songs.[15] The sacred ritual and the vernacular lyric tradition form the larger context in which these pieces are to be read; and as we saw in Chapter 2, the amorous discourse and imagery proper to the secular register were easily transposed into that of the spiritual. The flowery springtime landscape; the maidens decked out in jewelry and fine clothes, singing of their lovers; the ardent and desirous king or *sponsus* captivated by feminine beauty; the passionate, longed-for moment of the lovers' reunion—all these motifs are common to sacred liturgy and the corpus of vernacular lyric. Prominent in both registers are prayers for mercy—usually directed to an idealized female figure—and faith in the ennobling, salvific qualities of love. Needless to say, the two cannot be collapsed: the distinction between *caritas* and *cupiditas* remained fundamental for medieval readers and composers alike. But for poet-composers steeped in sacred and secular traditions, the points of contact between the two allowed allegorical and parodic transformations of the polysemous discourse of love and desire. The motet, in which sacred chant and vernacular lyric meet, was the perfect ground for such experimentation.

The Tenor *FLOS FILIUS EJUS*: Literal and Allegorical Flowers

"Stirps Jesse produxit virgam: virgaque florem. Et super hunc florem requiescit spiritus almus. ℣ Virgo dei genetrix virga est, flos filius ejus" (The stalk of Jesse produced a branch: and the branch, a flower. And upon this flower the bountiful spirit came to rest. ℣ The Virgin mother of God is the branch, the flower is her son [O16]). This responsory, source of the tenor *FLOS FILIUS EJUS* or *EJUS*, figures in the feast of Assumption and that of the Nativity of the Virgin; it is itself a citation of the famous messianic prophecy in Isaiah 11:1–2. The Tree of Jesse was a standard feature of medieval iconography, appearing frequently in Latin and vernacular texts, stained-glass windows, manuscript illuminations, and other works of art. It was well known to the medieval audience. Latin motets constructed on this tenor might develop either the Marian associations of the tenor's liturgical source or the messianic content of its biblical context; often the themes are developed in tandem.[16]

The presence of these thematics in vernacular motets is both less explicit and more complex. Some, it must be acknowledged, do not exploit the tenor's textual or liturgical associations, presenting at most a general contrast between the frustration, turmoil, or carnality of erotic love (in the upper voices) and the salvific qualities of divine love (in the tenor).[17] In other examples, however, the imagery of the tenor and its liturgical function in the worship of the Blessed Virgin are incorporated into the motet in a secularized form; a case in point is *Amours mi font souffrir peine a tort* (664) / *En mai, quant rose est florie* (663) / *FLOS FILIUS EJUS*.[18] In the opening line of the motetus, the image of the flowering branch has been completely secularized, fusing with the *début printanier* of the trouvère tradition:

> En mai, quant rose est *florie*,
> que j'oi ces oisiaus chanter,
> moi covient par druerie
> joie demener. (M, vv. 1–4)

In May, when the rose is *in flower*, when I hear these birds sing, it behooves me to pursue joyful dalliance.

The text continues with a plea for love designed to save the life of the lyric "I": "se je n'ai vostre aïe, / vostre amor . . . vos m'avés mort" (If I do not have your aid, your love . . . you have slain me [M, vv. 12–13, 15]). There is of course nothing unusual about a prayer for life-giving aid being directed to the Virgin. Indeed, a Latin contrafactum of this piece, *Flos ascendit de radice* (665) / *FLOS FILIUS EJUS*, moves from the flowering branch to a prayer for intercession on behalf of the Jews: a spiritualization of the progression in the vernacular motetus.[19] It would be difficult to argue, however, that the spiritual dimension was already present in the vernacular motetus; such words as *druerie* (v. 3) and the allusion to the lady in question as "brunete sans ami" (brunette without a lover [v. 15]) locate the text and its message of love in the secular rather than the devotional register. A similar effect obtains in the motet *Pensis, chief enclin* (677) / *FLOS FILIUS EJUS*.[20] Here the lyric "I" describes an encounter with a shepherdess "lés un aubespine, / dejouste un arbroie" (beside a hawthorne, next to a grove of trees [vv. 3–4]). Once again the image of flower and tree is secularized, and the lady, linked to the tree by metonymy, is eroticized; this time the register is the pastourelle. Perhaps the shepherdess's disinterest in the lyric protagonist and her refusal to answer him—she is more concerned with Robin, whose song she hears in the distance—carry humorous overtones by intensifying the difference between this maiden and the one celebrated in the tenor, whose love extends to all. In both cases, the configuration of flower, lady, and supplication in the name of love offer a secularization of the source responsory, setting up an amusing contrast within the motet as a whole; but the association is still somewhat loose, and the literary potential of the tenor is not fully exploited.

Most interesting, if less frequent, are those vernacular motets in which the specific textual and liturgical associations of the tenor *FLOS FILIUS EJUS* are of central importance to the overall dynamics of the piece. I will focus here on two such compositions, beginning with a four-part motet, *Plus bele que flor* (652) / *Quant revient fuelle et flor* (650) / *L'autrier joer m'en alai* (651) / *FLOS FILIUS EJUS*.[21] The conflation of erotic and spiritual discourse is apparent even within the quadruplum, in which the spiritual nature of the singer's love does not become clear until more than halfway through the piece:

> Plus bele que flor
> est, ce m'est avis,
> cele a cui m'ator.
> Tant com soie vis,

n'avra de m'amor
joie ne delis
autre mes la flor
qu'est de paradis:
Mere est au Signour,
qui si noz a mis
et nos a retor
veut avoir tot dis.

More beautiful than a flower, in my opinion, is she to whom I belong. For as long as I am alive, no one will have joy or pleasure of my love except the flower who is in paradise: she is mother of the Lord, who placed us here and wants us to return to him forever.

The motetus participates in the register of the pastourelle and presents a lady who is of this world and whose amorous desire is different from the Virgin's:

L'autrier joer m'en alai
par un destor.
En un vergier m'en entrai
por quellir flor.
Dame plesant i trovai,
Cointe d'atour.
Cuer ot gai,
Si chantoit
en grant esmai:
"Amors ai!
Qu'en ferai?
C'est la fin, la fin,
que que nus die, j'amerai."

The other day I wandered into a remote area to amuse myself. I entered an orchard in order to pick a flower. I found an attractive lady there, nicely dressed. She had a gay heart; she was singing with great feeling: "I have love, what will I do? It's the end, the end, whatever anyone says, I will love."

The triplum is a statement of love that is not clearly either secular or spiritual:

Quant revient et fuelle et flor
contre la seison d'esté,
Deus, adonc me sovient d'amors,
qui toz jors
m'a cortoise et doz esté.

Moult aim ses secors,
car sa volenté
m'alege de mes dolors;
moult en vient bien et henors
d'estre a son gré.

When leaf and flower return for the summer season, God, then I remember love,
who has always been courteous and sweet to me. I greatly value her succor, for it
is her will to alleviate my sorrows; great good and honor come to me for being in
her good graces.

The language is that of the courtly love lyric; yet it does not differ from
that applied to the Virgin in the quadruplum, and there are no statements or demands that would conflict with a devotional reading of the
text. This piece, in fact, exemplifies the ambiguous, equivocal nature of
the discourse of courtly lyric. The triplum—musically, the middle of the
three texted voices—mediates between spiritual devotion to the Virgin
(in the quadruplum) and the erotically suggestive encounter with the
lady (in the motetus). By seeming to point both ways simultaneously, the
triplum holds the motet together: here, in the lyric idealization of love,
the worlds of the quadruplum and the motetus can meet; here, the one is
translated into the other.

The interplay among the three texted voices, as well as their link to
the tenor, is heightened by the word *flor* in all three parts. In the quadruplum, the *flor* is first a standard of beauty, then a metaphor for the
Virgin: although not the same as the tenor, where the *flos* is Christ, the
quadruplum follows the tenor by using the flower in a spiritual sense.
In the triplum, the flower is naturalized as a phenomenon of the onset of summer. It does, however, function as a sign of love—spiritual or
erotic—since the return of flower and leaf causes the lyric protagonist to
remember his amorous sentiments. In the motetus, the *flor* is also a literal
flower. Yet the image of a man entering a garden to pick a flower, and
finding there an eagerly amorous lady, has unmistakable erotic overtones.
Although metonymy not metaphor associates the lady with the flower,
one cannot but see the possibility for a re-allegorization of the *flor*—
this time, with reference to the lady's sexual vulnerability rather than her
purity.

Despite the differences between quadruplum and motetus, the possibility exists for an allegorical reading of the motetus that would invest it
with spiritual significance. In isolation, this text does not invite allegorization; but in its present context—with the tenor an explicit link to the

Marian liturgy and with the triplum binding the motetus to the Marian text in the quadruplum, which appropriates the language of courtly lyric into a spiritual register—the allegorical impulse is not out of place. And the Marian liturgy from which the tenor FLOS FILIUS EJUS derives is replete with texts, derived from the Song of Songs, that would authorize such a reading: "Veni in hortum meum, soror mea sponsa, messui myrrham meam cum aromatibus meis" [22] (I went into my garden, my sister bride, I gathered my myrrh with my spices); "Veniat dilectus meus in hortum suum, ut comedat fructum pomorum suorum" [23] (Let my beloved come into his garden, that he may eat the fruit of his apples). These and other similar passages from the Song of Songs contain the same basic elements as the motetus: a man entering a garden, the gathering of flowers, and a female figure who gives voice to her powerful feelings of love.[24] The *hortus conclusus* of the Song of Songs is a standard topos for the Virgin in medieval art and literature, important also in the liturgy: "Hortus conclusus es, Dei Genitrix, hortus conclusus, fons signatus; surge, propera amica mea" (You are an enclosed garden, Mother of God, an enclosed garden, a sealed fountain; rise, hasten, my beloved).[25] The Marian reading of the lover entering his garden—the mystical marriage of human and divine, the Incarnation taking place within the body of the Virgin—is exploited in the motet *Descendi in ortum meum ut viderem poma convalli* (767) / ALMA REDEMPTORIS MATER (O48), a paraphrase of Song 6:10–12.

From the *virga* and *flos* of the tenor and its source text, then, we arrive at other biblical and liturgical passages in which tradition invests the imagery of flowering with a spiritual, and specifically Marian, sense. The motet as a whole encompasses a series of intricate movements between the literal and the figurative and between the sacred and the erotic. The heavenly flower, image of the Virgin, is translated into a literal flower, the plucking of which is both the occasion and the metaphoric representation of an erotic encounter; at the same time, the metaphor carries a latent possibility, brought out by the motet's intertextual play, for reinvestment with spiritual meaning. Although this textual construct could be considered parodic allegory—the motetus would not appear to contain religious allegory, if not for its context—this use of parody need not be interpreted as irreverent. The sudden realization that the amorous vignette of the motetus hides an allusion to the Marian liturgy and the Song of Songs could be a source of great amusement; it could also be a lesson in the importance of careful reading. To single out just one interpretation would be to destroy the fragile beauty and the subtlety of the motet, whose very nature consists in the simultaneous rendition of diverse texts and the suggestive play of meaning generated from their interaction.[26]

We can better appreciate the allegorical nuances by comparing the French motet to the Latin motets that use the same music. The quadruplum must be an independent composition, since it has no counterpart among the Latin motets or the source clausula; but the triplum and motetus were composed as contrafacta, and the music originally served for two different Latin double motets.[27] Central to the Latin pieces are the themes of Incarnation and Redemption, appropriate to the tenor's evocation of Mary as the mother of the Messiah. In *Stirps Iesse progreditur* (647) / *Virga cultus nescia* (648) / FLOS FILIUS EJUS, for example, the motetus praises the salvific qualities of the branch "Quam celestis gratie / ros imbuit" (which was imbued with the dew of celestial grace [M, vv. 3–4]); this branch brought forth the "fruit of glory," whereby "Trabeam / Carneam / Verbum induit" (the Word put on a robe of flesh [vv. 9–11]). The triplum also describes the flower that, perfected by the Holy Spirit, is a source of redemption: "Flos electos reficit, / Cuius odor mentium / Remedium" (The flower, whose fragrance heals minds, restores the elect [Tr, vv. 8–10]). The French texts translate the devotional motifs into the language of courtly lyric. Like its Latin counterpart, the triplum *Quant revient fuelle et flor* (650) opens with an image of flowering and moves quickly to the motif of a salvific love that soothes mental anguish and brings honor to its devotees. The motetus *L'autrier joer m'en alai* (651) goes farther in secularizing imagery, with its vignette reminiscent of the pastourelle. Yet as we have seen, the motif of a man entering a garden, one associated with an amorous lady, is present in the Song of Songs, which exegetical tradition interprets as an allegory for the entrance of the Holy Spirit into the Virgin, hence for the Incarnation. The French motet thus preserves the basic thematic structure of its Latin model, employing the flower motif at the beginning of each voice and focusing on Redemption and Incarnation in the triplum and the motetus, respectively, though the allegorical veiling increases as one moves from triplum to motetus. The importance of this underlying thematic structure, moreover, is further evidenced by its use in the other Latin three-part motet using this music, *Castrum pudicicie* (653) / *Virgo viget melius* (654) / FLOS FILIUS. Although this piece does not use the flower image, it does stress Redemption in the triplum and the Incarnation in the motetus.[28] Given this consistency, there is no reason to doubt that a clerical audience, familiar with the Marian liturgy and the Latin motets associated with it, would have seen the vernacular motet as a recasting of the same fundamental themes, expanded through the addition of a fourth voice. And superimposed on the structure of Marian devotion / redemptive love / amorous union are three levels of discourse: the devotional language of the quadruplum, the equivocal language of the triplum, and the parodic allegory of the motetus.

Before leaving this piece, we should note that not all manuscripts transmit the full composition: the quadruplum is lacking in three sources, and an additional two have only the motetus. The four-part composition appears only in the Montpellier and La Clayette codices. Without the quadruplum, the piece loses some of its richness; the allegorical play and the multiple transformations of the flower image are less elaborate. And although the motetus and tenor alone potentially present the play of sacred and erotic allegory, this reading is less openly indicated without the presence of the other voices. It is likely that the original composition included at least motetus and triplum, given the three-part clausula and Latin motets that lie behind it. There is no way of knowing, however, whether the quadruplum was original to the French piece—removed at some point in a desire for simplification—or whether it was added by a later composer who aimed for fuller and more complex exploitation of the underlying allegorical motif. What is clear is the fundamental importance of each voice in the motet's dynamic: the addition or subtraction of a single part alters the densely woven texture of the polyphonic construct.

The preceding example, though not entirely without Christological overtones, centers on the lady and on the movement between devotion to the Virgin and desire for the beautiful maiden. Its exploitation of the tenor rests on the word *flos* and on the tenor's liturgical context as celebration of the Virgin. I turn now to a three-part motet— *Quant define la verdour* (661) / *Quant repaire la dolçor* (662) / *FLOS FILIUS EJUS*—in which the intertextual play is not specifically Marian and can be linked to the biblical motif of the Tree of Jesse as a figure for the Incarnation and hence for the salvation of humanity.[29] The two texted voices share rhymes and many words. These parallels are preserved in the musical setting, in which rhyme words in the two upper voices sound simultaneously. The triplum presents winter, the death of leaf and flower, and the sorrowful departure of the birds; the motetus presents springtime, the birth of leaf and flower, and the joyful song of the birds; and both texts end with a statement of despair over the protagonist's lack of success in love:

Tr	M
Quant define la verdour,	Quant repaire la dolçor,
que muert la fuelle et la flour	que naist la foille et la flour
et par pré et par boscage	et par pré et par boscage
font cil oisiel grant tristour,	font li oiseil grant baudour,
qui n'i font point de sejour,	mon cuer est en grant tristor
lors ne me vient en courage	et me met en mon corage;
de servir en nul aage	car j'ai mis tout mon aage
bone amour.	en fine amor
Pour sa baudour	sanz nul retor.
ne nuit ne jour	Et nuit et jor
ne puis penser,	m'estuet penser,
[qui m'a doné,]	car j'ai doné,
Dieus, qui m'a doné	Dieus, quar j'ai douné
cors pensant et cuer amer.	cuer et cors pour bien amer.

Tr: When the greenery comes to an end, when leaf and flower die in field and forest, and the birds are in great sorrow and do not stay long, then it does not come into my heart to serve good love at any time. I cannot think of its joys by night or by day; [who has given me,] God, who has given me a pensive body and a bitter heart?

M: When the sweetness returns, when leaf and flower are born in field and forest, and the birds are in great joy, my heart is in great sorrow, which causes me to turn inward; for I have spent all my time in pure loving, with no returns. I have to think about it by night and by day, for I have given, God, I have given heart and body over to good loving.

Taken together, the two texts articulate the hopeless situation of the lyric protagonist, whose fortunes are detached from the natural cycle of seasons. Whereas the birds and the flowers experience a regular alternation between the bleakness of winter and the joyful rebirth of springtime—as indicated in the juxtaposition of the opening sections of triplum and motetus, respectively—he remains trapped in mournful meditation. The sense of futility and despair in love is heightened by the strategic location of the words *amour* and *amer*. The word *amour* sounds simultaneously in both voices just past the center of the motet (v. 8), appearing in rhyme position and further highlighted by the occurrence in all three voices of a cadence and rest. This brief pause and hint of closure at the word *amour* clearly mark it as the focus of the motet: the evocation of sorrowful winter and joyous spring alike leads to meditation on love. As the piece begins again after the momentary pause, the simultaneous statements of amorous despair and dedication lead once more to the explicit naming of love, this time in a play on words at the end of the motet: the word *amer* sounding simultaneously in both voices, but meaning "bitter" in the triplum and "love" in the motetus. This wordplay is so ubiquitous in the Old French courtly tradition that it cannot be seen as an allusion to any particular text; it refers, rather, to an entire constellation of passionate but doomed lovers. Here it underscores the impossibility of resolution: throughout the year the protagonist finds no relief from the unrelenting love that he can neither escape nor consummate. The impression of stasis and stagnation finds expression in the interweaving of the texts: death and life, grief and joy, departure and return exist in an eternal balance that allows neither progression nor retreat, and leads only to the obsessive realization of the bitterness of love.

Once again both texts are tied to the tenor through the repetition of the word *flour*. And the presence of the tenor and its biblical associations suggests the way out of the dilemma posed in the two upper voices. Returning to the passage in Isaiah that is the ultimate source for the responsory *Stirps Jesse. Virgo*, we find the juxtaposition of the death and the reflowering of the forest:

> Et subvertentur condensa saltus ferro;
> Et Libanus cum excelsis cadet.
> Et egredietur virga de radice Iesse,
> Et flos de radice eius ascendet. (Isa. 10:34–11:1)

And the forest groves are felled with the axe; and Lebanon falls in its glory. And there will come forth a shoot from the root of Jesse, and a flower will rise from his root.

The tenor ("The flower is her son"), an exegesis of the biblical passage, reminds us of the flower that is born, dies, and is reborn; one in whom all love comes to rest, with no possibility of refusal for those whose love is genuine. The destruction of the forests of Lebanon, the sprouting of a new flower, signal the end of the old order and the beginning of the Age of Grace. The Incarnation marks a turning point in history, the definitive end of one era and the beginning of another: a linear progression that spells release from the otherwise inescapable circle of sin and death. Even the play on *amer* participates in this new vision, since the bitterness of Christ's Passion allows the full consummation of divine love and the victory over worldly desire and death. The allegorical leap from *flos* to *filius*, stated in the tenor, allows a resolution that was not possible as long as we remained within the literal meaning of the texts.[30]

The relationship of the texted voices to the tenor is somewhat different in *Plus bele que flor / Quant revient fuelle et flor / L'autrier joer m'en alai / FLOS FILIUS EJUS*. The intertextual play pointed to the possibility—though not the necessity—of an allegorical reading of the motetus text. The play of hidden meanings, the rich capacity of poetic language to signify the erotic, the idealized, and the sacred, lay at the heart of that piece. In *Quant define la verdour / Quant repaire la dolçor / FLOS FILIUS EJUS* the two texted voices do not themselves carry an allegorical sense; they remain in the realm of worldly love. They seem to set up a contrast, yet in the end their message is the same. In this case the piece turns on the opposition of the two texted voices, taken as a unit, to the tenor, understood as an abbreviated exegesis of a well-known biblical passage. What is at issue is not the allegorization of the *flour* of the texted voices or of the love described therein, but the movement from those literal flowers and that worldly love to the allegorical flower of the tenor and the divine love that it represents.

The Gradual *Propter veritatem. Audi filia* and the Motif of the Dance

"Propter veritatem, et mansuetudinem, et justitiam: et deducet te mirabiliter dextera tua. V Audi, filia, et vide, et inclina aurem tuam: quia concupivit rex speciem tuam" (For truth, and mercy, and justice: and your right hand will lead you marvelously. V Listen, daughter, and behold, and incline your ear: for the king has desired your beauty [M37]). This gradual for the feast of Assumption, originating textually in Vulgate Psalm 44, is the source of several tenors.[31] Within the Latin corpus, motets built on these tenors are exclusively Marian; the vernacular examples reflect the irresistible opportunities for parodic secularization inherent in the liturgical expression of desire for a beautiful girl. Such is the use of the above tenor in the miniature motet *A vous pens* (457) / *PROPTER VERITATEM* (M37). The motetus is "A vous pens, bele douce amie, de cuer verai" (I think of you, beautiful sweet friend, with a true heart).[32] The simple refrain closes with an echo of the tenor, and it offers a rephrasing, in the language of vernacular lyric, of the gradual from which the tenor derives. The same effect is created in the motets *Biaus cuers desirrés et dous* (477) / *AUDI FI[LIA]* (M37) and *M'occirés voz, dous frans cuers et gentis* (476) / *AUDI FILIA* (M37). In both cases the motetus is a love plea addressed to a woman; the tenor literally asks her to listen to her lover's words. The appropriation of the liturgical phrase into a secular context is reminiscent of Latin biblical and liturgical parodies, such as those cited in Chapter 2, where the statement "Man does not live by bread alone" becomes a justification for indulgence in drink or where the Pater noster is rewritten as an erotic *salut d'amour*. Indeed, the phrase "Audi, filia, et vide" is the theme of an early-sixteenth-century *sermon joyeux* on a bride's nuptial duties, showing that the parodic readings cultivated by motet composers were still flourishing centuries later.[33]

The possibilities for parodic allegory in the manner of the "Fair Aelis" and "Violete" sermons are intriguing in the piece *C'est la jus par desouz l'olive* (482) / *QUIA CONCUPIVIT REX* (M37).[34] The tenor, a statement of desire, accompanies a poem conjuring up an amorous idyll:

> M: C'est la jus par desouz l'olive,
> je menrai ma tres douce amie;
> fontenele i couroit serie.
> Or charolais,
> je menrai ma tres douce amie
> aval les pres.
> T: QUIA CONCUPIVIT REX

M: It is down there under the olive that I will lead my sweetest beloved; there a little fountain flows clear. I was caroling; I will lead my sweetest beloved across the fields.

T: FOR THE KING HAS DESIRED

The language and the imagery of the motetus are typical of the refrains and rondeaux associated with the carol. The text is well suited to an eroticized reading of the tenor. But anyone wishing to read allegorically, to bring the motetus into line with the tenor's liturgical function, would find fertile ground. The refrain of verses 2 and 5 is similar to one Christ sang in the *Court de Paradis* as he led Mary Magdalene and the Virgin into the dance: "G'en main par la main m'amie, s'en vois plus mignotement" (I lead my beloved by the hand, thus I go more gaily [v. 470]). The image of both olive and fountain can contribute to a Marian reading, since they appear in Ecclesiasticus 24, the Epistle for Assumption: "Quasi oliva speciosa in campis, et quasi platanus exaltata sum iuxta aquam in plateis" (Like a beautiful olive tree in the fields, and like a plane tree in public squares I am exalted beside the water [Ecclus. 24:19]). In a sermon for Assumption that explicates Ecclesiasticus 24:17–20, Hugh of St. Victor explains that the olive is a symbol of mercy, hence of the Virgin;

the olive's location in the fields reflects her accessibility to all people.[35] The fountain is an image for the Divine Grace that infuses the Virgin: "quasi donis irrigata divinis in bonis operibus dilatata semper fuit" (she was always expansive in good works as if irrigated by divine gifts [*PL* 177:1028]). Alternatively, the olive tree might be a symbol for the Cross; one traditional view held that the Cross was made of palm, cypress, cedar, and olive wood. The olive is also glossed as a figure for God the Father in two other sermons by Hugh;[36] and we have seen the fountain glossed as a figure for the Incarnation in the "Violete" sermon. Any combination of these readings could allow an allegorical interpretation of the motet as figuring the mystical marriage of Christ and Ecclesia or of God and the Virgin.

I offer these allegorical readings as a speculative example of how a clerical audience might have understood the motet as signifying on two levels; since no gloss survives for this piece, we cannot be certain that it actually was allegorized in this manner. But the procedures that I have used are the same as those in the two sermons that we saw in Chapter 2; the reading adheres to the conventional interpretation of the tenor text. If this or some other allegorical meaning was discerned in our motet by its medieval performers or audience, however, it could only have been in a spirit of play. The allegorical reading allows a deeper, more complex appreciation of the piece; its identity as a vernacular dance song expressing untroubled, easily fulfilled desire remains to infuse the allegorical interpretation with irony and humor.

In fact, the motet *C'est la jus par desouz l'olive* / QUIA CONCUPIVIT REX takes on an interesting light when read in conjunction with another thirteenth-century text featuring parodic allegory: the discourse of Genius in Jean de Meun's continuation of the *Roman de la Rose*. In his much commented-on exhortation to the troops of love, Genius conjures up a vision of the Heavenly afterlife awaiting those who engage in procreation: a flowery pasture with a fountain—the triune fountain of life—and an olive tree, which bears the "fruit de salu" (fruit of salvation [ed. Lecoy, v. 20493]). Those who pursue fruitful love can look forward to an eternity of pleasant recreation in these meadows:

> lors irez ou champ deliteus,
> par trace l'aignelet sivant,
> en pardurableté vivant,
> boivre de la bele fonteine
>
> . . .

ainz irez par joliveté
chantant en pardurableté
motez, conduiz et chançonnetes,
par l'erbe vert, seur les floretes,
souz l'olivete querolant. (vv. 20618–21, 20625–29)

Then you will go to the delightful field, following the lead of the lamb, living for
eternity, to drink from the beautiful fountain. . . . Thus you will go joyfully, forever singing motets, conductus, and little songs, through the green grass, among
the little flowers, dancing under the olive tree.

Genius's version of Heaven is similar to the scenario in *C'est la jus par
desouz l'olive*, itself highly formulaic: joyous dancing and the bliss of love,
in a meadow beside a fountain and beneath an olive tree. The same details
appear in numerous other rondeaux as well.[37] This does not mean, of
course, that Jean de Meun modeled his text on our motet or on a specific
rondeau, but he did construct it from elements that are instantly recog-
nizable as belonging to the rondeau register, whatever other associations
they may have. As a result, the *biaus parc* Genius described must be read
with a double focus. It presents a view of Christian Heaven: the eternally
verdant scene of joyous celebration, centered around the life-giving fountain whose three streams are one — an obvious symbol for the Trinity —
and the tree with its salvific fruit, which might represent either the Virgin
or the Cross, both of whom bore the Savior.[38] At the same time, the
context of Genius's presentation colors our reading: it follows upon a
condemnation of both homosexuality and celibacy and a critique of the
Garden of Delight with which the *Rose* opens, now associated with the
narcissism and sterility of impossible desire and courtly flirtation. Stressing that this Heaven is open to all who engage in procreative sex — hardly
the canonical view of spiritual salvation — Genius invites a simultaneous,
alternative reading of the park as an erotically charged idyll, superior to
the Garden of Delight not because it represents spiritual devotion and
charity but because it stands for the fulfillment rather than the frustration
of sexual desire.[39] Again, the deformation of conventional textual figures
is reminiscent of the parodic *Sequencia leti evangelii secundum Lucium*, in
which the justification for adultery — presumably procreative — is "Maledicta enim arbor que non facit fructum" (For cursed is the tree that does
not bear fruit [ed. Lehmann, p. 70]). Genius's sermon employs allegorical
discourse for parodic purposes, fusing the carefree eros and pastoral setting of the rondeau repertoire with the ecstatic consummation of spiritual
desire in the metaphoric pastures of Heaven.

The discourse of Genius thus provides an important analogue for the motet *C'est la jus par desouz l'olive* / QUIA CONCUPIVIT REX. The complex play of allegory and parody, of spiritual and erotic exhortation, which occupies more than a thousand lines in Genius's sermon, is highly condensed in the motet. There is no room for elaborate textual comparisons and exegesis; such matters are left to the reader, performer, or listener. But the juxtaposition of the rondeau with a suggestive tenor derived from the liturgy of one of Christendom's most important feast days, and ultimately from a well-known psalm, would be enough to invite playful interpretive speculation in the educated circles where motets flourished—probably, indeed, the same circles that formed the original audience for the *Roman de la Rose*.[40]

The motif of festive dance, combined in the motetus with a rondeau format, is also used in our next example, *Li jalous par tout sunt fustat* (467) / *Tuit cil qui sunt enamourat* (468) / PROPTER VERITATEM (M37).[41] This one focuses on the "queen" who presides over the festivities and on the boisterous exclusion of those unworthy to participate:

Tr	M
Li jalous par tout sunt fustat	Tuit cil qui sunt enamourat
et portent corne en mi le front;	viegnent dançar, li autre non.
par tout doivent estre huat.	La regine le commendat
La regine le commendat,	(tuit cil qui sunt enamourat),
que d'un baston soient frapat	que li jalous soient fustat
et chacié hors comme larron.	fors de la dance d'un baston.
S'en dançade veillent entrar,	Tuit cil qui sunt enamourat
fier le[s] du pie comme garçon.	viegnent avant, li autre non.
T: PROPTER VERITATEM	

Tr: The jealous ones are completely driven away and wear a horn on their fore-
     heads; they should be mocked by everyone. The queen commands that they
     be beaten with a stick and chased away like thieves. If they want to join in
     the dance, kick them away like knaves.

M: All those who are amorous come and dance, the others no. The queen com-
     mands (all those who are amorous) that the jealous ones be driven away
     from the dance with a stick. All those who are amorous come forward, the
     others no.

T: FOR TRUTH

The two texted voices are closely related, with the motetus conforming to a standard rondeau format (ABaAabAB). The triplum, observing the same rhyme scheme and using many of the same lines and phrases, is

more loosely constructed and lacks the recurring refrain lines characteristic of the rondeau. The repertoire is the songs of May and dance songs,
where love is freely expressed and where women are not afraid to pro-
claim their amorous desire or their dissatisfaction with their husbands. At
first glance, these two rondeaux have little in common with the Marian
liturgy that produced the tenor. The refrain on which the motetus is
built, however, appears in a context that links it to spiritual devotion: the
Court de Paradis, where it is sung by none other than the Virgin Mary.[42]
The dance to which she invites all amorous souls is the carol in Heaven,
led by Christ; and, as we saw in Chapter 2, the idea of a Heavenly carol is
not unique to that text.

If we choose to read the motet with reference to the carol in Heaven,
most details fall into place. The jealous cuckolds who are opposed to love
can be identified with the enemies of the faith or with those who, like
the foolish virgins, are unworthy to participate. The separation of lovers
from nonlovers, a frequent motif in the refrain repertoire, is easily applied
to the distinction of the saved and the damned. In the *Court de Paradis*,
for example, Saint Peter, instructed by Christ to keep all uninvited guests
out of the Heavenly carol, sings the refrain: *Vos qui amez, traiez en ça, | En
la qui n'amez mie* (You who love, come over here, you who don't love go
over there [vv. 391–92]). And in the "Fair Aelis" sermon, a similar exclusion of those who do not love is glossed as an allusion to the damnation
of Jews, Saracens, and heretics: "Talibus debemus dicere *trahez vos en la,
qui n'amez mie* .i. 'Ite maledicti in ignem eternum'" (To such we should
say *go over there, you who do not love*, that is, "Go cursed ones into the
eternal fire").[43] The May queen who rules over the dance can be identified with the Queen of Heaven. Those with sufficient knowledge of the
liturgy might connect the invitation proffered to lovers—*viegnent dançar,
viegnent avant*—with the summons to the Beloved issued repeatedly in
the Song of Songs and echoed in the alleluia *Veni electa mea* (M54), used
with the gradual *Propter veritatem. Audi filia* for both Assumption and
the Common of Virgins.[44]

More generally, the scene evoked in the motet as a whole is a lively
recasting of the wedding festivities alluded to in Psalm 44. These, too, are
presided over by a queen: "Astitit regina a dextris tuis in vestitu deaurato"
(The queen stood at your right, clothed in gold [Ps. 44:10]). Although
there is no reference to a dance, the arrival of the bride in her finery,
accompanied by her entourage of maidens, clearly indicates a court celebration: "Omnis gloria eius filiae regis ab intus, in fimbriis aureis. . . .

Adducentur regi virgines post eam, proximae eius afferentur tibi. Afferentur in laetitia et exsultatione" (In all her glory the king's daughter enters, dressed in gold. . . . Behind her the maidens are led to the king, her companions are brought to you. They are brought to you in joy and exultation [Ps. 44:14, 16]). The bride is instructed to embrace her new life with the king: "Et obliviscere populum tuum, et domum patris tui" (And forget your people, and the home of your father [Ps. 44:11]). This allusion to the casting off of the forefathers is traditionally interpreted as a figure for conversion from pagan idolators; it also suggests the exclusivity of the joyous dance in celebration of love.

Even the *baston* used to drive the jealous ones away finds its parallel: "Virga directionis virga regni tui" (The scepter of your rule is a rod of direction [Ps. 44:7]). Those with sufficient knowledge of the biblical text might find in the king—normally interpreted as a figure for divinity—a fortuitous resemblance to the God of Love: "Sagittae tuae acutae, populi sub te cadent, in corda inimicorum regi" (Your arrows are sharp in the hearts of the king's enemies, people fall under your sway [Ps. 44:6]). Both the Christian God and the pagan God of Love wield allegorical arrows, powerful weapons to conquer the hearts of their devotees or punish disbelievers.[45] Indeed, the image of suffering from an invisible arrow wound, which only the love object can cure, is appropriated from the discourse of erotic love and applied to the love of God in a thirteenth-century *chanson pieuse*:

> Il m'a si navree d'un dart,
> Mais que la plaie n'i pert.
> Ja nul jour n'en guariré
> Se par li non.
> *Li debonnaires Diex m'a mis en sa prison.* (vv. 7–11)[46]

He has thus wounded me with a dart, but the wound doesn't show. Never will I recover except through him. *The noble God has placed me in his prison.*

Again, sacred and profane discourses of love meet in the iconography shared by both: the arrow-wielding divinity, the dance of love, the amorous queen of the dance, the existence of a strict code that determines who is admitted to the dance and who is not.

In fact, therefore, the dance songs making up this motet are relevant to the biblical text that produced the tenor. Although the texts stand on their own and do not need allegorical interpretation, the elements they contain, when brought into contact with the psalm through their juxtaposition with PROPTER VERITATEM, translate the biblical text into contemporary language and imagery. This allows a range of interpretive possibilities. The rowdy *fête champêtre* the texts describe might be a humorous contrast to the royal marriage with mystical significance celebrated in the liturgy; or it might be an allegorical representation of that same event. Like the psalm itself, the motet can be read in two different ways, making sense both literally and allegorically. And like *C'est la jus par desouz l'olive* / QUIA CONCUPIVIT REX, the present example retains its element of humor: the two levels of meaning are resolved, ultimately, when we understand it as parodic allegory.

The foregoing discussion has examined the play of allegorical and parodic meanings inherent in vernacular motets by focusing on the polyvalence of key motifs important in both sacred and erotic poetry—in particular, the flower and the dance. I now turn to the maiden herself, not only as the object of masculine desire but also as desiring subject. Feminine desire does not play a major role in the corpus of the *chanson courtoise*, but it is prominent in "popular" lyric genres, such as the rondeau, the *chanson de toile*, and the *chanson de mal mariée*. And feminine passion and desire for mystical union with God are important themes in hagiographical literature and, as we have seen, in the liturgy of the Virgin and the virgin saints. I wish to establish a context for the desiring female subject—as positive and negative figure—through a brief survey of motets featuring the *mal mariée* and employing a variety of tenors. I will then return to the Marian tenor VERITATEM, examining the use of contrasting female figures in the bilingual motet *In salvatoris nomine* (452) / *Ce fu en tres douz tens de mai* (452a) / *In veritate comperi* (451) / VERITATEM (M37).

A Love Beyond Marriage: Adultery and Virginity

The motif of marriage does not often enter the amorous discourse of vernacular lyric; when it does it is usually negative, as in the *chanson de mal mariée*. With the exception of the narrative *chansons de toile*, some of which feature a heroine eager to marry her lover, vernacular lyric nearly always treats marriage as an obstacle to love, though rarely an insurmountable one. One finds a greater range of attitudes in courtly romance, in which marriage is often presented as the natural culmination of love and the goal toward which the narrative inexorably moves. Nonetheless, adulterous love remains an important romance theme; it frequently appears in texts with a strong lyric association, such as the *Ro-*

man *du Castelain de Couci* or the various romances of Tristan and Iseult.
This hostility to marriage takes on an interesting character in the motet,
with its ties to sacred texts and music. Although the mystical marriage
is an important liturgical and devotional theme, and marriage itself is a
sacrament of the Church, the cult of virginity also produces a literary
topos of resistance to marriage. Hagiographic literature celebrates countless young men and women who refused marriage, albeit not for the
same reason as the personae in popular lyric. The love that motivates a
resistance to marriage may be either adulterous or virginal, and certain
antimarital motets exploit this dichotomy.

I begin with *Ja ne mi marierai* (367) / *AMORIS* (M27), which exemplifies
the equivocal nature of the idealized language of love. The motetus, only
four lines long, is constructed out of refrains:

> M: Ja ne mi marierai,
>   mais par amors amerai.
>   Ne vous mariez mie,
>   tenez vous ainsi.
> T: AMORIS[47]

M: Never will I marry; rather, I will love. Do not marry, keep yourself this way.
T: OF LOVE

The tenor comes from an alleluia for Pentecost week: "Alleluia. Veni
sancte spiritus, reple tuorum corda fidelium, et tui amoris in eis ignem
accende" (Alleluia. Come, Holy Spirit, fill the hearts of your faithful ones,
and kindle the fire of your love in them [M27]). This motet expresses
the ideal of extramarital love to which so many medieval songs are devoted; it conjures up the world of the pastourelle, or of the songs of May
and popular dance refrains, with their complaints about the restrictions
of marriage and the abuses perpetrated by jealous husbands. The refrain
that constitutes the first two lines of the motetus is used in precisely
this context in *Chançon vueill faire de moi* (R1669), a satirical *chanson de
femme* in which the persona explains that she is incapable of fidelity or
of returning the love of a good man, and she vows not to marry any of
her suitors unless she finds one who can adapt to her carefree style.[48] The
antifeminist and decidedly nonspiritual tone of the song is reflected in its
refrains: for example, "Je sui fame a droit, / Car je n'amai onques celui qui
m'amoit" (I am a woman indeed, for I never loved the one who loved me
[vv. 18–19]) and "J'ai plus menti que voir dit / A celui qui m'aime" (I have
told more lies than truth to the one who loves me [vv. 27–28]).

The antifeminist context is missing, however, from the motet, as is any indication of gender. And given the associations of the tenor, the motetus *Ja ne mi marierai* could just as easily refer to abstinence from marriage for the sake of consecrating oneself to God. Indeed, the Holy Spirit is invoked in precisely such a context in a macaronic pastourelle, "En may, quant dait e foil e fruit," each stanza of which ends with the opening line of a Latin hymn.[49] Repelling the narrator's sexual advances, the girl explains that she has dedicated her life to virginity and voices the prayer: "Mun pucelage me gardez: / Veni creator Spiritus" (Preserve my virginity: come, creator Spirit [vv. 47–48]). Several Latin hymns begin with this line; representative is that by Rabanus Maurus.[50] This hymn includes a supplication for the divine love the Holy Spirit brings—"Infunde amorem cordibus (Infuse hearts with love [str. 4, v. 2])—as well as a prayer for aid in overcoming temptation and adversity:

> Hostem repellas longius
> . . .
> Ductore sic te praevio
> Vitemus omne noxium. (str. 6, vv. 1, 3–4)

You keep the enemy at bay. . . . That with you leading the way, we may shun all that is harmful.

The love bestowed by the Holy Spirit, in other words, is both inspirational and salvific, conducive to leading a chaste and holy life. This understanding of the Holy Spirit is reinforced in the pious contrafactum of "En may, quant dait e foil e fruit"—the poem "L'autrier matin, el moys de may," associated with Saint Louis—where "Veni creator Spiritus" now closes a stanza in which the Virgin Mary advises the narrator to abandon his sinful ways.[51]

If we read the motet *Ja ne mi marierai* / AMORIS as a statement of dedication to the love celebrated in its tenor, then the motet as a whole is a lyricized recasting of Saint Paul's famous advice: "Dico autem non nuptis, et viduis: bonum est illis si sic permaneant, sicut et ego" (But I say to the unmarried and to widows: it is good for them to remain that way, like me [1 Cor. 7:8]). The phrase "par amors amerai" (v. 2), expressing the lyric persona's dedication, can be translated "I will be in love" or "I will love wholeheartedly." It often refers to erotic love, as in the refrains "Bien doit quellir violete qui par amours aime" (One who loves does well to gather violets) and "Il pert bien a mon viaire que l'aim par amors" (It shows in my face that I love him/her).[52] But it could also refer to divine love, given the easy appropriation of amorous language into the spiritual register. Gérard de Liège, for example, uses the term as a translation for Pauline *caritas*: "caritatem autem non habeam, id est *se je n'aime par amours*, nichil michi prodest" (but if I do not have *caritas*, that is, *if I do not love par amours*, it gains me nothing [*Quinque incitamenta*, 3.4.3]). In the motet, the qualifying phrase "par amors" serves only to distinguish an absolute love from that determined by the state of marriage; it does not specify whether this passion is erotic or spiritual. In spite of its extreme brevity, this motet encompasses two distinct readings, entailing an allegorical and a parodic relationship between motetus and tenor. Its humor as well as its artistry lie in the unresolved tension of the dual references: Christian celibacy, filled with the love of the Holy Spirit; and amorous freedom, under the tutelage of the God of Love.

A livelier antimarital complaint appears in the motet *Pour quoi m'avés voz douné* (353) / *[DO]CEBIT* (M26), in which a girl upbraids her mother for forcing her into marriage. The unhappy bride's grievance is that she was not allowed to marry her lover:

> Car ja par mon gré
> ne fust ainsint,
> qu'a autre fuisse dounee
> qu'a celui, qui j'ai de moi seisi,
> qui tant m'a honouree. (vv. 3–7) [53]

For never according to my will would it have happened that I was given to anyone other than the one to whom I gave myself, who has so honored me.

The tenor derives from another Pentecost alleluia: "Alleluia. Paraclitus spiritus sanctus, quem mittet pater in nomine meo, ille vos docebit omnem veritatem" [54] (Alleluia. The Comforter, the Holy Spirit, which the father will send in my name, he will teach you every truth [M26]). The background this lament implies is recounted in various *chansons de toile* or in other narratives, such as Marie de France's *Lai de Milun*: an amorous couple broken up by the forced marriage of the girl. The closing line suggests a daughter who feels betrayed by her mother's abandonment of what had been a certain complicity with the love affair: "Ja saviés vous bien, qu'avoie ami!" (You knew very well that I had a boyfriend! [v. 13]). In a fully secularized reading, the tenor—s/HE WILL TEACH—might imply that the girl will find a way around the restrictions of marriage: that the spirit of love, or perhaps even the mother herself, will instruct her in the myriad ruses that can enable a wife to keep a lover.

Although the motetus can be read as alluding to a familiar narrative pattern, the alternate reading, emanating from the tenor's sacred origins, is still possible. Many a virgin martyr refused marriage—often in violent opposition to her parents—because she had already pledged herself to the Heavenly Bridegroom. The statements in the motetus are not inappropriate to the hagiographic model: that the lovers belonged to each other, that the girl's beloved had honored her, and that he deserved her love. In fact, the reproach to the mother unhappy over her daughter's refusal to marry appears in a famous—and certainly serious—praise of virginity and the celibate life, Saint Jerome's epistle to Eustochium: "Quid invides, mater, filiae? . . . indignaris, quod noluit militis uxor esse, sed regis? Grande tibi beneficium praestitit: socrus Dei esse coepisti" [55] (Why do you envy your daughter, mother? . . . Are you indignant that she wishes to be the wife not of a soldier, but of a king? She has done you a great service: you have come to be the mother-in-law of God).

So powerful was the metaphor of Christ as Bridegroom/Lover that a girl's decision to be celibate is naturally cast in matrimonial terms. And even as devout a man as Saint Jerome could allow himself the pleasantry of referring to a consecrated virgin's mother as socrus Dei—perhaps the closest possible approach to the exalted mater Dei. Our motet could, in light of its tenor, be read in accordance with this model. The maiden confronting an unwanted marriage will be sustained and illuminated by the Holy Spirit in her commitment to chastity, just as many a virgin martyr was consoled, and her will strengthened, by a visitation from the dove of the Holy Spirit.[56] Like so many other examples that we have seen, this motet presents the possibility of both readings, drawing its humor from the dissonance between the images of the passionate adulteress and the righteous Bride of Christ.

Not all motets featuring the mal mariée use tenors that allude to the Holy Spirit. Some accentuate the parodic juxtaposition of chastity and adultery by using tenors that correspond to Marian feasts and the Common of Virgins. We have already considered Li jalous par tout sunt fustat / Tuit cil qui sunt enamourat / PROPTER VERITATEM, describing a dance that admits only the amorous and excludes jealous husbands. A clearer rejection of conjugal love appears in another motet with a shorter version of the same tenor: Je sui jonete et jolie (465) / Hé Dieus, je n'ai pas mari (466) / VERITATEM (M37). There is little possibility for the favorable allegorization of the young wife who speaks in both triplum and motetus of this piece.

The sentiment that moves her is *amer par joliété* (Tr, v. 4), a love characterized by high spirits and carefree pleasures. She freely acknowledges that her husband "would die of jealousy" (Tr, v. 9) if he knew of her activities, and she proposes that if he objects to her lover he should take one himself (M, vv. 12–13). Such statements could hardly apply to a pious maiden dedicated to chastity. Indeed, her husband's free access to her body emboldens the young wife:

> Quant il fait tout a son gré
> et de mon cors sa volenté,
> del plus mon plesir ferai. (Tr, vv. 14–16)

When he does everything he wishes and has his will with my body, all the more will I take my pleasure.

In this caricature, female sexuality is a force that marriage cannot contain; the husband, overwhelmed, reaps only shame in his cuckoldry. In a purely literal reading, this portrait of the willful wife—who seems to have stepped directly out of the fabliau tradition—contrasts humorously with the regal and virtuous bride celebrated in Psalm 44, textual source of the gradual *Propter veritatem. Audi filia.* The liturgical function of the source gradual leads us to the chaste marriage of the Virgin and the rejection of marriage by the virgin martyrs; the adulterous wife of the texted voices is now clearly a figure of lust, an Eve opposed to the Mary of the tenor. And the allegorization of the tenor text finally brings us to the mystical marriage of Ecclesia and Christ; a parallel allegorization of the texted voices would require us to read the wife as Synagoga, whose "adulterous" and "whorish" behavior is lamented in numerous Old and New Testament passages, or more generally as the unrepentant soul.[57]

A similar *mal mariée* figure is seen in two motets using the Assumption tenor PORTARE (M34a): *Nus ne set les biens d'amors* (286) / *Ja Dieus ne me doinst corage* (287) / PORTARE, which was discussed in Chapter 1, and *Si com aloie jouer* (288) / *Deduisant com fins amourous* (289) / PORTARE. The latter, in which triplum and motetus describe three women who sing gleefully of cuckolding their husbands and express hope for an imminent widowhood, is a typical caricature of the detrimental effects of untamable female sexuality. The tenor, from the Assumption alleluia *Dulcis virgo dulcis mater*, celebrates the ultimate paradigm of sexual purity: after living chastely even in marriage, the Virgin ascends to Heaven and is united in mystical marriage with Christ. Again, it would be difficult to imagine a greater contrast than that between the virginal wife of Joseph and immaculate Bride of God, and the lusty women who boast of their adulterous exploits.

The motets identified above represent a considerable variety in their treatment of the antimarital theme. In the first example the defense of love over marriage easily takes on spiritual significance; in the next two, although the parodic effects are stronger, the allegorical potential remains; in the last three the antifeminist satire dominates. The anonymous poets who produced these motets responded, with varying degrees of overt humor and irony, to the opposition of love and marriage that pervades courtly and popular lyric as well as hagiographic tradition. Although from one perspective the virgin and the adulteress are an absolute contrast, from another perspective they both exist outside normal marital bonds. Virginity and adultery disrupt lineage and subvert a social order founded on marriage. The ultimate violation of ordinary generational patterns is the Virgin Birth, and Marian poetry abounds with statements of the resulting paradoxes: Mary is not only a virgin mother but also the mother of the father, daughter of her own son, and the bride of both father and son. The unnatural character of this lineage is expressed—to cite just one of many possible examples—in the motet text *Mellis stilla maris stella* (808):

> virgo, paris
> patrem filia.
> Ordo stupet,
> cuius supplet
> vicem gratia. (M, vv. 8–12)[58]

A virgin, as daughter you gave birth to your father. The natural order is astonished, through grace it is made whole.

And a Latin hymn, *O mira creatura*, summarizes Mary's identity in a concise list of attributes: "Amica, sponsa, filia / Et soror creatoris" (Beloved, bride, daughter, and sister of the creator [ed. Dreves and Blume, vol. 2, p. 288, str. 1, vv. 5–6]).

The paradoxical transformations of normal lineage brought about by the Incarnation find an intriguing counterpart in the disrupting effects of incest as portrayed in pagan mythology. Here, too, the violation of lineage gives rise to linguistic play, as in Ovid's designation of Adonis—son of Myrrha and her father, Cynaras—as "ille sorore / natus avoque suo" (the one born of his sister and his grandfather [*Metamorphoses*, 10: 520–21]). These parallels did not pass unobserved by medieval commentators;

the *Ovide moralisé*, for example, glosses Myrrha as an incestuous woman, as the sinful soul, and as the Blessed Virgin.[59]

The pursuit of allegory, however, can be a dangerous game; it requires close attention on the part of the reader. If Myrrha is equivalent to Mary on one level of signification, it is essential to bear in mind that on another level she is diametrically opposed. Likewise, the conflict in a saint's life between earthly and heavenly husbands must be carefully distinguished from that erupting in the life of an adulteress. In Rutebeuf's *Vie Sainte Elysabel*, an allusion to what sounds like adultery or bigamy is quickly clarified as a statement of the young girl's religious devotion:

> Elysabel ot droit aage
> D'avoir l'ordre de mariage
> Mari li donent: mari a,
> Car cil qui bien la maria
> N'en douta gaires chevaliers
> Ne senechauz ne concilliers:
> Ce fu li rois qui tot aroie,
> Jhesucriz qui les siens avoie. (vv. 473–80) [60]

Elizabeth was of the proper age to be married. They give her a husband: yet she has a husband, for the one who married her has no fear of knights, seneschals, or counselors: that was the king who rules all, Jesus Christ, who protects his own.

Elizabeth acquiesces to the marriage, embracing a fully ascetic life only after she reaches widowhood; for other saints, however, the conflict between earthly and heavenly marriage is much stronger. The ordeals of such saints as Agnes, Christine, Margaret, or Euphrosina recall the young wife's lament in the motet *Pour quoi m'avés voz douné | [DO]CEBIT*.

The misreading of a virgin saint or of the Blessed Virgin as an adulteress is a source of humor that some medieval religious poetry in fact exploits. When Saint Agnes rejects her suitor on the grounds that she is already betrothed to one even better than he, both the young man and his father at first assume that she refers to an actual, earthly fiancé. The ensuing conversations are of great amusement for the audience, who understands what her would-be father-in-law does not:

> "Sire," dist ele, "jou ai m'amour donnee
> a un millour de cui sui afiee."
>
> . . .
>
> "Comment," dist il, "ames vous dont autrui?
> Vostre dangiers me torne a grant anui.
>
> . . .

Et nequedant, ki'st cil et dont est nes
Pour cui amour ensi vous demenes?"
Dist la puciele, "grans est ses parentes,
sollel et lune sormonte la biautes."
(ed. Denomy, vv. 146–47, 149–50, 153–56)

"Sir," said she, "I have given my love to a better man, to whom I am betrothed." . . . "What," said he, "then you love someone else? Your resistance
greatly annoys me. . . . Anyhow, who is he, and what is his lineage, this man you
insist on loving?" Said the maiden, "He is of noble birth, he surpasses the beauty
of the sun and the moon."

Similar scenarios take place in the lives of other virgin saints. More daring
is the motif of Joseph's Troubles with Mary, developed to great comic
effect in late medieval mystery plays but present in earlier lives of the
Virgin and, very briefly, in the Bible (Matt. 1:18–20). This episode draws
its humor from its evocation of the unthinkable: an eroticized reading of
the Blessed Virgin as an adulteress.[61] In order to accept Mary's pregnancy,
Joseph and the Temple priests must learn to distinguish the miraculous
from the natural, just as the would-be suitors of a virgin saint had to
learn to separate literal and figurative meanings in order to understand
her refusal of marriage.

The motets that we have just seen are to be understood against the
backdrop of this pervasive hagiographic motif: the pious maiden who
resists marriage because of a lover who turns out to be Christ, the Virgin
Mary pregnant through the intervention not of an adulterer but of the
Holy Spirit. Also contributing to the overall context for these pieces is the
conventional opposition of Mary/Ecclesia, the faithful Bride of Christ,
with Synagoga, the faithless and adulterous first Bride. Within the devotional model, resistance to marriage is motivated by a higher and nobler
love; true adultery—of the spirit—is defined as the violation of one's
bond with God.

The particular quality of the antimarital motet is illuminated through
comparison with the parodic use of the hagiographic motif in Boncompagno da Signa's *Rota Veneris*. In a letter providing the model for a woman
to dispose of her lover once she is married, the language of the *Gesta Sanctae Agnes*—used also in the liturgy of Saint Agnes, as in the responsory
quoted in the first section of this chapter—is appropriated and literalized
in such a way as to refer to actual marriage: "Amoris vestri vinculum per
effectum operum dissolvatur, quoniam nupsi viro, qui me maritali an-
nulo subarravit, *cinxit collum meum lapidibus preciosis deditque vestes auro*

et gemmis plurimum renitentes. Unde non possum nec debeo tecum more solito iocundari" (The bond of your love is dissolved through the effect of works, for I have married a man who has betrothed me with a marriage band, *he has girded my neck with precious stones and given garments of gold resplendent with many jewels.* Therefore I neither can nor should take pleasure with you as we were accustomed [ed. Bäthgen, p. 18; emphasis added]). Boncompagno's use of liturgical language rests on an analogy between earthly and spiritual marriage: the wife refuses an adulterous liaison just as the saint refuses a marriage that would violate her betrothal to Christ. What differentiates the motets we have examined here is their dependence on vernacular lyric. The *chanson de mal mariée* intersects with the hagiographic model not through a rhetoric of fidelity but through a common valorization of private passion: a love more noble, or at least more pleasurable, than that in institutionalized marriage. As the eroticized antitype of the consecrated virgin, the adulteress is a convenient figure for the parodic treatment of holy and unholy love.

A Bilingual Motet: The Virgin and the Harlot

My final example is a motet constructed around contrasting feminine figures, both spiritual and erotic: the four-part composition *In salvatoris nomine* (452) / *Ce fu en tres douz tens de mai* (452a) / *In veritate comperi* (451) / *VERITATEM* (M37) (Musical Example 3).[62] The Latin texts are clearly relevant to the Marian tenor, but the French triplum raises important questions of interpretation; it appears in only one source, the La Clayette manuscript.[63] The presence of this vernacular triplum turns a straightforward if elegant Latin double motet into a bilingual composition of greater complexity. In order to address the motet as a whole, I begin with an examination of the two Latin voices and then consider how the vernacular text affects our understanding of the motet.

The quadruplum is a text in celebration of the Incarnation, addressing the Virgin in her role as mother of God and *mediatrix*. Though conventional in its choice of language and imagery, the quadruplum is artfully constructed, incorporating texts relevant to the Incarnation from both pagan and Christian sources. The divine birth is announced in the quadruplum:

> Iam nova progenies
> Dilabitur

f. 378 v.

(452) In ___ sal-va-to-ris no-mi-ne, Qui san-gui-ne ___ Mun-do mun-dum

(452a) Ce ___ fu en tres douz tens de ___ mai Que de cuer gai Vont cil oi-seil-

(451) In ___ ve-ri-ta-te com-pe-ri, Quod sce-le-ri Cle-ri stu-det

M 37 Veritatem

ab-lu-it, ___ Ex-a-cto-ris e-ru-it Nos vo-ra-gi-ne, E-ius pi-e-

lon chan-tant. ___ En un ver-gier, pour lour chant O-ïr, m'en en-trai; Tant que, la-ïs!

u-ni-tas; Li-vor re-gnat, ve-ri-tas Da-tur fu-ne-ri. He-re-des lu-

Ge-ni-tri-ci Ma-ri-e Stu-de-a-mus psal-le-re. Er-go vir-go ___ vir-gi-num, ___

re-gar-dai En ce ___ jar-din, De-soz un pin Bien ra-mé, Pu-ce-le de grant bi-auté.

ci-fe-ri Sunt pre-la-ti, Iam e-la-ti Glo-ri-a; Mem-bra do-mant a-li-a ___

Cul-pis po-ne ter-mi-num Et nos ___ ti-bi ___ fac ___ pla-ce-re. Dum si-le-rent

Lon-gue-ment ot es-cou-té Tres-touz ces ois-se-lons chan-tant La dou-ce, la

Ca-pi-tis in-sa-ni-a; Ce-ci du-ces-que ce-co-rum, Ex-ce-ca-ti

(continued on next page)

Q: In the name of the Savior, who absolved the world with his blood and pulled us from the abyss of the executioner, let us attend to celebrating his holy mother Mary. Thus virgin of virgins, put an end to guilt, and make us pleasing to you. As all the world fell still and silent, your mellifluous word, O Father, came to earth from the regal seats. O what a mystery! Deity was wedded to flesh, and humanity was made cloak for Deity, divinity was veiled in the fragile veil of the flesh. Now a new progeny comes down, sent from the highest heaven, fair of face, but exhausted from the rigors of the Passion. He who holds the heavens in his hand, sustains the earth; free of all sin, he is sent and enclosed in the bosom of a virgin mother. O lily, protector of sinners, pray to your own son that, removing guilt, he call us back and gather us into the company of the saints.

Tr: It was in the very sweet season of May, when with a merry heart the little birds sing, that I went into an orchard in order to hear their song. And I went on until I saw in that garden, under a branching pine, a maiden of great beauty. The sweet one, the beauty with the bright face, listened for a long time to all those birds singing. I took a better look at her: she has a face of good color, a slender body, and blond hair in little ringlets; her eyebrows are well formed; her eyes are gray and laughing, her mouth small and pleasant, [she is] whiter than a gladiolus; nothing in her is ill formed. God put all his efforts into her beautiful appearance; no one could ever count or recount, without miscounting, the good things that are in her. Then she sang out with a cry: "*God give me a loyal sweetheart, if I have deserved it!*" Now all the birds left off their singing and sat around her. The nightingale leapt before her right away and asked for her love: "Lady in whom all good and valor are placed, for whom I am in great torment, lady full of sweetness, I am slain: know that I will die, if I have not your love."

M: *In truth* is found the unity of the licentious clergy; envy reigns, truth is given a burial. The light-bearing masters get preferential treatment, and are puffed up with glory; other bodily members rule in the insanity of the head; and blind leaders of the blind, given over to idolatry of earthly things, seek only their own gain; their hands are open and the benefits of the Cross are hidden. Weep, daughter of Syon! The fire in the tails of the foxes burns the fruit of the harvest. Appearing sorrowful through hypocrisy, simulated sanctity, like Tamar at the crossroads, shrivels up in the filth of idleness; she taints and weakens the whole world, to no profit; given to license, she pollutes chastity and casts aside charity, claiming thrift. She lies in wait for the sons of men, pillaging the poor and killing the just with swords of slander. There is not a one of them who does good, their conscience is a den of thieves; all-seeing God of vengeance, behold this evil.

T: TRUTH

Musical Example 3. From Gordon Athol Anderson and Elizabeth Close, eds., *Motets of the Manuscript La Clayette: Paris, Bibliothèque Nationale, nouv. ac. f. fr. 13521,* Corpus Mensurabilis Musicae, 68. © 1975 by American Institute of Musicology / Hänssler-Verlag, D73762 Neuhausen-Stuttgart. All rights reserved. International copyright secured. Legally protected. Duplications are not allowed.

Et mittitur
A supremo celo. (vv. 26–29)

Now a new progeny comes down, sent from the highest heaven.

This statement paraphrases a celebrated line in Virgil's Fourth Eclogue, interpreted in the Middle Ages as a prophecy of Christ: "iam nova progenies caelo demittitur alto" (now a new generation descends from heaven on high [v. 7]).[64] This allusion is carefully chosen to highlight the conversion from paganism to Christianity through its implicit evocation of the inspired pagan poet Virgil. The Fourth Eclogue, written just before the Incarnation, looks forward to the turning point of world history, the advent of the Age of Grace. Central to the New Dispensation is its universality, entailing the conversion and redemption not only of the Jews but also of the pagans. The recurrence of Christian prophecy within the pagan tradition was seen by medieval poets and theologians as a sign of this universality: the coming of the Messiah was felt, if indistinctly, even outside the realm of God's chosen people. The motif of conversion appears in the psalm that is the ultimate textual source for the tenor VERITATEM, in the evocation of the bride's new life (Ps. 44:11, 17). These verses are the source of the gradual Constitues eos. Pro patribus (M30), used in the feast of Saints Peter and Paul; in the traditional interpretation they refer to the establishment of the Church through the replacement of pagan "fathers" by apostolic "sons." The citation of a specifically pagan prophecy of the Incarnation in the quadruplum places the motif of conversion in the motet's very texture; the birth of Christ is implicitly linked to the "birth" and growth of the Church, his mystical body. The Virgilian text additionally highlights the phenomenon of inspired allegorical reading: Divine Grace illuminates new meaning that a text's original author could not have foreseen. As we will see, this idea itself is relevant to the interpretation of the four-part bilingual motet.

The Incarnation is also invoked in the paraphrase of an antiphon from the Christmas liturgy:

> Dum silerent
> Et tenerent
> Cuncta medium
> In terris silencium,
> Mellifluus
> Sermo tuus,
> Pater, a regalibus,
> Mundo venit sedibus.[65] (Q, vv. 12–19)

As all the world fell still and silent, your mellifluous word, O Father, came to earth from the regal seats.

This image of the birth of Christ as Incarnation of the Word—God "speaks," and the silent world "hears" and receives—is highly conventional, originating in the Gospel of John. But it has relevance to the motet at hand, implicitly recalling the language of the tenor's liturgical source: "Audi, filia, et vide, et inclina aurem tuam" (Listen, daughter, and behold, and incline your ear). The Virgin heard the greeting of the archangel; she conceived, the Word of God entering through her ear; the world fell silent to receive God's Word made flesh. And the manifestation of the Word entailed the unveiling of obscure prophecies: not only those of the Old Testament but also those uttered by inspired pagans who, like Virgil, could not themselves understand the full meaning of their own words. Overall, then, the quadruplum is intimately bound to the tenor VERITATEM. It celebrates the Virgin and her role in the Incarnation, using language that recalls Psalm 44 and its imagery of sacred marriage and birth; it invokes the profound mystery of God's birth and the New Age thereby begun. At its center, framed by liturgical and pagan accounts of the birth of Christ, is the most explicit statement of the Incarnation: divinity clothed in flesh, deity wedded to humanity in the womb of the Virgin. The text opens and closes with allusions to Passion and Redemption and to Mary as object of worship: to her one sings psalms, and through her one gains access to divine mercy.

The motetus laments ecclesiastical corruption. It is immediately apparent that the motetus is the antitype of the quadruplum. The latter centers on the image of divinity clothed in flesh, but the motetus has as a central image corrupted flesh cloaked in false sanctity. To the figure of the Blessed Virgin is opposed Tamar seated at the crossroads in the guise of a prostitute; idolatry replaces the images of conversion and reception of God's Word. The close relationship of these central portions of the two texts—verses 20–25 in both cases—is heightened by the shared rhymes -ium, -itas, and -o. To the motif of the body wedded to the divine spirit— of Christ, of the Virgin, or of the Church, a common figure of the Virgin and the allegorical body of Christ—is opposed that of the body out of control: "Membra domant alia / Capitis insania" (Other bodily members rule in the insanity of the head [M, vv. 10–11]). And whereas the quadruplum ends with a prayer for mercy and salvation, the motetus closes by beseeching God to take vengeance on unrepentant sinners. In this respect, the motetus expands on a different aspect of Psalm 44, the just but stern ruler who strikes terror into the hearts of his enemies: "Accingere gladio tuo super femur tuum, potentissime. . . . Sagittae tuae acutae, populi sub te cadunt, in corda inimicorum regis" (Gird on your sword above your thigh, most powerful one. . . . Your arrows are sharp in the hearts of the king's enemies, the people fall before you [Ps. 44:4, 6]).

As a Latin double motet, the piece is thus tightly woven, the two texted voices presenting alternate sides of the same fundamental themes, cast in imagery relevant to the biblical source of the tenor text. The vernacular triplum, situated between the celebration of *caritas* and the condemnation of *cupiditas*, transposes these themes and motifs into the language of the pastourelle or *reverdie*. Although at first reading the triplum clearly is a recasting of the thematics of the two Latin voices, the nature of these correspondences is less easy to determine. We can begin with the figure of the maiden. The musical setting of the piece is such that the phrase "pucele de grant biauté" (maiden of great beauty [Tr, v. 10]) parallels "ergo virgo virginum" (therefore virgin of virgins [Q, v. 9]), suggesting a possible equation. Yet the corresponding phrase in the motetus is "membra domant alia" (other bodily members rule [M, v. 10]), which might equally imply that the *pucele*, a figure of carnal desire, acts not on the rational mind, but on a different part of the body. This double reading of the triplum is strong in the crucial central portion of the motet (vv. 20–25), where the description of the maiden's beautiful, eroticized body and God's attention to her lovely face runs parallel to the accounts of the Incarnation and Tamar's corruption and harlotry. Even the *-ant*, *-ai*, and *-on* rhymes of the triplum in this section are somewhat similar to those of the two Latin texts, which also employ the vowels *a* and *o*. Other textual juxtapositions add to the bivalence of the triplum; for example, the narrator's absorption in the *pucele*—"Mielz l'en regardé" (I looked at her more closely [Tr, v. 14])—parallels the word *Ydolatria* (M, v. 14). The maiden's articulation of amorous desire and the immediate response of the birds, which leave off singing and gather around her, coincide in musical performance with the statement of the harlot's insidious influences on men—a parallel heightened by the similar rhymes *-i* and *-it* (Tr and M, vv. 30–35). And yet the prayer to the Virgin, "O lilium" (O lily [Q, vv. 39–46]), is concurrent with the nightingale's "prayer" for the maiden's love, which he claims will save his life. Depending on one's reading, the *pucele* of the triplum—seated in an orchard, listening attentively to the mellifluous song of the birds who desire her love, and attracting the attention of the male narrator—might be the deceiving temptress seated at the crossroads; or she might be the maiden—the Virgin, Ecclesia—of whom it is said, "Listen, daughter, and behold, and incline your ear: for the king has desired your beauty."

The orchard, too, is a bivalent image that lends itself to either interpretation of the triplum text. First, this *vergier*, well known from the pastourelle repertoire, is hardly an edifying place; most commonly, it is the scene of sexual escapades, ranging from flirtation to seduction to rape, involving the encounter of a shepherdess or a peasant girl with either a shepherd or a knight. Virgil's Fourth Eclogue—cited, we recall, in the quadruplum—opens with the suggestion of leaving the orchard groves: "Sicelides Musae, paulo maiora canamus. / non omnis arbusta iuvant humilesque myricae" (Sicilian Muses, let us sing a somewhat loftier strain. Not all do the orchards please and the lowly tamarisks [vv. 1–2]). Virgil's presumed prophecy of the Incarnation and the coming Age of Grace is thus explicitly distinguished from the other Eclogues, which are pastoral songs, appropriate to orchards. Yet the narrator of the triplum announces his entrance into an orchard, specifically because birdsong attracts him: "En un vergier, pour lour chant / Oïr, m'en entrai" (I went into an orchard in order to hear their song [Tr, vv. 4–5]). In addition, this is sung in juxtaposition to the statement of humanity's redemption, also phrased in spatial terms: "Exactoris eruit / Nos voragine" (He pulled us from the abyss of the executioner [Q, vv. 4–5]). One could easily read the triplum against the quadruplum: reversing the process of salvation, the narrator reenters the space of frivolity and cupidinous desire, encounters a decidedly eroticized maiden, and is seduced into an idolatrous contemplation of her bodily delights. By the end, he has projected his lustful fantasies onto the nightingale, lyric emblem of erotic passion, to such an extent that he imagines the bird voicing his own desire for the maiden's love.

At the same time, however, one cannot forget that the garden is a time-honored figure for the Virgin, and the amorous encounter in the garden a standard figure for the Incarnation. Even the nightingale is equally at home in religious poetry as a figure for Christ or as the embodiment of spiritual love.[66] The legend that it sings itself to death in amorous passion allowed the nightingale's poetic appropriation as a figure for Christ's Passion—or, more properly, for the soul consumed by contemplation of the Passion—in two important Latin poems, the *Philomena* of John of Hoveden (d. 1275) and that of John Pecham (d. 1292), as well as the Old French *Rossignol*. The nightingale is also a stock figure in Old French and Old Occitan poetry as the source of erotic (and poetic or musical) inspiration. In one thirteenth-century song, however, the nightingale inspires not erotic desire but the love of God:

> Rossignolet, bien faites vostre office,
> Les fins amans bien aprenez a vivre;
>   Ditez: Fuiez, fuiez,
>   Tout le monde laissiez. (vv. 10–13)[67]

Nightingale, you perform your office well, you teach true lovers well how to live; you say: Flee, flee, leave the world behind.

The lyric persona wishes to join the nightingale in the forest for a joyful celebration of love; but although the language is from courtly lyric, the imagined rendezvous is dedicated to the love of Christ:

> Rossignolet, par vo grant cortoisie
> Menez m'ou bois o vous en la gaudie.
>   La serons en deduit
>   Et le jour et la nuit,
>   Et si l'orons, celui
>   Qu'amours firent ocirre.
> Folz est li cuers qui Jhesum ne desirre. (vv. 18–24)

Nightingale, by your great courtesy, take me with you into the forest in joyful celebration. There we will experience delight both day and night, and we will pray to the one who was killed for love. Mad is the heart that does not desire Jesus.

"The one who was killed for love" might be either the nightingale or Christ. By the end of the poem the two have fused:

> Rossignolet, Jhesu de piteus estre,
> Assié nous tous delez toy a ta destre
>   En ce biau paradis (vv. 42–44)

Nightingale, merciful Jesus, seat us all beside you at your right, in that beautiful paradise.

Given this background, a spiritual reading of the triplum *Ce fu en tres douz tens de mai* is by no means impossible; the beautiful maiden enshrined in the garden, giving all her attention to the nightingale as it asks for her love, can easily be interpreted in allegorical terms. And if she is the Virgin, listening and receiving the Word of God, then the narrator who pauses to listen with her and to contemplate her beauty becomes a figure for the human witnesses to the Incarnation: those who fell silent to receive the mellifluous Word, those privileged to see the Blessed Virgin herself.

The fact remains that in spite of its erotic suggestiveness and its close ties to the pastourelle, the triplum cannot be reduced to a simple text of carnal desire; the possibility of an allegorical reading never disappears.

The motet as a whole makes an interesting comparison to a passage in the roughly contemporary *Rota Veneris* of Boncompagno da Signa. In this treatise on the art of writing love letters, Boncompagno suggests composing a dream narrative as a tool of seduction. He offers a model letter in which a man recounts an erotic dream and asks a woman to interpret it for him; she writes back, saying that if they meet that night in the garden, she can explain the dream in far more detail than is feasible in a letter. The setting of the dream narrative is similar to that of the triplum *Ce fu en tres douz tens de mai*. The narrator enters a beautiful orchard filled with blossoming trees and the song of nightingales; he encounters a "virgo speciosissima, cuius pulcritudinem non posset aliquis designare" (most beautiful maiden, whose beauty no one could describe [ed. Bäthgen, p. 17]), just as the narrator of the triplum discovers a *pucele de grant biauté* whose beauty is indescribable (Tr, vv. 10, 26–29). The encounter even takes place under a pine tree, as in the triplum. The dream narrative, however, proceeds rapidly beyond mere visual contemplation to embraces, kisses, and full sexual consummation.

Despite its overtly sexual content, Boncompagno's narrative contains several liturgical and biblical echoes. It begins with an allusion to the same Christmas antiphon cited in the quadruplum *In salvatoris nomine* (vv. 12–19): "*Dum medium silencium tenerent omnia* et dies iocundissimo tempore veris *suum perageret cursum*, causa venandi quoddam intravi pomerium" (*While all kept silent* and the day *was running its course* in the merry time of spring, being out hunting, I entered a certain field [ed. Bäthgen, p. 17; emphasis added]). And the description of the sexual encounter itself borrows imagery from the Song of Songs: "Post hec iocundiora et iocundissima exercendo . . . *introduxit me tandem in cubiculum suum, quod fulcitum erat floribus et malis stipatum*" (After that, behaving more and more delightfully . . . *she let me into her little room, which was supported with flowers and surrounded by apples* [ibid., emphasis added; see Song 2:5, 3:4]). The "little room," with its ivory and gold doorposts, crystal walls, and precious gems, also bears a fleeting resemblance to the Temple of Solomon, being decorated "cum celatura varia" (with varied carvings [ed. Bäthgen, p. 17; see Vulgate 3 Kings 7:31]). Through this accumulation of liturgical and scriptural allusions the narrator disguises his erotic vision as the mystical union of Christ and the Virgin or human soul, assigning himself the role of Heavenly Bridegroom. His entrance into the field on a spring day parallels the arrival of the *Sponsus* on a winter night; the maiden who greets him is the *Sponsa*; the scene of their union is a holy place. Just as the body of the Virgin is both nuptial chamber and temple, so this "virgin" admits her lover to a space that is at once temple and bedroom, as well as an obvious allegory for her body. The narrator's request for an explication of the dream is thus a teasing challenge to his female correspondent, who can in her reply either acknowledge the sexual nature of the request or divert the exchange into a discussion of spiritual devotion. By offering to meet the man at the scene of the dream she shows herself amenable to his eroticized use of Scriptural passages: in effect, she agrees to participate in a literal reenactment of the Song of Songs.[68]

The motet *In salvatoris nomine* / *Ce fu en tres douz tens de mai* / *In veritate comperi* / *VERITATEM* offers a similar exercise in interpretation. Framed by Latin texts of religious devotion and moral polemic, the vernacular triplum is deliberately ambiguous, casting in high relief the very process of reading and reminding us that "littera enim occidit, Spiritus autem vivificat" (2 Cor. 3:6). The unwary reader or listener can easily be led astray by this seductive text, as is graphically expressed in the motetus. Yet the possibility exists in the motet's intertextual dynamics for a redemptive reading of the triplum, an interpretation *in bono* of its imagery. Seated at the crossroads, Tamar seduced Judah precisely because he failed to recognize her; and this initial misreading, in which he mistook his daughter-in-law for a prostitute, led to a misinterpretation of her pregnancy.[69] Judah's unthinking act of fornication was at the same time a fulfillment of duty, one that could have been accomplished more honorably had he discerned the identity of the veiled woman before him. Indeed, in exegetical tradition Tamar becomes a figure not for harlotry but for Ecclesia: the allegorical woman who puts on new garb to become the Bride of Christ.[70] The central image of the motetus is a powerful reminder of the complexity of interpretation, the dangers of misreading: one can be deceived by a pious exterior covering inner depravity, but one can also be seduced by the beauties of the flesh, failing to discern the spirit within.

This last point is dramatized in the quadruplum, with its citation of the Fourth Eclogue: the words of the pagan poet Virgil contain an inspired meaning that he himself could not grasp, and that will be lost on those readers who fail to look beyond the textual surface. Indeed, the governing motif of the quadruplum—the Incarnation—is itself the ultimate example of a sacred "text," the Word of God, that was misread by all those unable to see beyond the flesh. And the tenor, with its ties to the liturgy, reminds us that an epithalamium for a royal wedding—or, for that matter, an erotic love poem—is to be read as a celebration of the Incarnation and the Virgin Bride of God. Similarly, the *reverdie* of the triplum, with its story of uninhibited sexual desire amid the birds and flowers, may be read as a representation of either *caritas* or *cupiditas*: its impact upon the reader is a function of his or her interpretive powers. The motet as a whole, like the others we have examined here, presents a puzzle—indeed, a challenge—to performers and audience alike: that of navigating a densely woven poetico-musical configuration without being seduced by the letter of the text or bewildered by the heady allegorical play of the spirit.

Chapter 4

The Pain of Separation and the
Consolation of Love

Oi, dous amis com longhement me laires uous en
estrengue pais. He pour diu trahe me post te.
O sweet friend, how long will you leave me in a foreign land?
Ha, for God's sake, draw me after you.
　　　　　　　　　　　—Gérard de Liège, *Quinque incitamenta*

I turn now to a different lyric motif, that of separation with its attendant emotional register of hope, pain, and consolation. In such songs the
male protagonist laments not his lady's resistance but her absence, and
the female protagonist is not a figure of joyous desire but one of sorrow,
grieving for her absent beloved. Related to this thematic are songs treating the moment of reunion, in which the pain of separation and absence
is contrasted with the euphoria of renewed presence.

The motifs of absence, separation, and reunion are also important
in two key moments of the extended Passion narrative: the Crucifixion,
reversed by the joyous reunion scenes after the Resurrection, and the Ascension, followed by the arrival of the consoling Holy Spirit on Pentecost.
In this chapter, I trace the thematics of bereavement, absence, and consolation in a series of motets employing tenors drawn from those feasts,
focusing on the grieving or hopeful maiden.

The maiden bereft of her lover—who may be dead, preoccupied with
another girl, or simply away on a journey—figures in the varied corpus
loosely referred to as *chansons de femme*. She is equally familiar in devotional literature, where she is identified with Mary or Ecclesia lamenting
the crucified Christ.[1] A song assumed to be a pious contrafactum of a
lost *chanson de femme*, for example, is constructed on a refrain employing
this image:

L'ame qui quiert Dieu de veraie entente
Souvent se plaint et forment se demente,
Et son ami, cui venue est trop lente
Va regretant, que ne li atalente.
Amis, amis,
Trop me laissiez en estrange païs. (vv. 3–8)[2]

The soul that seeks God with true intention often laments and grievously mourns, and regrets her beloved, to whom she is too slow to come, in her sorrow. *Friend, friend, you leave me too long in a foreign land.*

Gérard de Liège uses a version of the same refrain to express the insatiable quality of the soul's love for God: "Et ideo necesse habet cotidie in oratione ad amicum suum totis medullis cordis sui clamare et dicere: *Oi, dous amis com longhement me laires uous en estrengue pais. He pour diu TRAHE ME POST TE*"[3] (And thus every day in prayer to its beloved it [the soul] must cry out with all its heart and say: *Oh sweet friend, how long will you leave me in a foreign land? Ha, for God's sake, DRAW ME AFTER YOU*). The Latin phrase with which the soul ends its prayer is a citation of Song of Songs 1:3. The overall effect is not unlike a sequential version of a motet: vernacular lyric coupled with a brief Latin citation of a sacred text. And although no motet exists that contains this refrain and this Latin citation, one can find examples in which the motif of the lamenting maiden is combined with a tenor that evokes Christ's death or his separation from the Church. It is with such an example that my discussion begins.

The Virgin and the Cross

One of the central motifs of Christian art and literature is the Virgin as sorrowful witness to Christ's Passion. A brief survey of the topos of Mary's grief provides the background for our examination of a beautiful and subtle bilingual motet, *Au doz mois de mai* (275) / *Crux forma penitentie* (274) / *SUSTINERE* (M22).[4]

Christian tradition holds that the Virgin Mary was present at the Crucifixion. Her grief and bewilderment at this event are the subject of such poems as *Crux, de te volo conqueri* by Chancellor Philip of Paris (d. 1236) and the famous thirteenth-century Franciscan hymn *Stabat mater dolorosa*. Chancellor Philip's poem is a justification of the seemingly inexplicable harshness of Christ's Passion; here the Virgin accuses the Cross of unjustly robbing her of her "fruit" and inflicting a shameful death on one who did not merit such treatment.[5] The Cross replies, acknowledging the transfer of Christ's body from Mary to itself: "De tuo flore fulgeo, / De tuo fructu gaudeo" (I am resplendent with your flower, I rejoice in your fruit [5: 4–5]). This seeming injustice is resolved through the allegory of sacramental wine:

> Tu vitis, uva filius;
> Quid uvae compententius
> Quam torcular, quo premitur? (8: 1–3)

You are a vine, your son a grape; what is more fitting to the grape than the winepress by which it is pressed?

The movement from the body of the Virgin to the Cross is thus a natural process of growth, fruition, and harvest. The Cross replaces the Virgin as the locus for seeking God's son:

> Iam non pendet ad ubera,
> Pendet in cruce verbera
> Corporis monstrans lividi (10: 4–6)

He no longer hangs at the breast, he hangs on the Cross, showing the stripes of his livid body.

For the individual Christian, the message is that access to Christ can never be exclusively through the gentle and merciful Virgin, but must include a confrontation with and acceptance of the bitterness of martyrdom. The movement from vine to press, doubled in that from the image of Madonna and Child to the Crucifixion, reflects both the differences between the tender Virgin and the harsh Cross, and their link as the two poles of a natural and necessary progression. Indeed, beyond the figure of the winepress, the Cross is metaphorically equivalent to the Virgin. She is the vine on which the divine grapes grew, but the Cross itself is a tree:

> Quaerant in meo stipite,
> Sugant de meo palmite
> Fructum tuum (9: 7–9)

Let them seek in my stalk, let them suck from my sprout, your fruit.

The adversarial relation between Virgin and Cross has, by the end of the poem, become analogy and even metaphorical equivalence; the power of the poem lies in its ability to maintain the tension of this double focus.

Stabat mater dolorosa focuses more on the emotional experience of the Passion as it affected Mary and as it continues to affect all Christians.[6] Beginning with the figure of the afflicted mother, this poem encompasses a gradual movement that draws in the individual Christian soul—represented by the poetic persona—and reveals the true significance of the Crucifixion. The first half of the poem evokes Mary's great sorrow at the cruel death of her son. In the fifth of its ten stanzas, the poetic persona speaks:

> Pia mater, fons amoris,
> Me sentire vim doloris
> Fac, ut tecum lugeam. (5: 1–3)

Pious mother, fountain of love, make me feel the force of the sorrow, that I may grieve with you.

This identification with Mary's emotions soon develops into a fantasy:

> Iuxta crucem tecum stare
> Et me tibi sociare
> In planctu desidero. (7: 4–6)

I wish to stand with you beside the Cross and to be your companion in grief.

Merely witnessing the Crucifixion is not enough, however; the persona says:

> Fac me plagis vulnerari,
> Cruce fac inebriari
> Et cruore filii. (9: 1–3)

Cause me to be afflicted with his wounds, intoxicated with the Cross and with the blood of your son.

And this increasing identification with Christ's Passion culminates in a prayer for salvation:

> Quando corpus morietur
> Fac ut anima donetur
> Paradisi gloriae. (10: 4–6)

When the body dies, let the soul be given to the glory of paradise.

Opening with the experience of the Virgin, then, the poem closes with that of the individual Christian; and from imagery of pain, grief, and death, it moves toward a concluding vision of joy and eternal life. In this way it reenacts the cycle of the Passion itself—humiliation, death, and triumphant Resurrection—and its significance for the individual soul, which suffers in contemplation of Christ's death and rejoices in the hope of redemption.

Medieval exegesis easily identified the Virgin with Ecclesia as Bride of Christ, and in representations of the Crucifixion the figure of Mary standing to the right of the Cross was often replaced by or fused with Ecclesia, commonly depicted as catching Christ's blood in a chalice. The poetic lament for the crucified Christ could therefore also be voiced by the Church, personified as a maiden. Such is the case in the Old French poem *Quant li solleiz converset en Leon*.[7] The poem begins in the format of a typical pastourelle:

> Quant li solleiz converset en Leon,
> En icel tens qu'est ortus Pliadon,
> Per unt matin,
> Une pulcellet odit molt gent plorer
> & son ami dolcement regreter. (vv. 1–5)

When the sun moves into Leo, at the time the Pleiades rises, one morning, I heard a maiden weeping softly and sweetly lamenting her beloved.

The protagonist asks the maiden who her beloved is, and she replies in terms reminiscent of the Song of Songs: he is white and red (v. 19); he has described her lips as the sweetness of honey (v. 25); she sought him (v. 40), and the city guards beat her (vv. 43–48). Although this certainly invites an allegorical reading, it is only at this point that an explicit biblical allusion rends the narrative surface:

> Beles pulcelsz, fillesz Jerusalem,
> Por mei amor, noncieiz le mon amant,
> D'amor languis. (vv. 49–51)

Fair maidens, daughters of Jerusalem, out of love for me, tell my beloved that I languish with love.

From here on, the allegorical quality of the maiden is foregrounded. She explains that her beloved had a different girlfriend for five thousand years, whom he abandoned because of her iniquity (vv. 52–54), and lists the many Old Testament prophets who prepared the way by announcing his love for her. At the poem's conclusion, she states that when her beloved finally wanted to claim her ("Mei vult aveir" [v. 90]), "Il enveiad sun angret a la pucele" (He sent his angel to the virgin [v. 91]).

The movement in this poem, then, is somewhat different from that in *Crux, de te volo conqueri* or *Stabat mater*, for it involves a progressive unveiling of the allegory and an increasingly explicit commentary on the identity of the sorrowful maiden. The figure of the Virgin is not absent;

the poem opens with allusions to the season of Assumption and closes with the Annunciation, thereby invoking Mary's first encounter with divinity and her final reunion with Christ in Heaven. But instead of moving from the Virgin to the individual believer, *Quant li solleiz* begins with an unidentified maiden and reveals her as the image of the Church, the collectivity of all those who have loved Christ, suffered for him, grieved at his death, and yearned to be reunited with him. As in both Latin texts, the loss and grief with which the poem opens are gradually eclipsed, this time through the triumphant recollection of sacred history, which leads inexorably to the angelic salutation and the birth of the Messiah.

The lament of the Virgin/Ecclesia is not explicitly represented in *Au doz mois de mai | Crux forma penitentie | SUSTINERE*, but it is essential to an understanding of the piece (Musical Example 4). The treatment of the Virgin's lament is analogous to what we have seen in the poems discussed above; the crucial difference is structural. The motet operates not sequentially but simultaneously: although some linear movement may occur in a given motet text, it is primarily through textual juxtaposition and interplay that the motet generates meaning. Rather than moving forward from grief to joy or from allegory to explication, therefore, the motet offers a different vision in each of its texted voices. The motetus stresses the Cross as a figure of life, joy, and consolation, locus of the marriage of Christ and the human soul. The triplum is a pastourelle, narrating the male persona's encounter with a solitary shepherdess. In the motet as a whole, an allegorical reading of the triplum seems mandatory. The allegory is not unveiled explicitly as it is in *Quant li solleiz* or in pious contrafacta; here the girl consistently behaves like a shepherdess and at no time quotes the Bible, spouts religious dogma, or hints at a lover in Heaven. What is lacking in the triplum, however, is supplied by the motetus. The triplum, read on its own, is a conventional pastourelle; but the motetus and the tenor in praise of the Cross invite the allegorical reading.

Viewed in this way, the motet presents the two sides of the Passion: the grief of the Virgin or Ecclesia at the death of Christ and the (seeming) loss of the Beloved; the joyous transformation, in light of the Resurrection, of the instrument of death, bereavement, and pain into one of life, redemption, and glory. The dual aspect of the Passion is stated at the center of the motet, where two key phrases are sung simultaneously: " 'Robin, doz amis, perdu voz ai' " ("Robin, sweet lover, I have lost you" [Tr, vv. 7–8]) and "Sponsi le[c]tus in meridie" (bridegroom's nuptial couch at noon [M, v. 6]). Following this initial statement of the paradox of the Crucifixion,

Tr: In the sweet month of May I went into a flowering orchard. I came upon a shepherdess under a bush; she was guarding her sheep and grieving, as I will tell you: "Robin, sweet lover, I have lost you; I will depart from you in great sorrow!" I sat beside her and embraced her. I found her overwhelmed by her love for Robin, who had left her: she had great sorrow.

M: Cross, form of penitence, key of grace, staff of sin, source of mercy; root of the tree of justice, path of life, banner of glory, bridegroom's nuptial couch at noon, full light, chasing away the cloud of sorrow, clearing up the conscience: let humankind carry this, let them take comfort in it. One must bear the cross if one wants the joys of the true light.

T: TO BEAR

Musical Example 4. From Hans Tischler, ed., *Motets of the Montpellier Codex.* Recent Researches in the Music of the Middle Ages and Early Renaissance, 2–8 (Madison: A-R Editions, Inc., 1978–85).

the opposing emotions unroll in perfect juxtaposition: the shepherdess's statement of "grant dolor" (great sorrow [Tr, v. 9]) is sung against the characterization of the Cross as "Nubem luens tristicie" (washing away the cloud of sorrow [M, v. 8]), and the narrator's unsuccessful efforts to comfort the grief-stricken girl parallel the consolation and joy attributed to the Cross.

Triplum and motetus are distinguished not only by their perspective on the Crucifixion but also in language and poetic style. Either sentiment could, of course, be voiced in either language. But the list of attributes and allegorical figures in the motetus is a convention of Latin devotional poetry. There is no narrative and little integrated development, but the independent terms cumulatively create a doctrinal statement. In the first half of the piece, the Cross is evoked as a source of grace, life, justice; at the center is the marriage bed, a vivid reminder of the individual soul's access to the blessings that the Cross bestows; and the second half is the statement of what is available to those who bear the Cross.

The triplum forgoes this cascade of technical language and imagery and presents a narrative constructed out of familiar literary elements. The Passion is naturalized, vernacularized in the fullest possible sense of the word. In one sense, the texts could not be more different. And yet they work together within the motet. The French triplum deepens the pathos of the Crucifixion as a human event of pain, loss, and incomprehension; the Latin motetus provides the all-important perspective that allows us to transcend the limited understanding of the shepherdess, moving from grief to joy.

The tenor supports the positive view of the Crucifixion through its citation of an alleluia used for the Finding, Reception, and Exaltation of the Cross: "Alleluia. Dulce lignum, dulces claves, dulcia ferens pondera, quae sola fuisti digna sustinere regem caelorum et Dominum" (Alleluia. Sweet wood, sweet nails, bearing the sweet weight, you alone were worthy of bearing the Lord, king of Heaven [M22]). The same melody and nearly the same text are in an alleluia for Assumption, origin of the melodically identical tenor PORTARE: "Alleluia. Dulcis virgo, dulcis mater, dulcia ferens pondera, quae sola fuisti digna portare regem caelorum et Dominum"[8] (Alleluia. Sweet virgin, sweet mother, bearing the sweet weight, you alone were worthy of carrying the Lord, king of Heaven [M34a]). Through the body of Mary, Christ took on human flesh and entered the world; through the Cross, this flesh died and returned to life in order to complete the act of redemption. The parallelism of the two alleluias reflects the deep-seated analogy of the Virgin and the Cross, suggesting a metaphoric linking of the Crucifixion, scene of the Virgin's great sorrow, and the Assumption, occasion of her joyful arrival in Heaven. For anyone who knew both alleluias, the dual associations of the tenor would subsume the motet's disparate parts: the maiden grieving for her lost beloved, the King of Heaven united with his Bride.

If the period between the Crucifixion and the Resurrection constitutes the darkest and most fearful moment in Christian history, the much longer — indeed, still ongoing — period between the Ascension and the Second Coming is also a time of separation and widowhood for the Church as Bride of Christ. The current age is nonetheless marked by hope rather than despair: the Bridegroom has departed, but not without promising to return. In his absence the Church is comforted by the Holy Spirit. The sorrow at Christ's absence is thus tempered by the expectation of the Second Coming and by the presence of the Spirit, which infuses the hearts of the faithful: the Bridegroom is, literally, absent in body but present in spirit. The use of tenors drawn from the liturgy of Ascension and Pentecost enabled the composers of vernacular motets to exploit this rich thematic, at once erotic and eschatological. Following a brief overview of the thematic associations of Ascension and Pentecost, we will examine motets using tenors from the liturgy of those feast days.

Liturgical Contexts: Ascension, Pentecost, and the Spirit of Holy Love

Christ's Ascension and the subsequent descent of the Holy Spirit are distinct events celebrated on different days, but they are closely related. Central to these feasts are the fundamental themes of presence and absence, desolation and joy. In John 14–16, which contribute to the liturgy of both holidays, Christ addresses his disciples and speaks of his departure, promising eventually to return: "Non relinquam vos orphanos: veniam ad vos" (I will not abandon you as orphans: I will come back to you [John 14:18]). He acknowledges that his followers will experience sorrow and persecution — "Si me persecuti sunt, et vos persequenter (If they have persecuted me, they will persecute you also [John 15:20]) — but gives them this assurance: "Et vos igitur nunc quidem tristitiam habetis, iterum autem videbo vos, et gaudebit cor vestrum: et gaudium vestrum nemo tollet a vobis" (And so indeed now you have sorrow, but I will see you again, and your heart will rejoice: and no one will take your joy from you [John 16:22]). Christ explains that in the meantime his disciples—which is to say, the Church—will be comforted: "Paraclitus autem Spiritus Sanctus, quem mittet Pater in nomine meo, ille vos docebit omnia" (But the Paraclete, the Holy Spirit which the Father sends in my name, will teach you everything [John 14:26]). Christ's temporary separation from his followers is indeed necessary: "Expedit vobis ut ego vadam: si enim non abiero, Paraclitus non veniet ad vos" (It is best for you that I go: for if I did not go, the Paraclete would not come to you [John 16:7]). The Ascension, the Second Coming, and the Pentecost are thus interwoven as the aftermath of the Passion; and the two sides of the experience, inextricably joined, are suffering and joy, bodily absence and spiritual presence.

The same sermon in which Christ foretells his own departure and return and the descent of the Holy Spirit, is also the occasion for a discussion of love that operates on several levels: the love that binds the persons of the Trinity, the love shared between God and humanity, and that which unifies the community of the faithful. In effect, all the preceding are manifestations of one and the same love, conceived in terms of a hierarchy in which each form of love provides an analogy for the next: "Sicut dilexit me Pater, et ego dilexi vos. Manete in dilectione mea. Si praecepta mea servaveritis, manebitis in dilectione mea, sicut et ego Patris mei praecepta servavi, et maneo in eius dilectione. . . . Hoc est praeceptum meum, ut diligatis invicem, sicut dilexi vos" (As the Father has loved me, so have I loved you. Remain in my love. If you have kept my precepts, you will remain in my love, just as I have kept the precepts of my Father, and I remain in his love. . . . This is my precept, that you love your neighbor, as I have loved you [John 15:9–12]).

Humanity and divinity are thus joined in a circle of love: by obeying the commandment to love one another, the faithful demonstrate their love for God—"Qui habet mandata mea, et servat ea: ille est qui diligit me" (He who keeps my commandments and serves them, is the one who loves me [John 14:21])—and receive God's love for them, itself an extension of the love that conjoins Father and Son. This divine love is the Holy Spirit, whose descent to earth follows Christ's Ascension into Heaven. Thus earthly and heavenly love are intimately linked, the one an expression of the other; and the relationship between the two is realized corporeally in the body of Christ—the absent Bridegroom, soon to return—and spiritually in the Paraclete, the spirit of divine love that enlightens and comforts the hearts of the faithful.

The liturgy of Ascension stresses its nature as preparation for the de-

scent of the Holy Spirit, which is eagerly awaited during the period sepa-
rating Ascension and Pentecost. The Ascension hymn *Nunc sancte nobis
spiritus*, for example, looks forward to the arrival of the Spirit, as does
the antiphon "O rex gloriae . . . ne derelinquas nos orphanos, sed mitte
promissum Patris in nos, spiritum veritatis, alleluia" (O king of glory . . .
do not abandon us as orphans, but send the spirit of truth, promised
by the Father, into us, alleluia [*CAO*, no. 4079]). The Sunday following
Ascension includes the antiphon *Cum venerit Paraclitus quem ego mit-
tam vobis* (When the Consoler comes, whom I will send to you [*CAO*,
no. 2043]). The commemoration of Christ's departure from the earth
thus sets a mood of anticipation, looking forward to the illumination and
consolation the descent of the Spirit will bring.

The Holy Spirit is the most mysterious person of the Trinity, and
this is hardly the place for a detailed exploration of the relevant theological doctrine. A reading of the Pentecost liturgy and of sermons for
Pentecost, however, reveals the aspects of the Holy Spirit that would have
been familiar to those not specially trained in Trinitarian theology.[9] The
inspirational force of the Spirit, reflected in the disciples' glossalalia and
in subsequent occasions of prophecy and talking in tongues described
throughout the New Testament, is commemorated in the Epistle for
Pentecost (Acts 2:1–11) as well as in the responsory *Repleti sunt omnes
Spiritu Sancto. Loquebantur variis linguis Apostoli* (*CAO*, no. 7531), itself
constructed of phrases from the same passage. The consolatory function of the Paraclete, as well as its identity as the essence of divine love,
is clearly expressed in an alleluia that is the source of the motet tenor
AMORIS: "Veni sancte spiritus, reple tuorum corda fidelium, et tui amoris
in eis ignem accende" (Come, Holy Spirit, fill the hearts of your faithful
ones, and kindle the fire of your love in them [M27]). The identification
of the Holy Spirit with love and its association with the heart are also
expressed in a homily of Gregory the Great: "Hodie namque Spiritus
sanctus repentino sonitu super discipulos venit, mentesque carnalium in
sui amorem permutavit, et foris apparentibus linguis igneis, intus facta
sunt corda flammantia, quia dum Deum in ignis visione suscipiunt, per
amorem suaviter arserunt. Ipse namque Spiritus sanctus amor est"[10] (For
today the Holy Spirit with a sudden noise came upon the disciples, and
turned their minds from fleshly to holy love, and as it appeared outwardly
as fiery tongues, within their hearts were flaming: for while they received
God through the vision of fire, they were deliciously consumed with love.
For this Holy Spirit is itself love [*PL* 76, col. 1220]).

Hugh of St. Victor, in a sermon for Pentecost, describes the descent of the Holy Spirit as a corrective to the Fall. At the time of the Fall, he explains, human nature suffered two kinds of injury that estranged it from God: "In eo namque quod factus erat ad imaginem Dei secundum rationem, vulneravit eum per ignorantium boni. In eo vero quod factus erat ad similitudinem Dei secundum dilectionem, vulneravit eum per concupiscentiam mali"[11] (For inasmuch as [human nature] was made in the image of God with regard to reason, it was wounded through ignorance of the good. And truly inasmuch as it was made in the likeness of God with regard to love, it was wounded through the desire for evil [*PL* 177, col. 1120]). The Holy Spirit effects a renewal of the human race through intellectual enlightenment and redirection of desire: "Illuminaret ignorantiam, refrigeraret concupiscentiam; illuminaret ad cognitionem veritatis, inflammaret ad amorem virtutis" (It illuminated ignorance and quenched desire; it illuminated with the knowledge of the truth, enflamed with the love of virtue [*PL* 177, cols. 1121–22]). The representation of the Holy Spirit as a flame, for Hugh, symbolizes its dual function of enlightenment and amorous inspiration.

The infusion of the Spirit, which fills the heart with love, ennobles the character, provides consolation in the absence of the beloved, and inspires an outpouring of linguistic virtuosity, has several points of contact with secular love lyric. That love is the inspiration for song is perhaps the most widespread topos of courtly lyric: to love and to sing are virtually one and the same. Absence from the beloved is a common theme in courtly and popular lyric. The male lover is consoled in his passion by the love that fills his heart and sustains him, and the amorous experience is often heralded as a source of moral improvement. The maidens of the pastourelle and *chanson de femme* are often keeping faith with an absent lover whom they variously seek, summon, await, or lament. The lyric persona, whether male or female, is thus thematically analogous to the Church, whose Bridegroom is absent.

The idea of Pentecost as a festival of love appears in a poem from the first half of the fourteenth century, Jean de Condé's *Messe des oisiaus*. The poem, a dream vision, describes a Mass conducted by birds in honor of Venus. The officiating priest is the nightingale; the sermon—an exposition of obedience, patience, loyalty, and hope as the four cardinal virtues of love—is preached by the parakeet; and various other birds are responsible for different parts of the chant. The Host is a red rose, which miraculously remains whole even after petals are removed for Communion. The most solemn moment of the Mass—bodily union with Christ—is thus overlayed with a motif that carries unmistakable erotic associations. The inviolate rose is an image for the body of Christ, whole and indivisible, present in its totality in the Host or in any fragment thereof.[12] But given the context of a Mass in honor of Venus, and the powerful associations of the nightingale and the red rose with erotic love poetry, the image also expresses the fantasy of sexual consummation without loss of virginity, an eroticization of the Blessed Virgin, the *rosa sine spina*.

Several details identify the Mass with Pentecost: it takes place in May, there are two alleluias (one rendered in four-part polyphony) and a sequence, but no gradual.[13] The Kiss of Peace is administered by a dove bearing a green branch, "De coi maint amant conforta" (With which it consoled many a lover [v. 342]): an image of the consoling Holy Spirit, so often a dove in sacred art. Furthermore, after the Mass Venus holds a banquet for her followers at which is served a highly intoxicating drink; and in the gloss at the end of the poem, Jean identifies its effects with possession by the Holy Spirit. The sermon about love, the Host with its amorous associations, and even the presence of Venus herself are all part of the parody of Pentecost as a celebration of divine love, here eroticized. The narrator's closing comments, rounding out the gloss in which he transposes the elements of the poem into the devotional register, stress the importance of spiritual love:

> Or prions Dieu de cuer fin
> Que de la vraie amour sans fin
> Esprende nous cuers finement. (vv. 1577–79)

Now let us pray God with pure heart that he enflame our hearts nobly with true love without end.

These lines not only complete the movement from erotic to spiritual love; they also underscore the Pentecostal nature of this inspirational love by echoing the alleluia *Veni sancte spiritus*: "fill the hearts of your faithful ones, and kindle the fire of your love in them."

The tone of Jean de Condé's poem is as difficult to capture as that of many a vernacular motet. What are we to think of its seeming sacrilege: the eroticized Eucharist, the liturgical worship of a pagan goddess, the ardent speeches urging all, including nuns, to follow Nature by taking lovers? And how are we to interpret the gloss offered at the end, in which the whole becomes an allegory for sacred ritual and divine love? Did the medieval audience actually accept this strange poem as a moral piece featuring religious allegory? The many details about the erotic pleasures of Venus's banquet, as well as the impassioned defense of erotic love, make this unlikely. To my mind, Jean's poem tries to have it both ways: it is at once parody and allegory. It affords its audience a dual pleasure, combining the daring humor of the erotic Mass with the intellectual exercise—reassuringly edifying—of allegorical exegesis. And in this respect it is close in spirit to the motet, a genre in which, as we have seen, parody and allegory coexist in polytextual constructs that refuse to resolve themselves into a single reading.[14] Jean de Condé's humorous portrayal of an eroticized Pentecost in celebration of love is similar in spirit to the use of Pentecostal tenors in vernacular motets treating the pains and joys of love.

Absence and Consolation in the Vernacular Motet

Alleluia. Non vos relinquam orphanos: vado, et venio ad vos, et gaudebit cor vestrum. (M24)[15]
Alleluia. I will not abandon you as orphans: I go, and I return to you, and your heart will rejoice.

Alleluia. Paraclitus spiritus sanctus, quem mittet pater in nomine meo, ille vos docebit omnem veritatem. (M26)[16]
Alleluia. The Comforter, the Holy Spirit, which the father will send in my name, he will teach you every truth.

Alleluia. Veni sancte spiritus, reple tuorum corda fidelium, et tui amoris in eis ignem accende. (M27)[17]
Alleluia. Come, Holy Spirit, fill the hearts of your faithful ones, and kindle the fire of your love in them.

Each of these alleluias is the source of a tenor used in both Latin and French motets: ET GAUDEBIT (M24), ILLE VOS DOCEBIT (M26), and AMORIS (M27), respectively. Each employs a central image or idea that is fundamental to the liturgy of Ascension and Pentecost, but also applicable to the poetic celebration of erotic love. The first looks forward to the heartfelt joy of reunion with the Bridegroom; the second addresses the need for consolation and spiritual enlightenment in his absence; the third invokes the inspirational force of love through the compelling image of the heart afire. It is no surprise that the composers of vernacular motets were drawn to the tenors that carry these associations, so easily transferrable to love poetry.

Motets addressing the nature of the love experience could adopt a variety of perspectives, as we have seen. Love might be critiqued or praised, allegorized as holy, or viewed with ironic detachment; it might be the source of joy or sorrow, depravity or edification. Often, love was described in idealized language that mediated between the erotic and the spiritual; and it is with such an example that I begin. Emblematic of the ambiguous language of love is the piece *Amors m'a asseuré* (366) / *AMORIS* (M27):

> M: Amors m'a asseuré
> de gent secors,
> qu'a cele m'a assené
> qui est la flors
> et li estandars d'onors;
> car cortoisie et valors
> ierent banies, je crois,
> quant el les retint a soi;
> et puisque si haut don doi
> d'amors avoir, a tous jors
> a li m'otroi.
> Ja ne partirai d'amors,
> ne bone amors de moi!
> T: AMORIS [18]

M: Love has assured me of noble aid, for it has assigned me to her who is the flower and the standard of honor; for courtesy and valor were mustered, I believe, when she retained them for herself; and since I stand to receive such a noble gift from love, I pledge myself to her forever. Never will I depart from love, nor good love from me!

T: OF LOVE

This praise of love is difficult to categorize definitively. The motetus employs a high concentration of terms reminiscent of military and feudal service: *estandars d'onors, banies, retint, otroi.* The language of feudal obligation is central to the rhetoric of love in the courtly lyric tradition, in which the male persona typically represents himself as "vassal" of the lady he admires, or complains of having been "ambushed" by the weaponry of her beautiful body and held hostage in the "prison" of love.[19] And nothing in the motetus prevents it from being read as a declaration of earthly love and devotion. But there is also nothing to rule out the possibility of a spiritual reading: the "flower" to whom the singer directs his love, that paragon of honor and virtue, might be either earthly or heavenly.

Love is not portrayed as a source of suffering, as in so many secular love songs; instead, it is a source of succor, though whether this aid is erotic or spiritual in nature is not specified. The piece as a whole is truly equivocal. It celebrates an undying, honorable, and salvific love; and the audience is free to decide just what kind of love might fit that description.

In many motets, however, the theme of amorous separation is more clearly secular in nature, and its association with a tenor alluding to the Holy Spirit has decidedly humorous implications. In our next example, *A cele ou j'ai mon cuer mis* (368) / *AMO[RIS]* (M27), the lover's appeal to his lady is comically conflated with the Church's prayer to the Holy Spirit:

> M: A cele, ou j'ai mon cuer mis,
> mon cuer et mon cors li doi[n]g:
> tout mais a, ja!
> Ce poise moi,
> que trop m'est loi[n]g,
> car trop resoi[n]g,
> que ne me guerpist.
> Douce dame debonere,
> ne me lessiés ainsi,
> car se voz volés retraire,
> si m'avés traï.
> Car plus a d'un an,
> que je ne vi
> vostre dous viaire,
> qui si me redue,
> Dieus, que j'aim si.
> Dame, merci!
> L'en dit, qu'au besoi[n]g
> voit on son ami.
> T: AMO[RIS] [20]

M: I give my heart and my body to her, where I placed my heart: she has it forever and ever! It burdens me that she is so far from me, for I worry that she may abandon me. Sweet noble lady, don't leave me like this, for if you withdraw from me you have betrayed me. For it has been more than a year since I saw your sweet face, which haunts me, God, which I love so. Lady, have mercy! It is said that one recognizes one's friend in a time of need.
T: [OF] LOVE [*or*: I LOVE]

The motetus, in which the long-absent persona implores his lady not to withdraw her love, is combined with a tenor whose immediate function is simply to underscore the sentiments of love. Indeed, the two syllables used in the piece, if taken as a word in their own right, form a declaration of love in Latin: Amo (I love). Beyond its immediate linguistic associations, the tenor alludes to the alleluia (cited above) in which the Holy Spirit is invited to kindle the flames of love in the hearts of the faithful. Appropriated by implication into the motet, this prayer becomes an expression of hope that the lady's heart will remain aflame with love for her admirer. Here, the context of human love dominates and determines our reading of motetus and tenor alike. Like the somewhat disingenuous appeal to charitable friendship in the closing lines of the motetus, the tenor allows the lyric persona to ennoble his love by associating it with moral and spiritual values. The allusion to the sustaining love of the Holy Spirit, rather than prompting an allegorical interpretation of the motetus, only increases the sense of lighthearted melodrama that pervades the piece.

The motif of amorous separation and hope of reunion implies a chronology, a narrative of departure and return; and the possibilities for narrative and temporal play are heightened by the presence of future-tense verbs in the tenors *[ILLE VOS] DOCEBIT* and *ET GAUDEBIT*. I begin with *Au departir plorer la vi* (349) / *DOCEBIT* (M26), in which the motetus offers a first-person narrative by the male lover:

> M: Au departir plorer la vi,
> la plus envoisie,
> qui onques nasqui;
> quant me regarda,
> mon cuer tresperça
> presque parmi.
> Et doucement soupira
> de cuer asoupli,
> qu'en priant merci
> li cuers me failli.
> Et tout voiant li,
> tout pasme chei;
> ne me respondi,
> mais de grant pitie plora.
> Ainc puis mes cuers ne l'oblia.
> T: DOCEBIT[21]

M: In departing I saw her weep, the gaiest one ever born; when she looked at me, it pierced my heart nearly all the way through. And sweetly she sighed with a soft heart, so that in begging for mercy, my heart failed me. And seeing her I fell into a faint; she did not answer me, but she wept with great pity. Never since then did my heart forget her.

T: s/HE WILL TEACH

The male persona describes his lady's grief at his departure, and his own pain at witnessing her sorrow; the tenor carries a promise of consolation. The implied narrative structure of the piece as a whole is expanded by the play of tenses between tenor and motetus. The motetus, constructed on a series of preterites, narrates the moment of separation as a past event. The protagonist has never forgotten that moment, but the use of the preterite suggests that he has in some sense moved away from it: it is sealed in his heart as a self-contained image, not an ongoing context for his actions. The future tense of the tenor contrasts markedly with the motetus. If the two parts are taken as integral parts of a whole, then we see that the story is not yet over: there is a promise of consolation or resolution. In the larger context of the motet as a whole, the protagonist is suspended between the event recorded in his memory and the future moment when his grief will be resolved through some unspecified revelation. The tenor thus reopens the closed narrative of the motetus, just as Christ's prophecy of the Pentecost, and eventually of the Second Coming, dissolves the false sense of closure created by his Ascension into Heaven.

In spite of the structural parallels with the biblical narrative, however, the motet cannot be read as an allegory for Christ's Ascension. The unhappy lover who fainted in grief at leaving his lady and who can only meditate on his memory of her reciprocal grief, can hardly be a figure for the triumphant risen Christ. Rather, his tale emerges as a parodic recasting of the motifs of spiritual loss and replenishment represented by the tenor. The implied analogy of the grieving maiden with Ecclesia, or of the departing lover with Christ, adds a dimension of humor that the motetus does not have on its own. The associations contributed by the tenor heighten the emotional intensity of the piece, again imparting a melodramatic quality to lyric expressions.

I complete this discussion of narrative structures in motets of separation, and of the allegorical or parodic readings that they invite, with two motets that draw on the *chanson de toile* repertoire: *En une chambre cointe et grant* (328) / ET GAUDEBIT (M24) and *Seule se siet bele Aie* (348) / ILLE VOS DOCE[BIT] (M26). The source alleluia for the tenor ET GAUDEBIT, *Non vos relinquam*, belongs to the time between Ascension and Pentecost; it corresponds to the period when the Church was without its Bridegroom and had not yet received the consolation of the Paraclete, a time at once of bereavement and anticipation. These associations are playfully exploited in the motetus scenario:

> M: En une chambre cointe et grant
> se sist bele Eglentine
> deseur un lit riche et plesant
> et enclos de cortine;
> en sospirant
> va regretant
> ce, qu'aime d'amor fine.
> Puis va disant:
> "Dieus, por qu'aim tant
> celui, qui tant va demorant,
> quant set, que j'ai dolor si grant,
> que nuit ne jor ne fine?
> Or n'i sai medecine,
> se plus atent."
> T: ET GAUDEBIT[22]

M: In a large pretty chamber sat fair Eglentine, on a rich and pleasant bed enclosed with a curtain. Sighing, she laments the one that she loves truly. Then she says: "God, why do I love so much the one who delays so long, when he knows that I have such great sorrow, without end, day or night? Now I know of no other cure if he waits any longer."

T: AND S/HE WILL REJOICE

The second employs a tenor associated with Pentecost, and again the motetus exploits the associations of consolation in the absence of the beloved:

> M: Seule se siet bele Aie
> souz un pin verdoiant.
> Por son ami s'esmaie
> qui tant vait demorant.
> Paor en a grant
> et dit en soupirant:
> "He, Dieus, donez moi tant
> qu'un jor en mon vivant
> solas et joie en aie."
> T: ILLE VOS DOCE[BIT][23]

M: Fair Aie sits alone under a green pine. She grieves for her beloved, who delays in coming. She has great fear and says, sighing: "Ha, God, grant me that one day while I am still alive I have solace and joy from him."

T: HE [WILL] TEACH YOU

In both cases the tenor provides a highly charged backdrop for the tale of feminine grief and desire. Its future tense—explicit only in the first example, but implied in the second, for anyone familiar with the motet repertoire—contrasts with the present tenses used throughout the motetus. Again, one may read the tenor as mitigating any sense of closure in the motetus narrative; it comments upon the central scenario, looking ahead to a denouement. And once again, its intertextual associations raise the possibility of allegorical readings. Fair Aie might be a figure for the widowed Ecclesia; in that case, the tenor is an answer to her prayer for consolation. Alternatively, the tenor might be secularized as a promise of solace in the earthly realm, as is offered, for example, in numerous pastourelles in which the male protagonist attempts to comfort—or to take advantage of—a lonely shepherdess. Or one could imagine an ironic relationship between motetus and tenor: perhaps Fair Aie suffers because she has devoted herself to the wrong sort of love, and will find solace and joy only when she opens her heart to the teachings of the Holy Spirit.

The motet of fair Eglentine is also susceptible of a double reading. Taken literally, it is the story of a maiden who fears that her lover has abandoned her; the tenor points to a favorable outcome, promising a joyful reunion. And read allegorically, Eglentine becomes a figure for the human soul awaiting the return of Christ. In this context, the bed where she meditates on her absent lover recalls the famous passage in the Song of Songs, interpreted tropologically as the soul's search for Christ through contemplation:

> In lectulo meo, per noctes,
> Quaesivi quem diligit anima mea.
> Quaesivi illum, et non inveni. (Song 3:1)

In my little bed, at night, I sought him whom my soul loves. I sought him, and did not find him.

And in the use of the word *enclos* (v. 4), one might find an echo of the *hortus conclusus*, figure for the Virgin or for the pious heart. Once again, motetus and tenor can be harmonized through the allegorization of the one or the secularization of the other; yet neither method of reconciling the two parts of the motet dominates.

The special qualities of the motet can be highlighted through comparison of *Seule se siet bele Aie* | ILLE VOS DOCE[BIT] with a *chanson de toile* featuring Fair Aie that appears in Jean Renart's *Roman de la Rose* (ed. Lecoy, vv. 1183–92):

Siet soi bele Aye as piez sa male maistre,
sor ses genouls un paile d'Engleterre,
et a un fil i fet coustures beles.
          Hé! Hé! amors d'autre païs,
mon cuer avez et lïé et souspris.

Aval la face li courent chaudes lermes,
q'el est batue et au main et au vespre,
por ce qu'el aime soudoier d'autre terre.
          Hé! Hé! amors d'autre païs,
mon cuer avez et lïé et souspris.

Fair Aie sits at the feet of her wicked mistress, an English cloth on her lap, and she works pretty stitches there with a thread. Hey! Hey! love from another country, you have bound and ambushed my heart. Hot tears flow down her face, for she is beaten morning and evening, because she loves a soldier from another land. Hey! Hey! love from another country, you have bound and ambushed my heart.

In Renart's *Rose* this song is sung by Lïenor, a young maiden who is herself sewing with her mother and who could thus be identified with the protagonist of her song. More important, Lïenor will soon be accused of sexual misconduct with a knight from another land: no less a personage than the emperor's seneschal, who invents the charges in an attempt to block her marriage to the emperor. These charges bring great shame and grief to Lïenor and her family—indeed, she is nearly murdered by a furious male relative—and she must go to some lengths to prove her innocence.

In the context of Renart's romance, then, the song of Fair Aie mirrors an aspect of the central narrative, intensifying and nuancing its depiction of the dangers of amorous intrigue. Within the framework of the romance, no allegorical reading is suggested; the *amors d'autre païs* can only be a foreigner, not an otherworldly spiritual Bridegroom. In and of itself, the motetus *Seule se siet bele Aie* is similarly the story of a lovelorn maiden. The presence of the tenor changes things, allowing not only a secular but also a spiritual reading. And the simultaneous recognition of these two readings constitutes the piece's aesthetic force as well as its humor. In the one case, the literalization of the tenor suggested a happy ending to the story hinted at in the motetus: Aie's lover will return. The other reading requires the allegorization of the motetus according to a clue in the tenor: Aie is the widowed Ecclesia, and the tree under which she sits might represent the Cross. Jean Renart placed the *chanson de toile* in a context that brought it into dialogue with a tale of love, court intrigue, and the politics of feudal marriage. But the motet of Bele Aie, like that of Eglentine, creates another dialogue, hermeneutically more complex, between the *chanson de toile* and a different register altogether: spiritual love, the intrigue of Passion and Redemption, the marriage of Christ and Ecclesia. The frequent appearance of amorous maidens in pious contrafacta underlies our willingness to consider an allegorical reading of these motets; familiarity with the *chanson de toile*, characterized by its frank representation of feminine erotic desire, prevents us from taking this implied allegory at face value. The motets of Aie and Eglentine are fine examples of poetic ambiguity, of simultaneous movement toward allegory and toward parody; in the fullest sense, works of literary polyphony.

The Lovers United

I close this survey of the theme of separation and absence with a brief examination of motets that treat the motif of amorous reunion. We have seen examples in which the motif of a maiden going to meet her lover is associated with tenors from the liturgy of Assumption. In other motets, however, the male lover effects the reunion by returning from afar or simply by appearing to his beloved. Given the strong associations linking the descent of the Holy Spirit and the promise of a Second Coming of Christ—the Paraclete sustains the faithful during the period of waiting, but in no way detracts from the eager anticipation of Christ's return—it is no surprise that the motif of reunion can sometimes be used in motets that employ tenors associated with Pentecost. Even more directly germane to the thematic of reunion, however, is the event of Christ's Resurrection. During this brief interlude, Christ was reunited with his Bride. The joyous moments in which he revealed himself to his followers—especially the emotionally charged encounter in the garden with Mary Magdalene—are evoked, with varying degrees of humor or irony, in certain motets built on tenors drawn from the Easter liturgy.

The motif of the returning lover figures in the trouvère repertoire as well, as can be illustrated by means of two songs by Adam de la Halle. The first, *Au repairier en la douche contrée*, employs the reunion motif as a means of introducing the central theme of the song: proximity to the loved one, and the opportunity to gaze upon her, heightens the pleasurable pains of love. The motif of return is limited to the opening stanza:

> Au repairier en la douche contrée
> Ou je men cuer laissai au departir,
> Est ma douche dolours renouvelée
> Qui ne m'i laist de chanter plus tenir.
> Puisque d'un seul souvenir
> Jolis estre aillours soloie,
> Pour coi chi ne le seroie,
> Ou je sai et voi cheli
> Qui me tient joli? (vv. 1–9) [24]

In returning to the sweet country where I left my heart at my departure, my sweet pain is renewed, which does not allow me to keep from singing. Since I managed to remain merry elsewhere from mere memory, why wouldn't I be so here, where I know and see her who keeps me merry?

There is no hint here of spiritual allegory or parody of any kind, no reference to any context other than that of human love. The song elaborates a conventional amorous psychology. Love is inspired by the visual spectacle of the beloved, intensified by her presence, nourished through the imaginative faculty of memory; the pain that it causes is a source of pleasure and joy.

Adam's other "reunion" song, *De tant com plus aproime mon païs*, is more complex, featuring bestiary imagery. By the late thirteenth century, the birds and animals of bestiary tradition—somewhat like the tenors of the motet repertoire—had been incorporated into the literature of erotic love. Richard de Fournival's *Bestiaires d'amours*, followed by the *Response du Bestiaire* and the *Dit de la panthère d'amours*, transposed the allegorical bestiary code from the spiritual to the amorous register. Adam's song, here quoted in its entirety, participates in this redefinition of the bestiary tradition:

> De tant com plus aproime mon païs,
> Me renovele amours et esprent,
> Et plus me sanle en aprochant jolis,
> Et plus li airs et plus truis douche gent.
> > Che me tient chi longuement,
> > Et chou aussi,
> Qu'en souvenir i choisi
> Dames de tel honneranche
> C'un poi de le contenanche
> De me dame en l'une vi,
> Si qu'a le saveur de li
> Me delit a se samblanche.

Si fait li tigre au mireoir, quant pris
Sont li faons, et cuide proprement
En li mirant trouver chou qu'ele a quis;
Endementieres s'enfuit chieus qui les prent!
 Ne faites mie ensement,
 Dame de mi,
Ne ne m'ouvliés aussi
Pour me longue demouranche;
Car ch'est en vo ramenbranche
C'au mireoir m'entrouvli,
Car a vous est, non pas chi,
Li cuers et li esperanche.[25]

The closer I come to my country, love renews and enflames me, and the prettier the place seems to me in approaching, and the sweeter I find the people. That keeps me here for a long time, and this too, that I selected for remembrance ladies of such honorable bearing that I saw a little of my lady's countenance in one of them, so that I delight, through her appearance, in my lady's aura.

Thus behaves the tigress with the mirror, when her cubs have been taken, and gazing there, she really believes herself to have found what she was seeking; meanwhile the one taking them runs away! Don't do the same, lady, with regard to me, don't forget me for my long absence; for it is in memory of you that I forgot myself in the mirror, for my heart and my hope are not here, but with you.

According to bestiary tradition, the tigress deceived by the mirror is an image for people who, distracted by earthly temptations — including beautiful women — fail to realize that the devil has stolen their soul. Richard de Fournival employs the tigress as a figure for the effects of the erotic vision: upon seeing his lady, he forgot all else (*Bestiaires d'amour*, ed. Segre, pp. 40–42). From this perspective, Adam's admission that he has gazed upon beautiful women like the tigress distracted by the mirror could be a moral comment on the frivolous, spiritually destructive nature of his amorous passion. In appropriating the bestiary image into his song, however, Adam divests it of its moralistic associations. Instead, the figure of the tigress is the basis for a complex meditation on memory and forgetfulness. Looking upon other ladies and imagining that he sees aspects of his own beloved, Adam avoids falling into the trap of deception: far from causing him to forget her, these spectral images only stir his memories and heighten his desire to be reunited with the lady he loves. If he forgot himself upon gazing into the mirror of love, it was only to replace self-absorption with a fixation on her beautiful image. Similarly, he hopes that his lady will continue to think of him and that she will not allow the distractions of the world to obscure the memory of her lover.

Insofar as the image of the tigress retains its associations with the bestiary tradition of moral and spiritual allegory, Adam uses it to elevate the love shared between him and his lady. In his song, the distracting mirror of the world is not an image for erotic love; it is, rather, a threat posed to that love. In the elaborate transference of the bestiary image from the moral to the amorous register, the noble and salvific love of the tigress for her cubs, emblematic of human love for God and for the salvation of the soul, comes to represent the bond conjoining lover and lady. This love, closely linked to love of the place where the couple is united, is posited as the basis for the intellectual and imaginative exercise of memory and as the source of general well-being. Through his incorporation of a powerful metaphor, Adam succeeds in establishing an analogy between erotic and spiritual love, whereby the former absorbs the salvific qualities of the latter.

The strophic *chanson* operates differently from the polyphonic motet. In the former, component parts of the poetic system are integrated: the piece moves in a single line from beginning to end, and the significance of the bestiary image is spelled out within the text. The motet's construction, however, is through juxtaposition rather than integration of parts; and it is generally more concise, operating through allusion rather than explication. One can see all these features in the brief motet *Lies est cil qui el pais va* (350) / *DOCEBIT* (M26):

> M: Lies est cil, qui el pais va,
>   ou il a bele amie,
>   quant ne l'a veue pieça.
>   Si bone compaignie
>   ne puet nus avoir, com il a.
> T: DOCEBIT[26]

M: Happy is he who goes to the country where he has a beautiful sweetheart, when he hasn't seen her in a long time. No one can have such good company, as he has.

T: S/HE WILL TEACH

The motetus, like Adam's songs and like Christ's prophetic words to the disciples, elaborates the motif of the returning lover. The tenor, with its promise of instruction from an unspecified source, refers to an education in love: the consoling spirit that will teach the lovers what to do is the mutual desire that brings them together. Yet even this interpretation hinges on a knowledge of the tenor's liturgical origins, its reference to the spiritual consolation and divine love brought by the Holy Spirit. Because the tenor is a direct quotation of the liturgy, its incorporation into an amorous motet retains more explicit irony than does Adam's use of the tigress metaphor. The motetus cannot be resolved into an allegory for either the Pentecost or the Second Coming, for the pleasure ascribed to the returning lover is not applicable either to the Paraclete—an entity to whom emotions are never attributed—or to the severe Christ of the Last Judgment. Rather, the tenor builds humorously on the motetus. As in other examples we have seen, it projects the implied narrative of homecoming and reunion into a future of amorous instruction; and as an explicit sign of the movement from the spiritual to the erotic register, it adds a humorous, somewhat irreverent note to the piece as a whole.

As noted earlier, the motif of the returning lover is most appropriate to the Resurrection narrative, and one can find a range of allegorical and parodic uses of tenors from the Easter liturgy. In the following example, *Chantez seri, Marot* (262) / *PRAECEDAM VOS* (M19), the vernacular motetus corresponds closely to the implied narrative context of the tenor:

> M: Chantez seri, Marot,
>   *vos amis revient;*
>   s'aporte un nouvel mot
>   de vous, car il convient,
>   que je de ce chant et not,
>   dont plus souvent me souvient.
>   Et je l'ai fet si mignot,
>   que, quant on l'ot,
>   il demande, qu'on le lot.
>   *Donc chantez, bele, mignotement,*
>   *que vos amis revient.*
> T: PRAECEDAM VOS [27]

M: Sing brightly, Marot, *your sweetheart returns*; and I bring a new verse about you, for it is fitting that I sing and make music about that which most stirs my memory. And I made it so lovely that, when anyone hears it, he has to praise it. *So sing merrily, beautiful one, that your sweetheart returns.*

T: I WILL GO BEFORE YOU

The tenor derives from an alleluia for Easter week: "In die resurrectionis meae, dicit Dominus, praecedam vos in Galilaeam" (In the day of my Resurrection, says the Lord, I will go before you into Galilee). The words are based on Christ's prophecy of the Resurrection as he spoke to the disciples in Gethsemane, shortly before his arrest: "Postquam autem resurrexero, praecedam vos in Galilaeam" (But after I am raised up, I will go before you to Galilee [Matt. 26:32]). These words are echoed by the angel who informs Mary Magdalene and the other Mary of the Resurrection and instructs them: "Et cito euntes, dicite discipulis eius quia surrexit: et ecce praecedit vos in Galilaeam: ibi eum videbitis: ecce praedixi vobis" (Then go quickly and tell his disciples that he has risen from the dead, and behold, he is going before you to Galilee; there you will see him. Lo, I have told you [Matt. 28:7; see also Mark 16:7]).

This enunciation of the Resurrection—to the Apostles and to Mary Magdalene—is combined with a motetus in which a maiden, her name a popularized version of Mary, is summoned to meet her returning lover. Mary Magdalene was not the sole recipient of the angel's message, but she is certainly one of the most important witnesses of the Resurrection; in three accounts, she is the first to see the risen Christ (Matt. 28:9; Mark 16:9; John 20:11–18). And just as Mary was instructed to spread the joyful news of Christ's Resurrection, so Marot is invited to express her joy in song. Finally, motetus and tenor share the first-person voice of the returning male lover, be he sweetheart or Heavenly Bridegroom. The motetus is a carefully crafted vernacularization of the biblical narrative. Mary Magdalene has become the shepherdess Marot, or Marion, known for her amorous passion and her propensity for song; and the risen Christ has taken on the image of the lover who sings joyfully of returning to the woman he loves. Although the motetus would not invite an allegorical reading in and of itself, its conjunction with the Easter tenor PRAECEDAM VOS invests it with new meaning. There is no sense of parodic jest or ironic disjunction. Rather, the motetus focuses on the human side of the Resurrection story: on Mary Magdalene as a woman who deeply loved Christ, for whom his death was tragic and his return profoundly joyous, and on Christ himself as a figure of love and empathy.

A parodic element does appear in our second example of a motet with an Easter tenor, *Quant voi la fleur en l'arbroie* (250) / *ET TENUERUNT* (M17), in which the pastourelle setting is now explicit:

M: Quant voi la fleur en l'arbroie
     au commencement
     de la seison qui verdoie,
     que comunement
     mainent oisiaus joie,

par moi seulement,
loing de toute gent
mon chemin erroie.
Pastourele
gente et bele
trovai grant joie fesant;
si chante et frestele
et si rapele
en fleütant
Robin, qui s'ombroie.
D'autre part la voie,
et quant il l'entent,
il li respont maintenant
en chantant:
"Veez la, ma douce amie
desouz l'olivier m'atent,
la bele aus euz veirz, rians,
au cors gent,
la bele, la blonde.
Espringués legierement,
que li soliers ne fonde!"
T: ET TENUERUNT [28]

M: When I see the bloom in the woods at the beginning of the season of greenery, when the birds are all joyful, I take my path alone, far from all people. I found a shepherdess, fair and beautiful, expressing great joy; she sings and plays her flute, and thus in fluting she calls Robin, who is in the shade across the way. And when he hears her, he replies by singing: "See there my sweet beloved waiting for me under the olive tree, the fair one with gray eyes, laughing, of noble bearing, the beautiful blonde. *Spring lightly, so that your shoe does not press down!*"

T: AND THEY CLASPED

The motetus remains within the conventional framework of the pastourelle corpus, which abounds with simple narratives of the frolics, both musical and sexual, of Robin and Marion. But the scenario can also be a transposition of the encounter between the risen Christ and the Marys, as described in the Easter alleluia that is the source for the tenor: "Alleluia. Surrexit Dominus et occurens mulieribus ait: Avete; tunc accesserunt et tenuerunt pedes ejus" [29] (Alleluia. The Lord arose and, running up to the women, said: Hail. Then they came up to him and clasped his feet).

A maiden seeks her lover; when he calls out to her, she runs up to him.

Other details, though entirely at home in the repertoire of pastourelle or *reverdie*, contribute to the possible allegorical reading of the motetus: the spring season is that of Easter, the verdant setting recalls the garden where Mary Magdalene encountered the risen Christ. Even the olive tree can, as we have seen, hint at an association of the shepherdess with the Bride of Christ. Again the idyll represented in the motetus offers a secularized version of key elements of the biblical narrative, reconstructed in the familiar image of the amorous, singing shepherds of the pastourelle. And again it is only through contextualization within the motet that one sees the parallel between the vernacular text and the biblical model; the juxta-position of motetus and tenor causes us to read both a little differently. This example differs from the preceding, however, in that many details locate it in the pastourelle's erotic register. Thus the correspondences that emerge between motetus and tenor are more attenuated; the effect is humorous, a parodic exploitation of allegorical parallels.

I close with *Hui main au doz mois de mai* (122) / *HEC DIES* (M13), in which the motetus presents a narrative scenario that explicitly parodies the biblical event celebrated in the tenor:

> M: Hui main au doz mois de mai,
>   desouz le solau levant,
>   en un vergier m'en entrai.
>   Desous un pin verdoiant
>   une pucele i trovai
>   roses coillant.
>   Lors me trai vers li;
>   de fine amour li pri.
>   Ele me respondi:
>   "A moi n'atoucherés voz ja,
>   quar j'ai mignot ami!"
> T: HEC DIES [30]

M: This morning in the sweet month of May, as the sun was rising, I went into an orchard. Under a verdant pine I found a maiden gathering roses. Then I went up to her; I asked her for true love. She replied: "You will never touch me, for I have a handsome lover!"
T: THIS DAY

The scene is a conventional one within the pastourelle genre: the male protagonist enters an orchard, finds a maiden gathering flowers, asks for her love, and is refused on the grounds that she loves another. But the tenor, whose words are echoed at the beginning of the motetus, adds a new dimension to our reading of the text. It derives from the Easter gradual *Hec dies. Confitemini Domino* (M13): "Hec dies quam fecit Dominus: exsultemus et laetemur in ea. Ⅴ Confitemini Domino, quoniam bonus: quoniam in seculum misericordia eius" (This day that the Lord made: let us exult and rejoice in it. Ⅴ Praise the Lord, for he is good: for his mercy endures forever).

Both the motetus and the gradual refer to the crucial events that took place *on this day*. Might the two stories be linked? If one looks at the motetus as a recasting of the Easter story, many details take on a new light: as on that first Easter morning, a man and a woman meet in a garden, at dawn, in the springtime. And the refrain sung by the maiden suddenly appears as a lyricized version of the famous words spoken in the garden by Christ to Mary Magdalene, "Noli me tangere" (Do not touch me [John 20:17]). Yet the motetus cannot be resolved into an allegory for the Resurrection scene, since the genders of the two participants are reversed. Any effort to construct an allegorical reading of the male protagonist as Christ founders at once on the maiden's appropriation of what should logically have been his line and, by extension, on her lack of interest in the entire encounter. At the same time, one can hardly imagine a pastourelle text in which the male protagonist, having met a beautiful maiden who approaches him eagerly, forbids her to touch him. Within the framework of the Passion narrative, the line must be spoken by the male persona while the expression of desire must come from the female figure. Within the framework of the pastourelle genre, the two roles must be reversed.

The motet *Hui main au doz mois de mai* / HEC DIES illustrates difficulties inherent in allegorizing the male lyric persona. The female persona moves easily between the realms of sacred and erotic. As object of desire or as desiring subject — grieving, yearning, or joyous — she can be Mary, Ecclesia, or the human soul, beloved Bride of Christ. The maiden who resists amorous advances can be interpreted *in bono* as the ascetic soul or virgin saint pledged to a Heavenly lover, or *in malo* as the faithless Synagoga. As a result, texts centered on the lady or the maiden are ambiguous; and in motets constructed of such texts, the tension between allegory and parody is often pronounced, allowing for considerable hermeneutic play. The identification of the male amorous persona with Christ, though not without precedent, is more limited in its applicability to vernacular lyric. Certain roles adopted by the male personae of vernacular lyric — for example, the adventurer who encounters an amorous shepherdess, or the adulterous lover who mocks or fears his lady's husband — cannot easily be adapted to the Christological model. Such figures are only for parodic effect, as the ironic counterpart or moral inversion of the sacred model.

Of the various stances adopted by the male lyric persona, however, one readily lends itself to allegorical use, whether serious or parodic. The figure of the suffering male lover, rejected by his lady and wronged by society, invites association with the motif of martyrdom, whether that of Christ or of the martyr saints. The pain of longing for an absent beloved is associated with the sorrow of Ecclesia or of the human witnesses to the Crucifixion; but the pain of rejection, humiliation, bodily torment, and false accusation is that of Christ, Man of Sorrows. The allegorical and parodic exploitation of the suffering male persona is the focus of the next chapter.

Chapter 5

Sweet Pain and Fatal Desire

Sextum signum est quod ille qui languet ex amore libenter sustinet
duras penas pro dilecto suo. Et illud signum ostendit hodie Christus.

The sixth sign is that he who languishes from love willingly endures
great pains for his beloved. And Christ showed that sign today.

—Sermon for Good Friday on *Amore langueo*

Ha, con m'a mort de debonaire lance,
S'einsi me fait morir a tel dolour!
De ses biauz ieuz me vint sanz desfiance
Ferir u cors . . .

Ah! how she has killed me with a noble lance, if she lets me die in such
sorrow! She ambushed me, striking my body a blow from her fair eyes.

—Châtelain de Couci

Among the most compelling and most frequently employed figures in
Christian allegory is that of Christ as Heavenly Bridegroom, with the role
of Bride alternately assigned to the Virgin, to Ecclesia, or to the individual
soul. In previous chapters we considered the maiden separated from her
lover, lamenting his absence or eagerly awaiting his return; and the Bride,
the *pucele de grant biauté* or queen of the dance whose celebration in
vernacular lyric provides a point of contact with the adoration, through
music, poetry, and ritual, of the Blessed Virgin. In this chapter the focus
is the male lyric persona for whom love is a source of joy and a painful
martyrdom. The figure of the suffering male lover provides another point
of contact between sacred and secular lyric. Whether his pain is caused by
the hard-heartedness or capriciousness of the lady he loves or by the malicious behavior of love's enemies, the lover's plight admits of moral and
spiritual readings that can identify him as the image of Christ, as a willing
martyr of love, or as an endangered soul in need of divine intervention.

The motets examined in this chapter are built on tenors from the liturgy of Christmas and that of the Passion (Easter or Holy Cross). The repertoire of Latin motets reflects the intimate relationship between these two events in sacred history. Normally the texts in a Latin motet are closely related to the tenor, elaborating on the sacred event or doctrinal point to which it refers. In a number of cases, however, we find that a tenor from the Easter liturgy is used for a Marian text or one about the birth of Christ; or conversely, though less frequently, that a tenor from the Christmas liturgy is used for a motet commemorating the Passion. For example, the Latin double motets *Salus virgini* (174) / *Hodie natus in Israhel* (175) / *IN SECULUM* (M13) and *Ut celesti possimus* (129) / *Cum sit natus hodie* (130) / *HEC DIES* (M13) combine texts devoted to the Incarnation and birth of Christ with tenors from the Easter gradual *Hec dies. Confitemini Domino.* Christmas and Easter are, of course, the central events of the Incarnation, when Christ is celebrated as Savior, Bridegroom, and King; and the moments when Nature was confounded through the Virgin Birth and the triumph over death. Crucial to these events are two icons of Christianity: the Virgin and the Cross, each of whom bore the body of Christ. These two figures, who provided the point of departure for our examination of the motifs of loss and separation, now initiate our discussion of love's martyrdom.

The Suffering Lover and the Man of Sorrows

In the *Court de Paradis*, discussed in Chapter 2, the martyr saints recall their bodily mortification through the refrain

> Cil doit bien joie mener
> Qui joie atent
> Des max qu'il sent (vv. 291–93) [1]

He should be joyful who expects joy from the pains that he feels.

The suffering caused by love is an age-old and ubiquitous topos of love poetry, present in the Ovidian tradition as well as the Song of Songs and central to vernacular lyric. The popularity of this topos allowed another point of contact between sacred and secular paradigms: erotic love and spiritual love are forms of martyrdom. In hagiographic tradition, bodily mortification replaces sexual gratification as the focus of the saint's desire: the imitation of Christ's Passion through martyrdom is the consummation of the soul's mystical marriage. Countless virgin martyrs refused sexual penetration and chose instead the bodily violation and dismemberment of martyrdom. The liturgy of Saint Andrew, to cite but a single example, is pervaded with his joyful expressions of desire for the Cross, as in the antiphon: "O bona crux, diu desiderata et concupiscenti animo praeparata, suscipe discipulum ejus qui pependit in te" (O good cross, long desired and prepared for the yearning soul, take up the disciple of the one who hung on you).[2]

In the previous chapter, we examined the contrasting figures of Virgin and Cross as background for the motet *Au doz mois de mai* (275) / *Crux forma penitentie* (274) / *SUSTINERE* (M22). The pervasive juxtaposition of the Virgin and the Cross allows an exploration of the Crucifixion as an event in the temporal, limited realm of human life on earth and in the eternal realm of the spirit. The contrast between these two icons embodies two sides of Christian spirituality: the joy of salvation and the infinite mercy of God, for which the Virgin serves as conduit; and the harshness of martyrdom, the devastating price to be paid for sin. Ultimately, the ecstatic union of spiritual Bride and Bridegroom is possible only in conjunction with the painful mortification of the flesh; and in this light, the Virgin and the Cross are fundamentally analogous figures. In the language of medieval allegory, the body of Mary is the nuptial chamber in which the marriage of human and divine was consummated; in the words of Cassiodorus, commenting Vulgate Psalm 18:6, "*Et ipse*, Christum Dominum dicit, qui *tamquam sponsus* Ecclesiae suae, *processit de thalamo suo*, id est de utero virginali" (*And he*, this means Christ the Lord, who *as the bridegroom* of his church *proceeded from his bridal chamber*, that is, from the virginal womb).[3] It is on the Cross—*sponsi le[c]tus* (nuptial couch [M, v. 6]), in the words of the above-mentioned motet—that this marriage is consummated in the bodily passion of the Crucifixion. Philip the Chancellor similarly states:

Hic est lectus praeelectus,
Ex electis est confectus
Liliis convallium. (3: 4–6)[4]

Here is the preeminent bed, it is constructed from select lilies of the valley.

Both sequence and motet identify the Cross with the nuptial bed of the Song of Songs, "Lectulus noster floridus" (Our couch is of flowers [Song 1:15]). And the reference to noon (*in meridie*, v. 6) in the motetus recalls the *Sponsa*'s appeal, "Indica mihi . . . ubi cubes in meridie" (Show me . . . where you lie at noontime [Song 1:6]). In this way noon, the hour of the

Crucifixion, is redefined as the moment in which the marriage of Christ and Ecclesia was consummated. The Cross is thus a place of refuge and of amorous and erotic tryst.[5]

The parallel roles of the Virgin and the Cross—as privileged spaces within which the drama of Redemption was enacted through the marriage of human and divine—can be derived from textual correspondences such as those elaborated in the sequence *Crux, de te volo conqueri* (see Chapter 4). It is more explicit in the anonymous sequence *Lignum vitae quaerimus*.[6] Here the Virgin and the Cross are the two loci where the fruit of life must be sought, and hence two manifestations of the tree of life. Each embodies a paradox that is part of the sacred mystery of the Incarnation and Redemption:

> Hic virgo puerpera,
> Hic crux salutifera,
> Ambae ligna mystica;
>
> Haec hysopus humilis,
> Illa cedrus nobilis,
> Utraque vivifica. (st. 5–6)

Here is the child-bearing virgin, here the salubrious cross, two mystical trees; this one a humble hyssop, that one a noble cedar, and both life-giving.

The parallelism of the Virgin and the Cross, figures of sterility and death miraculously transformed into figures of life and salvation, is visually stressed in the treatment of the sequence *Lignum vitae quaerimus* in the *Vergier de soulas*, a compilation of allegorical texts, figures, and diagrams representing various aspects of Christian doctrine. A full page is devoted to the Latin poem and its French translation (fol. 3v; see figure). In the upper left-hand section of the page, the text is disposed around a vertical series of images of the Virgin and Child; lines treating the Virgin are on the left and those treating the Cross are on the right, with text commenting on both figures appearing in the middle or split between the two sides of the page. Text and miniatures form a cross, whose vertical post is made up of images of the Virgin and whose crosspiece is provided by the images of biblical and monastic authorities who have commented upon the salutary effects of both Virgin and Cross. This "cross" built out of the Virgin's body echoes the image of Christ on the Cross that appears at the right. Thus although the representation of the Passion in the lower register stresses Mary's role as sorrowful witness, both the text and the layout of illustrations in the upper register reflect the deep-seated analogy

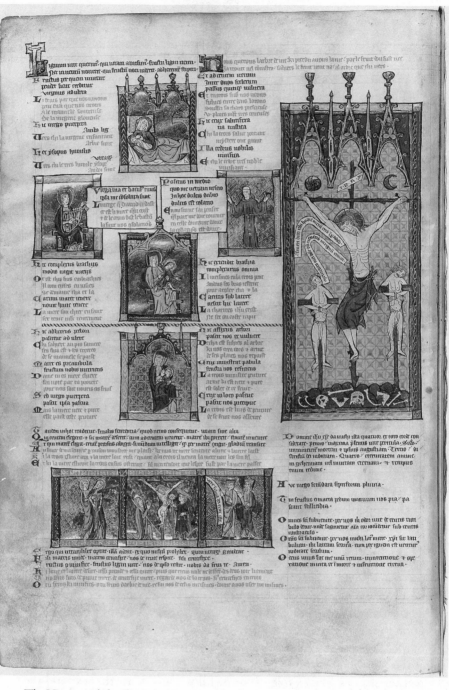

The Virgin and the Cross, as portrayed in the *Vergier de solas*. Paris, Bibl. Nat. fr. 9220, fol. 3v.

between the Virgin and the Cross as bearers of Christ and instruments of salvation.

The close association of Virgin and Cross, the image of Christ as at once Victim and Bridegroom and the allegorical identification of Cross and marriage bed, imply a profound linking of joy and pain, desire and death. These correspondences bear an intriguing relation to the representation of the lady in secular love lyric, variously a seductress, a cruel tormenter, and the source of mercy and beneficence. Erotic desire is represented as a wound that is at once painful and delightful, which the lady causes and she alone can cure:

> Amare
> crucior,
> morior,
> vulnere, quo glorior.
> Eia, si me sanare
> uno vellet osculo,
> que cor felici iaculo
> gaudet vulnerare![7]

Bitterly I am tormented, I die, from the wound in which I am glorified. Oh, if she only wished to heal me with a kiss, she who delights in wounding my heart with a blissful dart.

But if the lover's passion is cast in language reminiscent of martyrdom, the reverse happens as well: the Passion of Christ is expressed through the image of the pains of love. The metaphoric wound of love is applied to the Crucifixion, for example, in commentaries on Song of Songs 4:9, "Vulnerasti cor meum, soror mea, sponsa; vulnerasti cor meum in uno oculorum tuorum, et in uno crini colli tui" (You have wounded my heart, my sister bride; you have wounded my heart in one of your eyes, and in a hair of your neck). The commentary of Honorius of Autun is exemplary:

Ita Christus amore Ecclesiae vulneratus est in cruce. Prius vulnerasti cor meum, quando causa amoris tui flagellatus sum, ut te facerem mihi sororem, scilicet regni cohaeredem, iterum vulnerasti cor meum, quando amore tui in cruce pendens vulneratus sum, ut te sponsam mihi facerem gloriae participem, et hoc *in uno oculorum tuorum et in uno crine colli tui*. Similitudo est ab illo, qui capitur pulchritudine oculorum, vel crinium, puellae.[8]

Thus Christ was wounded on the Cross for love of the Church. First you wounded my heart, when I was beaten for your love, in order to make you my sister, that is, a partner in the kingdom; again you wounded my heart, when for your love I was wounded hanging on the Cross, in order to make you my bride and participant in glory, and this was *in one of your eyes and in one of the hairs of your neck*. This is in the figure of one who is captured by the beauty of the eyes or the hair of a maiden.

It is on the Cross that Christ fulfills the promise of the mystical union first formed within the body of the Virgin, thereby consummating his betrothal to his true Bride, Ecclesia: the Crucifixion is a sort of love service, a voluntary suffering undertaken in honor of the beloved. At the same time, Christ's Passion is necessary in the first place because of sin introduced into the world by Eve; the more immediate cause is the treachery of his first Bride, Synagoga. This fundamental motif is exploited in numerous homilies and other devotional texts featuring the image of Christ as lover and chivalric champion of the human soul, itself personified as a lady who may be either devoted or hard-hearted.[9] The Passion is thus simultaneously linked to the virtue and the perfidy of a configuration of literal and allegorical women; the paradigm encompasses the dichotomous view of women so often attributed to medieval society.

This construct finds its mirror in vernacular lyric, with its endless evocations of *li douz maus d'amer* (the sweet pains of love) — without which no joy of love is possible, just as the joy of Redemption is impossible without the Crucifixion — and the lady who has "wounded" her lover, usually, as in the Song of Songs, with a glance from her beautiful eyes.[10] Like Eve, the lady causes her admirer pain and turmoil because her erotic nature makes her inherently desirable, a temptress. Yet she may also cause him to suffer because she refuses to yield to his desire; in the Christological model, she corresponds to Synagoga, of whom the poet of *Quant li solleiz converset en Leon* comments, "Lei ad laisiét, quar n'ert de bel serviset" (He left her because she did not serve him well [v. 53]). And the *douz maus d'amer* can become a metaphor for sexual pleasure, just as the saint's martyrdom represents a sublimated consummation. Thus the suffering male lover admits of more than one moral or allegorical reading: the spiritually damaged victim of seduction, the martyr who accepts bodily suffering as the means to a higher love, and even the betrayed and suffering Christ himself.

The ubiquitous motif of amorous suffering, as developed by the trouvères, can be illustrated by one of the Châtelain de Couci's songs, *Mout m'est bele la douce conmençance*. It is constructed around the conflicting emotions of desire and pain, joy and fear. The first three stanzas suffice to demonstrate the development of these motifs:

Mout m'est bele la douce conmençance
Du nouvel tanz a l'entrant de Pascour,
Que boiz et pré sunt de mainte samblance,
Blanc et vermeill, couvert d'erbe et de flour;
Et je sui, las, du tout en tel balance
Qu'a mainz jointes aour
Ma bele perte u ma haute richour,
Ne sai lequel, s'en ai joie et paour,
Si que souvent chant la u du cuer plour,
Car lons respis m'esmaie et mescheance.

Ja de mon cuer n'istra maiz la samblance,
Donc me conquist as mos plainz de douçour
Cele qui j'ai du tout en ramembrance,
Si que mes cuers ne sert d'autre labour.
Ha, franche rienz, en qui j'ai ma fiance,
Merci pour vostre honour!
Car s'en vous truis le samblant menteor,
Mort m'avrïez a loi de trahitour;
Si en vaudroit mout mainz vostre valour,
Se m'ociiez einsinc par decevance.

Ha, con m'a mort de debonaire lance,
S'einsi me fait morir a tel dolour!
De ses biauz ieuz me vint sanz desfiance
Ferir u cors, que n'i ot autre tour;
Mout volontiers en preïsse vengance
—Par Dieu le Creatour!—
Tel que mil foiz la peüsse le jour
Ferir u cuer d'autretele savour;
Ne ja certes n'en feïsse clamour,
Se j'eüsse de moi vengier poissance.[11]

Very beautiful to me is the sweet beginning of the new season at the approach of Easter, when forest and field are of varied appearance, white and red, covered with grass and flowers; and I, alas! am caught in the balance, such that with clasped hands I adore my beautiful loss or my great wealth, I don't know which. Thus I often sing while my heart weeps, for long delay and misfortune dismay me.

Never will there leave my heart the image of her who conquered me with sweet words, she whom I hold entirely in my memory, such that my heart knows no other labor. Ah! noble creature, in whom I place my faith, have mercy, for your honor's sake! For if I find your appearance to be false, you will have killed me like a traitor; and your worthiness will be depleted if you kill me through deception.

Ah! how she has killed me with a noble lance, if she lets me die in such sorrow! She ambushed me, striking my body a blow from her fair eyes without further ado. How gladly I would take vengeance—by God the Creator!—by striking her in the heart a thousand times a day with a similar sweetness. Nor, to be sure, would I complain, if I had the power of avenging myself.

The song is set in the period before Easter. This season, encompassing both the transition from winter to spring and the passage from Lent to Easter and Pentecost, is appropriate to the conflicting emotions of the lyric persona, balanced as he is between despair and hope, death and renewal. The motif of the lover's impending death has certain associations with Christ's Passion: it is a death suffered willingly in the name of love, it is effected through betrayal by the one he loves, the murder weapon is a lance (albeit a metaphorical one). At the same time, his worshipful attitude invites the association of the all-powerful lady, object of adoration, with Christ the Savior. She withholds or dispenses mercy; her image sustains the supplicant's heart and memory; her sublime and all-pervasive presence is subtly echoed in the flowering landscape, whose colors—red and white—are conventionally associated with feminine beauty. The poet here draws on the ideological framework of Eastertide in order to enrich his language of adoration and desire. But there is no consistent allegorical development. Neither lover nor lady can actually be identified with Christ, nor does the persona move toward a renunciation of tormented erotic love in favor of spiritual devotion. The tension lies in the simultaneous movement toward death and renewal, joy and despair, that characterizes the persona's ongoing state of desire, and not in the crafted interplay of spiritual and erotic registers that is the motet's domain.

The equation of desire, pleasure, and pain that informs both spiritual and erotic discourse is embodied in the unicorn, a conventional image for Christ: drawn to the lap of a beautiful maiden, it falls victim to hunters—generally portrayed as stabbing the beast while it lies with its head in the maiden's lap—just as Christ descended to the womb of the Virgin and, having become man, was captured, crucified, and stabbed in the side. The maiden holding the unicorn in its moment of death is truly a fusion of the Virgin and the Cross, Eve and Ecclesia: object of desire and instrument of death, temptress and virgin, endowed with an aura of beauty that is a sign of purity and a fatal attraction. The unicorn is also an image for the courtly lover, as in Thibaut de Champagne's famous song:

> Ausi conme unicorne sui
> Qui s'esbahist en regardant,

> Quant la pucele va mirant.
> Tant est liee de son ennui,
> Pasmee chiet en son giron;
> Lors l'ocit on en traïson.
> Et moi ont mort d'autel senblant
> Amors et ma dame, por voir:
> Mon cuer ont, n'en puis point ravoir.   (vv. 1–9) [12]

I am like the unicorn that becomes overwhelmed as it gazes, looking upon the maiden. It is so delighted in its suffering, it falls unconscious into her lap; then it is killed through treachery. Truly, love and my lady have killed me in the same way. They have my heart, and I can never have it back.

On the surface, the unicorn's death represents the agony of unrequited desire. But there is also a deeper erotic significance to the physical passion of the unicorn/lover as he collapses onto the lady. In the Christological model, the virgin who lures the unicorn to its death is at the same time the bride with whom he is united through that very death. In its larger implications, the allegory of the unicorn suggests not so much the frustration of desire as its ultimate consummation.

The double significance of the unicorn is apparent in Richard de Fournival's *Bestiaires d'amour*. The unicorn figures in an account of the lover's progress through the first three stages of love—sight, hearing, and smell—and it is the model for the third stage: attracted by the "scent of virginity," it falls asleep in the maiden's lap and so is killed by the hunters. Initially, the lover's torment does appear to be frustration:

Et Amors, ki est sages venerres, me mist en mon cemin une pucele a qui douc[h]our jou me sui endormis et mors de tel mort com a Amor apartient, c'est desperance sans atent de merci. (ed. Segre, p. 44)

And Love, who is a wise hunter, placed in my path a maiden at whose sweetness I fell asleep and died such a death as pertains to Love, that is, despair without expectation of mercy.

Only a few lines later, however, the sleep-induced death of love is more fully explained:

Et se je parfusse pris as autres .ij. sens: a gouster en baisant et a touchier en acolant, dont parfusse jou a droit endormis. Car adont dort li hom, quant il ne sent nul de ses .v. sens. Et de l'endormir d'amors vienent tout li peril. Car a tous les endormis suit la Mors, et a l'unicorne ki s'endort a la pucele et a l'homme ki s'endort a la seraine. (ed. Segre, pp. 45–46)

And if I had come to be captured through the other two senses—taste in kissing and touch in embracing—then I would truly have fallen asleep. For a man sleeps when he feels none of the five senses. And from the sleep of love come all the perils. For to all those who sleep comes Death, to the unicorn lulled to sleep by the maiden and to the man put to sleep by the siren.

In this equation, the perilous sleep of love and the death that it brings can only be the loss of rational consciousness at the moment of sexual climax; and the virgin whose purity tames the fierce unicorn is conflated with the erotic temptress who lures sailors to their death. Unicorn and siren together function to express the paradoxical fusion of desire and fear, pleasure and pain, that characterizes human passion.

The correspondences between human and divine passion, and the perception of the female body as locus of erotic pleasure and of painful torment, are exploited in motets that concentrate on the predicament of the suffering male lover. I begin with two examples using tenors that derive from the same source as that of the motet discussed at the beginning of Chapter 4, *Au doz mois de mai* (275) / *Crux forma penitentie* (274) / SUSTINERE (M22), an alleluia for the Finding of the Cross: "Alleluia. Dulce lignum, dulces claves, dulcia ferens pondera, quae sola fuisti digna sustinere regem caelorum et Dominum" (Alleluia. Sweet wood, sweet nails, bearing the sweet weight, you alone were worthy of bearing the Lord, king of Heaven [M22]). We recall that the tenor SUSTINERE is melodically indistinguishable from the tenor PORTARE, presumably taken from an alleluia for Assumption that is musically identical, and textually nearly identical, to the above: "Alleluia. Dulcis virgo, dulcis mater, dulcia ferens pondera, quae sola fuisti digna portare regem caelorum et Dominum" (Alleluia. Sweet virgin, sweet mother, bearing the sweet weight, you alone were worthy of carrying the Lord, king of Heaven [M34a]). In our first example, the tenor designation varies in the sources: *Ne sai tant amour servir* (283) / *Ja de bone amour* (282) / SUSTINERE (M22) or PORTARE (M34a).[13] Both motetus and triplum are statements of steadfast devotion to love combined with grief at finding no favorable response:

Tr	M
Ne sai tant amour servir	Ja de bone amour
Que me veille guerredoner	Mes cuers ne se departira,
Ce qu'ai mis en bien amer,	Mes sanz nul sejor
Quant ele m'a en despit	Adés la servira,
Qui tant me fait la nuit soupirer;	Quant qu'a ma dame plera
Si que quant je mi doi reposer,	Qui tant a de valour,
Ne me sai de cele part tourner	Dont ja a nul jour
Que penser ne me face fremir,	Mes cuers joie n'avra.

Qu'ele me tiegne en mon lit,   S'en sui en dolor,
Amours, quant je mi doi dormir.   Pour ce que ne la vi pieça
                                             S'en chanterai par douçor:
                                             Hé, Dieu! la verrai je ja,
                                             La bele qui mon cuer a?[14]

Tr: I don't know how to serve love enough for her to be willing to grant me recompense for what I have invested in good loving, when she who causes me to sigh all night long despises me, so that when I should be resting, no matter which way I turn, the thought makes me tremble *that she holds me in my bed, Love, when I should be sleeping.*[15]

M: My heart will never depart from good love, but I will always serve her without respite, in whatever way it may please my lady who has such worth, and of whom my heart will never have joy. Thus I am in sorrow, because I haven't seen her for a long time. Thus I will sing sweetly: *Hey, God! will I ever see her, the fair one who has my heart?*

The texts both employ a male voice and both are declarations of undying love in spite of the pain that it brings. They differ in that the triplum is more focused on the turmoil of unrequited desire—rejected by the lady, the lover is reduced to nocturnal fantasies—while the motetus treats the frustration of separation without specifying that it is caused by the lady's resistance. The two tenor designations, in turn, are apparently a function of the motet's double focus: SUSTINERE is appropriate to the triplum, and PORTARE, though working well with both texts, brings out an added dimension of the motetus.

The tenor SUSTINERE, associated with Christ's Passion, suggests a humorous identification of the suffering lover with Christ, the Bridegroom rejected and crucified by his chosen people. The link to the tenor is especially strong in the fantasy with which the triplum closes. Through the etymological correspondence of *tiegne (tenir)* and *sustinere,* Christ's Passion on the Cross, marriage bed of the Divine Bridegroom, fuses with that of the lovesick man tormented by erotic dreams; the effect is comic melodrama.[16] Those versions using the Assumption tenor PORTARE achieve a similar effect through the allusion to the Virgin, who held the body of Christ within her body, a spiritual version of the erotic fantasy that haunts the lover's dreams. Moreover, the refrain at the end of the motetus echoes the Assumption motif of amorous reunion. The tenor's dual identity thus reflects the two themes of the motet as a whole, male passion and the lady as object of desire and adoration. The lover's torment and its hoped-for denouement parodically refigure the motifs of Passion and

Assumption that are simultaneously present in the tenor melody. The complex play of the motet would appeal strongly to an audience familiar with both alleluias, people who could recognize the dual associations of the tenor melody; but the humor could be appreciated even if only one of the sources was known.

The dual function of the alleluia melody is similarly at issue in the interpretation of *En non Diu, Dieus, c'est la rage* (271) FERENS PONDERA (M22/M34a). The motetus, attributed to an unidentified monk of Saint Denis, is a statement of amorous torment:

> M: *En non Diu, Dieus, c'est la rage,*
>   *que li maus d'amer*
>   *s'il ne m'asoage;*
>   ne puis souffrir son outrage,
>   mon courage en retrairai,
>   de lui partirai.
>   Mes n'est pas en moi,
>   quar *quant la voi, Deus, la voi, la voi,*
>   *la bele, la blonde, a li m'otroi.*
> T: FERENS PONDERA[17]

M: *In the name of God, God, it's madness if I have no relief from the pains of love*; I cannot suffer this outrage, I will withdraw my affections, I will depart from love. But I don't have it in me, for *when I see her, God, when I see her, see her, the fair one, the blonde, I give myself to her.*
T: BEARING THE WEIGHT

Since the tenor—unique in the motet repertoire—involves words that appear in both versions of the alleluia, one cannot actually tell whether the reference is to the Cross or to the Virgin; all possibilities are open. Most literally, the tenor might simply be a comment on the burden borne by the lovesick man.[18] As an allusion to the Crucifixion, it adds to the comic intensity of his protestations of pain. Since the abbey of Saint Denis possessed one of the holy nails, veneration of the instruments of the Passion was strong there; though it is not certain that the entire motet is the work of the monk, it may be that a member of that community composed this humorous little motet honoring the sweet pains of a different sort of passion. Yet the composer perhaps chose the tenor for its allusion to Assumption as well: with reference to the Virgin it contributes to the fantasy of union with the woman who will "bear the weight" of her lover's body. A double reading of the tenor suggests that the pains to which the lady subjects her lover are merely the prelude to an ecstatic union: again, a parody of the sacred paradigm of Passion, Resurrection, and Assumption.

Slanderous Spies, Perfidious Women: The Lover Embattled

To continue the exposition of the allegorical and parodic treatment of the male lover, I turn to a series of examples using tenors from the Easter gradual *Hec dies. Confitemini Domino* (M13): "Hec dies quam fecit Dominus: exsultemus et laetemur in ea. ℣. Confitemini Domino, quoniam bonus: quoniam in seculum misericordia eius" (This day that the Lord made: let us exult and rejoice in it. ℣. Praise the Lord, for he is good: for his mercy endures forever). The source for the gradual is Vulgate Psalm 117:24, 29. The psalm is a hymn of thanksgiving to the Lord for salvation from enemies. Its relevance to Easter is obvious: on this day the Church celebrates Christ's act of Redemption, whereby humankind was saved from the dominion of the devil and the prison of Hell. The composers of vernacular motets recognized numerous possibilities latent in the gradual and its dual context of Easter and of the psalm itself. Not every motet using a tenor from this gradual exploits its biblical or liturgical associations. Some composers chose their tenors more for musical reasons than for textual ones. And in other instances, the tenor with its allusion to Easter might simply reinforce the lyric associations with springtime. Such is the case, for example, in *L'autre jour* (200) / *Au tens pascour* (201) / *IN SECULUM* (M13) or *Dieus, de chanter maintenant* (176) / *Chant d'oisiaus et fuelle et flor* (177) / *IN SECULUM* (M13)—both discussed in Chapter 1—where the tenor supports the seasonal setting given in the motetus. The tenor *IN SECULUM* (FOREVER) also underscores the motif of undying love, without necessarily implying any additional levels of meaning. In other instances, however, the tenor plays a more important thematic role; at the end of Chapter 4, we saw that a parodic recasting of the Resurrection scene is played out in *Hui main au doz mois de mai* (122) / *HEC DIES* (M13). The tenors drawn from the gradual *Hec dies. Confitemini Domino*—*HEC DIES, DOMINO, QUONIAM,* and *IN SECULUM*—carry associations with the Easter story and with the themes of salvation, mercy, the dangers of earthly or infernal enemies, the faithlessness of humans, and the absolute reliability of God.

The resulting thematic nexus offers a rich field for allegorical or parodic exploitation by motet composers. A lighthearted adaptation of the Man of Sorrows motif is found in *Bons amis, je vos rendrai* (193) / *Qu'ai je forfait ne mespris* (192) / *IN SECULUM* (M13):

<table>
<tr><td align="center">Tr</td><td align="center">M</td></tr>
</table>

Tr	M
"Bons amis, je vos rendrai	"Qu'ai je forfait ne mespris,
les desperz et les corros,	dame, envers voz?
que vos avés endurés	Vostre amor mi destraint si,
comme loiaus amorous;	que je languis et muir toz.
si me rent et doins a voz."	Haro, je voz pri merci,
	biaus fins cuers doz!"

T: IN SECULUM[19]

Tr: "Good friend, I will recompense you for the hardships and afflictions that you have suffered like a loyal lover; thus I yield and give myself to you."
M: "How have I misbehaved or done wrong, lady, toward you? Your love so constrains me that I languish and will soon die. Help, I beg you for mercy, beautiful sweet noble heart!"
T: FOREVER

The motet is a secular recasting of the basic paradigm of the suffering lover conjoined, through eternal love and mercy, with his bride. The motetus is the male persona's plea for mercy from his lady; the triplum is the lady's acknowledgment of her lover's afflictions and her submission to his desire. Most literally, the motet contrasts the male lover's suffering with the eventual fulfillment in love that this suffering brings; the tenor is perhaps a comment on the undying quality of love. A consideration of the tenor's biblical source—a psalm of thanksgiving for divine mercy— turns it into an ironic commentary on the lover's self-indulgent cry for sexual "mercy." The contrast between spiritual adoration and erotic desire is further underscored in the term that expresses the male persona's love-longing, "je languis" (I languish [M, v. 4]), an echo of the famous "quia amore langueo" (for I languish with love [Song 2:5]) of the Song of Songs.

Finally, if the tenor's more immediate origin in the Easter liturgy is taken into account, the motet could be a parodic recasting of the Passion model: the Man of Sorrows speaks in the motetus, and the *Sponsa* in the triplum declares her love and submission. The dialogue of reproachful lover and devoted beloved is paralleled in the Good Friday liturgy, in which Christ and his people speak during the Adoration of the Cross.[20] In this ceremony, performed as responses between soloists and choir, Christ offers reproaches in which he contrasts the favors he has lovingly bestowed with the harsh betrayal of the Crucifixion; each reproach is answered with an expression of praise and devotion. The dialogue begins:

Popule meus, quid feci tibi? Aut in quo contristavi te? Responde mihi. ℣. Quia eduxi te de terra Egypti: parasti crucem Salvatori tuo.

Agios o Theos, Agyos yschiros, Agios athanatos, eleison ymas.
Sanctus Deus, sanctus fortis, sanctus immortalis, miserere nobis.

My people, what have I done to you? Or how have I grieved you? Answer me. ℣.
For I led you out of Egypt: you have prepared a cross for your Savior.
Holy God, holy and mighty, holy and immortal, have mercy on us.
Holy God, holy and mighty, holy and immortal, have mercy on us.

The opening words of Christ's reproach closely resemble those of the motetus. The emotive intensity of the liturgical model and the importance of the ceremony to which it belongs give it a prominence that facilitates recognition of the parody, lending a melodramatic quality to the lover's plea.

The motet, in short, functions coherently on three levels. Literally, it presents the motif of reciprocal desire and everlasting love; tropologically, it is a cry for mercy to a powerful figure capable of ending the supplicant's torments, cast as analogous to the suffering soul's appeal to God; and allegorically, it is an image for the crucified Christ and his repentant Bride. For the two figurative readings, however, it operates in an ironic mode that makes it a fine example of the polysemous parody we have come to expect from vernacular polyphony.

In our next example, *Vilene gent* (124) / *Honte et dolor et ennui et haschie* (125) / *HEC DIES* (M13), the lover cries out not in an appeal to his beloved, but against the enemies of love (Musical Example 5). Both upper voices appear to emanate from the same persona, who declares his commitment to love and calls for vengeance against spies and slanderers; the primary distinction between the two texts is that love's enemies are addressed directly in the triplum, and the motetus refers to them in the third person until the last line. The two voices are linked throughout by shared rhymes; in addition, the calls for vengeance—Tr, vv. 4–5 and M, vv. 3–4—are nearly identical. Framing the appeal to vengeance, in triplum and in motetus, are a reiteration that the behavior of the *vilene gent* will not dissuade the persona and his lady from continuing to love (Tr, vv. 1–3, 8–9), and an implied opposition of the *griez maus* wished on love's enemies with the *doz maus* felt by lovers (M, vv. 1–2, 5–8).

The correspondences between the two texted voices are emphasized by the musical structure.[21] The motetus uses nearly the same melody for verses 1–2 and 3–4, echoed in the triplum in an overlapping pattern. The melody for the first six syllables of motetus v. 1 is repeated in the first six syllables of triplum v. 2; a similar repetition marks the first six syllables of motetus v. 3 and triplum v. 4. In addition, the last six syllables of motetus

(translation and caption follow on bottom of facing page)

v. 4 and triplum v. 5, textually identical, employ almost the same melody, as does the phrase *vilene gent* at the end of motetus v. 2 and the beginning of triplum v. 1. A similar feature appears toward the end of the piece with the overlapping musical echo "gent, fausse gent" and "vileine gent" (Tr, v. 7 and M, v. 7). The placement of rests, moreover, allows the phrases *griez maus* (M, v. 4 and Tr, v. 5) and *les maus* (M, v. 5) to sound alone, causing these terms to stand out in performance. The rapid-fire reiteration of pain alternates between the two voices, moving from the double allusion to the suffering wished on love's enemies to the counterexample of the lover's own amorous suffering. In this way both the punishment of the *vileine gent* and the contrast between their experience and the lover's are emphasized. The phrase *vileine gent* itself is strategically placed at the beginning of the piece (Tr, v. 1), midway through the first statement of the tenor melody (M, v. 2), and midway through its second statement (Tr, v. 7), where it introduces an extended apostrophe to the lover's adversaries (Tr, v. 7 and M, v. 7); successive rests in motetus and triplum highlight the words *fausse* and *vileine*. Textual and musical correspondences together thus stress the false, scurrilous nature of love's enemies and the ills wished upon them.

The motet is an amusing parody of the serious dangers described in the psalm that is the ultimate source for the tenor: "Circumdederunt me sicut apes, et exarserunt sicut ignis in spinis; et in nomine Domini quia ultus sum in eos" (They surrounded me like bees, and flared up like fire among thorns; and in the name of God I took vengeance on them [Ps. 117:12]). And just as the psalmist pledges his devotion to God— "Deus meus es tu, et confitebor tibi" (You are my God, and I praise you [Ps. 117:28])—so the persona of the triplum vows that he and his *amie*

Tr: Villainous people, never will we leave off loving loyally because of your slander and your spying. Moreover, as love constrains me, may grievous pains and torments come quickly to you, villainous people, false people! We will love, my sweetheart and I, merrily.

M: May all villainous people have shame and sorrow and bother and anguish! Moreover, as love masters me, may grievous pains and torments come to them at once! They don't feel the pains that often grip me on account of my sweetheart. *Villainous people, you never feel them, the sweet pains that I feel.*

T: THIS DAY

Musical Example 5. From Hans Tischler, ed., *Motets of the Montpellier Codex.* Recent Researches in the Music of the Middle Ages and Early Renaissance, 2–8 (Madison: A-R Editions, Inc., 1978–85).

will persevere in their devotion to love: "Ja ne lairons a amer loiaument" (Never will we leave off loving loyally [Tr, v. 2]). The lament concerning the treacherous, slanderous enemies of love also recasts the motif of Christ's betrayal, an important theme of the Passion liturgy, as exemplified in the Easter responsory: "Locuti sunt adversum me lingua dolosa, et sermonibus odii circumdederunt me; pro eo ut diligerent me detrahebant mihi. Ego autem orabam, et exaudisti me, Domine Deus meus. ℣. Et posuerunt adversum me mala pro bonis" (They spoke against me with a lying tongue, and surrounded me with words of hatred; they betrayed me because of those who loved me. But I prayed, and you heard me, my Lord God. ℣. And they gave me back evil for good [*CAO*, no. 7095]).

The motet *Vilene gent* / *Honte et dolor* / HEC DIES does not present an allegory of Christ's Passion; its simple rhetoric of steadfastness in love and anger at love's enemies includes no specific details that would allow an identification of the lyric persona with Christ. Through its association with Easter, however, the tenor emphasizes the themes of betrayal, martyrdom, and faith—and ultimately the hope for salvation as a result of unwavering dedication to love—central to the two texted voices. And the allusive quality of the tenor transforms this portrait of amorous martyrdom into a parody of Christian martyrdom.

The model of Christ's Passion—betrayal by Synagoga, atonement for Eve's seduction of Adam—also informs the rare instances of antifeminist motets. Interesting examples are the contrafacta motets *Deo confitemini* (131) / DOMINO (M13) and *Mout est fous qui fame croit* (132) / DOMINO (M13). A comparison of the Latin and French texts brings out the parallels between the two models:

> M: Deo confitemini
>   qui sua clementia
>   carnem suo numini
>   iunxit in Maria
>   ut Abrahe semini
>   promissa ferret auxilia.
>   Se conformans homini
>   sic subiectum crimini
>   seductum hostis malitia
>   redemit morte pia.
> T: DOMINO [22]

M: Praise God, who in his mercy joined flesh to his divinity in Mary, that promised help be brought to the seed of Abraham. Conforming himself to man, he thus redeemed through his pious death the one subject to crime, seduced by the malice of the enemy.

T: THE LORD

> M: Mout est fous qui fame croit
> et qui l'aime et qui la sert.
> Sache bien quel que i soit
> qui plus i met, plus i pert.
> A peine aime ce qu'el doit
> ce puet l'en voer tout en apert
> ainçois engigne et deçoit
> ce que de li sorpris voit
> s'il servise tornent a depert.
> Pis a cil qui plus desert.
>
> T: DOMINO [23]

M: Very foolish is he who believes a woman, and who loves her and serves her. Know well that no matter what, the more he puts into it the more he loses. She will hardly love what she should, that can be seen clearly; she sooner tricks and deceives the one that she sees captivated by her; his service is turned to loss. The one who deserves most has the worst of it.

T: THE LORD

The Latin motet, in keeping with the Easter tenor, celebrates Redemption. Its opening line, "Deo confitemini," corresponds closely to the source gradual: "Confitemini Domino" (Praise the Lord). And like the psalm from which the gradual derives, the motet cites both an act of persecution—in this case, the primeval treachery that corrupted the human race—and God's merciful act of salvation. The French motet is an erotic reading of the motifs of seduction and betrayal suggested by the tenor and elaborated in the Latin motet. *Mout est fous qui fame croit* focuses on the figure of Fallen Man, seduced by Eve; the embattled protagonist of Psalm 117, victim of human perfidy, becomes the male victim of female sexual duplicity. The tenor points to the only means of redemption available to those caught in the web of destructive eros: the renunciation of worldly entanglements and an absolute faith in God.

As is often the case with contrafacta, it is difficult to determine which text came first. But correspondences between the texts suggest that one was written with the other in mind, not merely as words fit to a pre-existing melody. The French text elaborates on the motif of seduction, which the Latin text cites as the source of the Fall. The opening line of each text announces its principal theme—faith in God and distrust of women; subsequent lines stress divine mercy and feminine perfidy. The "promised help" brought by Christ and his act of Redemption contrast with women's lack of recompense to the ones who serve them. Indeed, the plight of the man deceived by a woman and held in thrall—"de li sorpris" (captivated by her [v. 8])—is a figure for the fallen human race, "subiectum crimini / seductum hostis malitia" (subject to crime, seduced by the malice of the enemy [vv. 8–9]). What is at issue, therefore, is not an allegorical reading of the betrayed or rejected lover as Christ, but a moral reading of erotic love itself as the image of Original Sin.

Our examples thus far have illustrated considerable variety in their use of the Passion model. The torments of the lovesick male persona can be a form of eroticized martyrdom, ironically contrasted with the martyrdom of Christ on the Cross; this conceit rests on the double reading of the Crucifixion as a tortured death and a mystical marriage consummation. The dialogue of sorrowing lover and lady can also become an implied analogy for the dialogue between Christ and his people; the lady as cause of her lover's suffering and as loyal beloved implies a subtle play on Synagoga—Christ's first, unfaithful Bride—and Ecclesia, his true Bride. The embattled lover can also suffer at the hands of the world at large; in this model, his "martyrdom" is less an erotic consummation than a simple instance of unjust persecution, and the focus shifts from his fixation on the lady to his adversarial relationship with love's enemies. Finally, the lady herself may be cast in the adversarial role with the emphasis on her erotic allure not as a source of pleasure but as the means by which she corrupts and deceives. In this model, the tribulations of love are no longer a source of erotic excitement nor an ennobling martyrdom, but a sign of moral blindness. Thus far, these themes have appeared singly. In closing, I consider a motet family whose members offer more complicated perspectives on erotic and spiritual passion.

Sponsus/Agnus: The Joys and Pains of Love

"Descendit de celis missus ab arce patris; introivit per aurem virginis in regionem nostram indutus stola purpurea et exivit per auream portam; lux et decus universe fabrice mundi. *V.* Tanquam sponsus Dominus procedens de thalamo suo et exivit" (He descended from Heaven, sent from the ark of the father; he entered through the ear of the Virgin into our world, clothed in a purple stole, and he went forth through the gate of gold; the light and ornament of the created world. V. The Lord went forth like a bridegroom proceeding from his bridal chamber [O2]).

The family of motets to which we now turn is built on the tenor TAN-QUAM, taken from a responsory for Christmas Matins that uses language from Vulgate Psalm 18 to stress Christ's role as Bridegroom. At the heart of the motet family is a conductus motet, *Tanquam suscipit vellus* (636) / *TANQUAM* (O2).[24] Expanding from this basis, we have the Latin double motet *Tamquam agnus ductus ad victimam* (640) / *Tamquam suscipit vellus* (636) / *TAMQUAM* (O2) and the musically identical bilingual motet *Quant naist la flor en la pree* (637) / *Tanquam suscipit vellus* (636) / *TANQUAM* (O2). The latter composition is also transmitted with a French quadruplum, *Qui voudroit fame esprover* (639) / *Quant naist la flor en la pree* (637) / *Tanquam suscipit vellus* (636) / *TANQUAM* (O2). The four-part bilingual motet is paralleled in a French motet that, aside from the transposition of motetus and truplum, is musically identical: *Qui voudroit fame esprover* (639) / *Deboinerement atendrai merci* (638) / *Quant naist la flor en la pree* (637) / *TANQUAM* (O2).[25] As a group, this family of motets offers a variety of perspectives on the figure of the male lover and on the joys and dangers of love.

The original Latin motetus, appropriate to the Christmas tenor, treats the Virgin Birth. In the Latin double motet, this motetus, a conventional meditation on the mystery of the Incarnation, is combined with a text focusing on the Passion:

M	Tr
Tamquam suscipit	Tamquam agnus ductus ad
vellus pluviam,	victimam,
ita percipit	crucem subit Christus,
dum concipit	sanctissimam
virgo propriam	animam
Domini graciam.	tradens, ut redimeret peccatores.
Novus usus per Mariam	Inferni fregit fores;
novi partus incipit,	resurrexit Dominus; psallite,
in qua naturam decipit,	plausus agite,
dum sic concipit	hympnos Deo dicite,
intra viri nesciam	nec in vobis sit facinus.
hominis substanciam,	Cunctorum redemptori
rex, qui per iusticiam	cum floribus
corripit	occurrite,
omnem maliciam	ligno nacionibus

Et peccatum eripit   regnare Deum dicite.
Et dat veniam.
T: TANQUAM

M: Like the fleece absorbed the moisture, the Virgin received God's own Grace
    when she conceived. A new order began through Mary with a new birth, in
    which she deceived nature. For thus, knowing no man, she conceived the
    substance of man, the king, who with justice vanquishes all evil, takes away
    sin, and grants forgiveness.
Tr: Like a lamb led to sacrifice, so Christ suffered the Cross, relinquishing his
    most holy spirit, in order to redeem sinners. He broke down the gates of
    Hell; the Lord arose; sing psalms, give praise and sing hymns to God; may
    you be without sin. Come running with flowers to the Redeemer of all,
    proclaim that God rules all nations through the Cross.
T: LIKE

The motet coheres around the Messiah, in three parallel similes of
tenor, motetus, and triplum: *Tamquam [sponsus]* (Like [a bridegroom]),
Tamquam suscipit vellus pluviam (Like the fleece absorbed the moisture),
and *Tamquam agnus ductus ad victimam* (Like a lamb led to sacrifice).
Christ's dual identity as Bridegroom and sacrificial victim accompanies
an allegorical statement of his miraculous conception. The source responsory is constructed on the motif of Christ's entry into the world through
the body of the Virgin, a metaphorical bridal chamber: within her the
spirit took on flesh and emerged like a bridegroom who has just consummated his marriage. This motif is doubled in the motetus, which employs
a different allegorical figure for the Virgin—the fleece of Gideon—and
stresses Christ's identity as king and redeemer. The triplum develops the
theme of Christ the redeemer and thereby replaces the Virgin with the
Cross, focusing not on the conjoining of flesh and spirit within the Virgin
but on their temporary disjoining as Christ passes through the Crucifixion and descends into Hell, only to arise again triumphant. The motet
as a whole presents the Virgin and the Cross as parallel figures. Each is
a locus of the consummation of the marriage of Christ and his Church,
representing the overturning of the old order through a miraculous violation of nature—the Virgin Birth and the Resurrection. Implicit in this
juxtaposition is a contrast between the dramatic and joyous arrival of
the Bridegroom—at Christmas and at Easter—and the grievous suffering
embraced by the sacrificial Lamb of God.

The three-part bilingual version, musically identical to the three-part Latin motet, combines the motetus *Tanquam suscipit vellus* with the French triplum *Quant naist la flor en la pree*:

M	Tr
Tanquam suscipit	Quant naist la flor en la pree,
Vellus pluviam,	Que l'erbete a la rousee
Ita percipit	Contre le soleil resplent,
Dum concipit	Lors doit joie estre menee
Virgo propriam	De la gent
Domini graciam.	Qui d'amors ont bon talent.
Novus usus per Mariam	Car la saison est tornee
Novi partus incipit,	En rejovenissement,
In qua naturam decipit.	Si est joie asaisonee
Dum sic concipit	A ceus qui maintienent jovent.
Intra viri nesciam	En droit moi nomeement
Hominis substanciam,	N'ert elle ja oubliee,
Rex, qui per iusticiam	Car ne sai vivre autrement;
Corripit	*Je m'en vois si mignotement.*
Omnem maliciam	
Et peccatum eripit	
Et dat veniam.	
T: TANQUAM	

M: [see above]

Tr: When the flower is born in the meadow, when the grass glitters with dew in the sunlight, then those who wish to love should be joyful. For this season brings rejuvenation, and joy is sharper for those who are youthful. And certainly it will never be forgotten by me, for I know no other way to live: I go along so gaily.

T: LIKE

When read against the musically identical Latin triplum *Tamquam agnus ductus ad victimam*, the French text may be seen as a recasting of the Passion motif: Easter is the occasion of spiritual renewal and the lyric season of regeneration through love and song. The flowers and joyful song associated in the Latin triplum with the celebration of Christ's Resurrection are here transposed into the flowers that herald the coming of spring and the joy of young lovers.

The French triplum is not incongruous as accompaniment to the motetus. We have seen other examples in which a statement of love, phrased without explicit erotic overtones, accompanies a devotional text and can be read as translating spiritual love and devotional imagery into the secular language of courtly lyric, perhaps with allegorical significance. In the bilingual version of the motet the contrast of birth and martyrdom, central to the Latin double motet, is absent; instead, both texts focus on the theme of joyful renewal. Indeed, the allusion to the birth of flowers is a subtle doubling of the birth of Christ celebrated in the motetus,[26] and the reference to dew echoes the moisture on Gideon's fleece, with which the motetus opens. The closing refrain of the French triplum — *Je m'en vois si mignotement* (I go along so gaily) — even provides a vernacular, secularized version of the psalm text that produced the tenor, "Tanquam sponsus procedens de thalamo" (Like a bridegroom proceeding from the bridal chamber): in both cases a lover goes on his way. Whereas the Latin triplum offered a development of Christ as Heavenly king and redeemer, the French text focuses on the motifs of birth, joy, renewal, and love that the motetus and the tenor implicitly or explicitly invoke.

A more complex version of the motet appears in the La Clayette manuscript, where the bilingual motet has a quadruplum:

> Qui voudroit fame esprover
> N'i porroit trover
> Loialté, car tout adés est preste de fauser.
> Biau semblant sevent moustrer
> Pour musart fere muser;
> Mes quant l'en voient tourner,
> Dont font leur joie, ne font ci que chifler.
> Mar s'i voudra nus fier:
> Trestout le mont la devroit eschiver.
> Qui plus est a son gré
> Et loialment l'aime et tient en chierté,
> C'est cil que plus het et que plus tient en vilté.
> Por ce lo ceus qui l'ont acoustumez
> Qu'il s'en retraient, si feront que senez.

He who wanted to test a woman could never find loyalty in her, for she is always ready to dissemble. They know how to put on a fair appearance to bemuse the dreamer; but when they see him turn, having had their pleasure, they just make fun of him. Woe upon him who would trust a woman: all the world should flee her. The one most to her liking, who loyally loves and cherishes her — that's the one she most hates and reviles. Therefore I counsel those who have frequented women to withdraw from their company: thus they will act wisely.

This antifeminist text adds a startling dimension to the motet, which now turns on an elaborate series of contrasts. The stern warning against association with women contradicts the enthusiastic endorsement of love in the triplum; the figure of the Virgin in the motetus stands in clear opposition to the deceiving temptresses of the quadruplum. The motet as a whole now embodies an opposition between erotic love—dangerous and deceptive—and the pure, salvific love of the Virgin and Christ.

Each of the three voices contributes a different perspective on the central topic, resulting in a configuration of diverse but interlocking texts. The motetus presents a form of love that "deceived nature" (*naturam decipit* [v. 9]) because it superseded natural law; this supernatural birth absolved humankind of sin and ushered in a new age, that of Grace. The quadruplum focuses on a different sort of deception, the wiles of women. It thereby expands on the theme of salvation developed in the motetus, for the wiles of Eve, primeval temptress, are the basis of Original Sin and the fatal corruption of nature. Quadruplum and motetus thus treat of Fall and Redemption, of the violation of nature through sin and the transcendence of nature through divine grace. And the triplum offers a view of humankind in perfect harmony with nature, experiencing joy and rejuvenation in conjunction with the resplendent renewal of springtime.

As is sometimes the case with four-part motets, the triplum is the most ambiguous and the one that mediates between the two other texted voices. A secular reading of the triplum as a conventional *reverdie* reveals it as a statement of the amorous insouciance warned of in the quadruplum: bewitched by springtime, the lyric persona is a classic *musart* ready to fall prey to the feminine *biau semblant* (Q, vv. 5, 4). A spiritual reading, however, links the triplum with the motetus as an elaboration on the theme of renewal; if we wish to find a medieval precedent for such a reading we need look no further than the sermon *Renovamini spiritu*, which quotes a conventional *strophe printanière* in illustration of the statement that "l'ame se doit renouveler autresi come li tens se renouvele contre la nouvele seson" (the soul should renew itself just as the world renews itself for the new season).[27] The intertextual dialogue within the motet is of considerable complexity. The triplum transposes the motetus into the language of secular lyric, with subtle parallels to the text that produced the tenor; the quadruplum warns of the dangers of taking this idyllic discourse literally and falling into the trap of worldly temptations. And both motetus and tenor are there to remind us of the solution for anyone who does fall prey to worldly snares: the Virgin, antidote to Eve, and Christ the Redeemer. What is crucial in this poetic game is the careful distinction of the literal and the allegorical.

The presence of the quadruplum changes our reading of the male personae who figure in the triplum and the motetus and, by implication, in the tenor. In the three-part bilingual motet, love is unproblematic, a source of joy linked to the natural cycle of growth and renewal, associated implicitly with imagery of flowering, light, and fecundity. These naturalistic images are the basis for the allegorical representation of the Incarnation in the motetus and in the tenor's source responsory. The amorous persona of the triplum thus appears as the human counterpart of the Heavenly Bridegroom, a participant in the earthly manifestation of cosmic love. And given the widespread technique of appropriating both courtly lyric and popular refrains into devotional texts, his song could even be understood as that of Christ himself; it is not, for example, so different from the refrains that Christ sings, and the way that he addresses the Heavenly court, in the *Court de Paradis*. The addition of the quadruplum renders this easy equation more problematical, reminding us that spiritual love and erotic love are to be carefully distinguished. The male lyric persona may still function poetically as an image of Christ, but the love that he celebrates is the distortion rather than the reflection of divine love; it can be redeemed only through allegorical sublimation.

The elaborate allegorical play that characterizes the bilingual motets is largely absent from the four-part French motet *Qui voudroit fame esprover* (639) / *Deboinerement atendrai merci* (638) / *Quant naist la flor en la pree* (637) / *TANQUAM* (O2). This piece, as noted above, is musically identical to the four-part bilingual motet except for the reversal of triplum and motetus. The new French triplum, in other words, uses the same melody as the motetus *Tanquam suscipit vellus* (636):

> Deboinerement
> atendrai merci
> [de la bele, qui]
> cors a bel et gent;
> n'a si avenant
> de Paris
> dus qu'a Gant.
> Mes de s'amor vers moi m'esprent,
> que je sui son fin amant
> et son bienvoellant,
> son serjant.
> Mes li mesdisant
> la m'ont esloignie[e]:

si ont fait vilanie.
A mains jointes si la pri
[et] quier merci:
Alegiés vostre ami,
car ja en tout mon vivant
n'amerai fors li!

I will courteously await mercy from the beautiful one of fair and noble bearing; there is no one so lovely from Paris to Ghent. I am inflamed by her love for me, for I am her true lover and her well-wisher and her servant. But the slanderers have estranged her from me: they do a despicable thing. With clasped hands I implore her and seek mercy: Grant relief to your sweetheart, for never in all my days will I love any but her!

With the absence of the Latin text the spiritual element all but disappears from the motet, remaining only in the single word of the tenor and in the music itself, which still carries associations with the Latin double motet and with the source clausula. The motet now presents a layered meditation on the human experience of love. The motetus offers an idealized statement of joyous amorous devotion; the love described in the triplum is more problematic, but the lyric "I" still retains his faith in love and in his lady, blaming her recalcitrance on slanderers. The quadruplum outlines the most cynical view: women themselves are to blame for love's misfortunes, for they do not value the loyalty that is the centerpiece of the male lover's concept of amorous integrity. The tenor does offer a solution, reminding us that all three views are limited; the only real escape from betrayal, the only true assurance that one's love will bear fruit, lies in turning to the Heavenly *Sponsus*. But the presence of this message in the motet is greatly reduced in comparison with the versions that contain the Latin text *Tanquam suscipit vellus*.

With its various French, Latin, and bilingual compositions, this motet family is a fascinating example of the ways that parallel motifs can be employed in devotional and secular contexts. The joyful lover presented in *Quant naist la flor* contrasts with his unhappy counterparts in *Deboinerement* and *Qui voudroit fame*, victims of malicious lies and of the fickleness of the beloved, respectively. This same fundamental contrast is established in the Latin double motet, with its juxtaposition of the Incarnation and the Passion: the King of Heaven, like the lyric persona, is both triumphant bridegroom and suffering victim. The varying contexts created by the different combinations of texts result in different readings. *Quant naist la flor en la pree*, for example, has a strongly allegorical quality in the three-part bilingual motet that pairs it with *Tanquam suscipit vellus / TANQUAM*. The four-part bilingual motet opens up a double reading of the French triplum. The Latin motetus remains key to the allegorical significance of *Quant naist la flor en la pree*: here the sacred truths that lie hidden under its veil of springtime imagery and amorous delight are revealed. And the French quadruplum offers an interpretive key to the moral reading of the triplum: it explodes the illusions of love's pleasures and shows the stark realities of amorous deception. The four-part bilingual motet embodies two opposing readings, two lessons about two different kinds of love, either of which can be derived from a decoding of *Quant naist la flor en la pree*. And in the French four-part motet, the idealized vision of *Quant naist la flor en la pree* serves as the basis for a meditation on the pleasures and dangers of worldly love.

Motet composers, juggling different combinations of texts and composing new ones to accompany the texts they knew, explored the varied meanings inherent in the polysemous language of love. As a text passed from one context to another, it took on new significance and opened up fresh perspectives on the shared language and imagery of sacred and profane love. The myriad of contrafactual and recombinant versions found in some motet families is in part the result of adaptations directed at different performance contexts that demanded — or allowed — alterations in the ideological and aesthetic qualities of a given motet. And it is also a manifestation of the strong spirit of play and experimentation that characterizes the vernacular motet in the thirteenth century.

Conclusion
Allegorical Play and Textual Polyphony

Littera enim occidit, Spiritus autem vivificat.
For the letter kills, but the spirit gives life.
—2 Corinthians 3:6

At the beginning of this study I posited a dual context for the vernacular motet, that of sacred music and vernacular lyric. In its very fabric the French motet with Latin tenor is a hybrid genre: its overall form originated in sacred polyphony, its tenor leads ultimately to the liturgy and often to the Bible, and its texted voices draw on the secular lyric tradition. Having established this much, however, we naturally proceed to the question of how the component parts of the motet relate to one another, what sort of harmonious whole is created. Medieval techniques of literary analysis, developed through biblical exegesis, mythography, and other forms of textual commentary, teach us that seeming conflicts, blasphemies, and incongruities in the Letter of the text are to be resolved through a discernment of the Spirit, the hidden meanings—for there can certainly be more than one—that lie within. The search for textual meaning, however, must still be informed by some sort of interpretive context, some sense of the text's overall purpose. And in a composite text like the vernacular motet, any attempt to unite the disparate parts is frustrated by the difficulty of determining the dominant interpretive context. Are we to read the motet in light of its devotional associations or its secular ones? Efforts to resolve the tensions within the motet lead only to a new division, that of interpretive method. This division can be expressed generally as the distinction between the moralizing and Christianizing techniques of the exegetical and mythographic traditions on the one hand, and the humorous and eroticizing techniques of scriptural and liturgical parody on the other.

According to the first method of reading, the key to the motet lies in the tenor, whose meaning is dependent on its liturgical and scriptural origins. The tenor is assumed to carry the associations of its ritual source. If it is textually derived from the Bible, as much of the liturgy is, then it additionally contributes the meaning(s) normally ascribed to the source passage, as determined through the standard techniques of exegesis. The various ritual, tropological, and allegorical meanings borne by the tenor thus provide the interpretive context within which the upper voices are to be read. This method in no way limits the motet to a single meaning. Like passages of Scripture, the texted voices may be susceptible of various figurative readings; and like pagan mythology, they may be interpreted both *in bono* and *in malo*. All such readings, however, are ultimately subservient to the devotional framework of the tenor. If the upper voices are interpreted as declarations of erotic desire, for example, then they contrast unfavorably with the spiritual love expressed in the tenor, which creates an implicit moral commentary on the frivolity of amorous pursuits. If the same declaration of desire is to be redeemed, it can only be through an allegorical reading that transposes it into a spiritual register, turning the motet into a hymn of love for God, a drama of Assumption, or the like.

The other interpretive method, diametrically opposed to the first, locates the key to the motet in the upper voices. These in turn draw their meaning, not from the techniques of allegorical exegesis, but from the vernacular lyric tradition itself. The motet may participate in a single lyric register or in more than one; it may praise love or lament its painful effects; its personae may be courtly, clerical, or pastoral. In all cases, however, it is a secular composition focused on human love, erotic desire, the beauties of the natural world. It is this secular context—usually amorous, though sometimes social or political—that provides the overall interpretive framework for the motet. Within this framework the tenor is divested of its devotional meaning; if its source texts are part of the interpretive process they, too, receive a secularized reading. The tenor IN SECULUM, for example, now refers to undying love or to erotic mercy; the tenor ET GAUDEBIT promises the joyful fulfillment of earthly desire. The secularization—indeed, the eroticization—of sacred text violates the principles of exegesis, which taught that no scriptural passage could be interpreted in conflict with the ideal of charity or with doctrinal truths. But such techniques are abundantly illustrated in parodic texts, with their subversions, distortions, and eroticizations of prayers, of the Mass, even of the Bible itself.

The transgressive and parodic nature of the motet is apparent, in fact, whichever way we read it. Medieval thought posited love as the basis for all human experience and behavior. Disordered, excessive, or otherwise inappropriate love, manifested in sin, is still a shadow—however distorted—of the divine love that permeates the cosmos. That these different forms of love have a common language was equally well established. Nonetheless, charitable love and cupidinous love were not to be confused. Augustine, contrasting the destructive force of *cupiditas* with the salvific effects of *caritas*, exclaimed: "Quid similius et quid dissimilius? Affectus sunt, amores sunt; immunditia spiritus nostri defluens inferius amore curarum, et sanctitas Spiritus tui attolens nos superius amore securitatis, ut sursum corda habeamus ad te" (What is more similar and what more dissimilar? Both are affections, both are loves; the uncleanness of our spirit flowing down with a love of worldly cares, and the sanctity of your Spirit raising us up with a secure love, that we may lift up our hearts unto you [*Confessions*, 13: 7.8]).

Though acknowledging that sin and salvation alike are motivated by forms of love, Augustine stresses the essential difference between these loves. The same point is made by Origen, who states unequivocally: "Est quidam amor carnis de Satana veniens, alius amor spiritus a Deo exordium habens, et nemo potest duobus amoribus possideri"[1] (There is one love of the flesh, coming from Satan, and another love of the spirit originating in God, and no one can be possessed of two loves). Profane love may be linked to sacred love as its imperfect shadow, its perverse distortion; this, indeed, is what enables the former to act as a figure for the latter in allegorical writings. But the two forms are nonetheless firmly distinguished, and the hierarchical relationship is absolute. The vernacular motet violates this fundamental principle by combining the two registers in such a way that either one may act as interpretive context for the other. The motet, constructed around similarities in the language and iconography of sacred and profane love, subordinates spiritual difference to literary equivalence.

Whether the motet is read from the spiritual or the secular perspective, the resolution of its parts entails an element of parody. The moral and allegorical interpretation of vernacular lyric, though not unparalleled in other literary genres, is itself a parody of exegesis. The opening lines of the "Fair Aelis" sermon, discussed in Chapter 2, clearly identify what follows as an intellectual game, playfully executed as a means of redeeming a popular but unedifying song: "Legimus quod de omni verbo occioso reddituri sumus Deo rationem in die iudicii. Et ideo debemus . . . prava in bonum exponere, vanitatem ad veritatem reducere"[2] (We read that we will be obliged to give account to God of all idle words in the Day of Judgment. Therefore we must . . . expound lewd things into good, and lead vanity back to truth). There can be no question with such pieces as the "Fair Aelis" or "Violete" sermon of uncovering hidden meaning deliberately placed in the text by the author, or even—as mythographers sometimes argued on behalf of pagan texts—of rescuing half-formed truths, gleaned by the author from his insights into the natural world or the human psyche and recorded in ignorance of their full implications. As the sermon states, *Bele Aalis* is a frivolous and utterly profane text: it is *verbum occiosum, prava, vanitas*. Its transformation into a Marian hymn is a playful exercise that tests the limits of allegorical interpretation. The secularization of sacred text is likewise a parody of exegesis, albeit one that moves in the opposite direction. The imposition of a spiritual reading operates through the fragmentation of the text into units that, thus decontextualized, can be correlated individually with familiar Christian imagery. The equation of Ovid's Myrrha with the Blessed Virgin, for example, rests on certain narrative elements: Myrrha's union with a father, resulting in a son who suffers a violent death. But the Marian reading excludes other equally important aspects of the narrative, such as the erotic nature of Myrrha's passion, her use of deception, and that same father's murderous rage when he discovers her identity. Similarly, the fragmentation of sacred text results in the creation of decontextualized units that can be assimilated into a profane framework.

In the motet, sacred chant and secular lyric are present. But both have been detached from their usual context, and in combination each potentially becomes the context for the other. From the interaction of musical and literary registers is generated not one but multiple meanings. This is the true sense of textual, or literary, polyphony as developed in the vernacular: not merely a chorus of voices, but a proliferation of poetic languages, a plethora of interpretive lenses through which the composition takes on now one aspect, now another. In its most intricate manifestations, the vernacular motet is characterized by a free play of allegory, a simultaneous presence of figurative readings both sacred and profane, none of which excludes the others.

This study has concentrated on the thirteenth-century motet, but its conclusions apply to fourteenth-century motets as well. Guillaume de Machaut, the greatest French poet-composer of the fourteenth century, continued to explore the tension between allegorical and parodic readings generated by the textual dynamics of the motet. Although the Latin tenors that he used do not appear in the thirteenth-century corpus, their relation to the vernacular texted voices is in keeping with the Old French tradition. Sometimes the secular context of the upper voices predominates, as in his motet 14, *Maugré mon cuer, contre mon sentement / De ma dolour confortés doucement / QUIA AMORE LANGUEO.*[3] The upper voices detail the joys of love for which the lyric protagonist wishes in vain; the tenor is from the Assumption antiphon *Anima mea liquefacta est* (*CAO*, no. 1418), itself slightly adapted from Song of Songs 5:6–8. The motet as a whole can be seen as contrasting the dissatisfactions of erotic desire with the salvific spiritual yearnings of mystical love. Nonetheless, the theme of unrequited longing dominates the motet. Even the source antiphon draws on a moment of tension within the Song of Songs, the separation of the lovers and the Bride's anxious quest: "Quaesivi et non inveni; illum vocavi et non respondit mihi" (I sought and did not find him; I called him and he did not answer me [see Song 5:6]). In constructing his motet around the theme of frustrated desire, Machaut has extracted and secularized a key phrase, transforming the soul's languishing back into courtly lovesickness.

In other motets, however, the spiritual context of the tenor plays a more important role in determining the overall meaning of the piece. For example, in the upper voices of motet 4, *De Bon Espoir, de Tres-Dous Souvenir / Puis qu'en la douce rousée / SPERAVI,* the lyric protagonist laments the suffering that his desire causes him and vows to maintain hope in spite of his lady's refusal to grant mercy. The tenor is from the Introitus "Domine, in tua misericordia speravi: exsultavit cor meum in salutari tuo" (Lord, I hoped in your mercy: my heart exulted in your aid [first Sunday after Pentecost; see Vulgate Ps. 12:6]). From the perspective of the upper voices, the tenor underscores the lyric protagonist's determination to continue hoping for amorous mercy. But from the devotional perspective of the tenor's source, the erotic *Bon Espoir* and *mercis* of the upper voices are unmasked as false hope and fruitless mercy, superseded by the spiritual hope and divine aid that are the only real source of salvation. If the upper voices are to be redeemed, it must be through an allegorical reading that equates *bonne Amour*—the lover's ally in his struggle against

Desir—with divine assistance and rewrites courtly *Espoir* as spiritual hope in God.[4] In this piece Machaut thus creates a delicate balance between courtly and devotional readings that is reminiscent of the techniques of thirteenth-century composers.

The term *polyphony* is sometimes applied to other literary works of the later Middle Ages: to Jean de Meun's *Roman de la Rose*, for example, or to Machaut's *Voir Dit*.[5] Insofar as such works are polyphonic, it is not simply through the juxtaposition of lyric, narrative, and prose—as in the *Voir Dit*—or through the sheer multiplication of speakers, as in the *Rose*. True textual polyphony, as developed in the vernacular motet, involves the simultaneous presence of different literary codes and interpretive contexts. If the *Rose* is polyphonic, this is not only because it presents a series of speeches, but because each of the major discourses embodies a well-defined perspective, within which the key themes of the poem are recast in a particular configuration and with a particular polemic intent. Alain de Lille's Natura and Boethius's Philosophia, for example, are transformed, vernacularized, and parodied in different ways in the successive figures of Reason, the Old Lady, and Nature. Without stretching things too far, one could see the *Rose* as a giant polyphonic structure, in which the implied "tenor" of Jean's Latin sources is endlessly rewritten, both respectfully and parodically, in the "upper voices" of the poem's major discourses.

This study has not addressed what may be the most profound question of all concerning the vernacular motet: how and why such a form ever arose in the first place.[6] Hybrid in nature; often effecting the most improbable of combinations; constructed in part from musical and textual fragments; built of deceptively simple and conventional texts, whose interaction can be complex and inventive; seemingly designed to pose the maximum difficulty for the listener intent on unraveling its verbal play—the vernacular motet is peculiar, perhaps even baffling. Many examples of the genre are so short that they hardly seem suited to formal performance. Among the numerous medieval French romances and *dits* with intercalated refrains and chansons of all kinds, only the version of the *Roman de Fauvel* transmitted in Bibl. Nat. fr. 146—an idiosyncratic compilation, to say the least—contains polyphonic motets, and most of these are in Latin.[7] The vernacular motet is an enigmatic and challenging form, about which much remains to be learned. Nonetheless, as I have shown, the motet did not develop in isolation from other literary forms, nor does it lack either poetic or intellectual rigor. The musical and phonetic complexity of the corpus as a whole, its appeal to the ear, is matched overall by the wit and complexity of its poetry and its appeal to the intellect. Challenging and humorous, playful and inventive, the vernacular motet is a fascinating mirror of the intellectual and literary ferment of the thirteenth century.

Reference Matter

Notes

Introduction

1. R. Smith argues for the orality of the motet in "Music or Literary Text?" She shows that musical setting and execution must be taken into account in order to understand motet versification, and that a distorted view results if the motet is treated as a written text intended to be read. Page also stresses the performative aspects of the motet and argues that phonics are more important than semantics in its artistry, in *Discarding Images*, pp. 85–111. Although I do not agree with Page's dismissal of verbal meaning and intertextual play within the motet, I do readily acknowledge the importance of sound—verbal echoes, alliteration, rhyme, assonance—in the overall aesthetics of motet texts. For a well-reasoned argument showing that the juxtaposition of texts in the performance of a motet can actually enhance the play of meaning, see Butterfield, "Language of Medieval Music."

2. For a list of tenors used in motet composition through the late thirteenth century, including complete texts of each liturgical source, identification of the feast day with which that portion of the chant is associated, and a list of motets using each tenor, see Tischler, *Style and Evolution*, vol. 2, pp. 39–62.

3. The only exception is the conductus motet, in which each of the upper voices carries the same text. The conductus motet is not treated in this study.

4. On the relationship between clausulae and motets, see N. Smith, "Earliest Motets" and "From Clausula to Motet." On the early development of Notre Dame polyphony and the rise of the motet, see Sanders, "Medieval Motet"; and Yudkin, *Music in Medieval Europe*, pp. 357–431. For comments on the problems of establishing a chronology for thirteenth-century motet composition in both Latin and French, see Everist, *French Motets*, pp. 3–12.

5. On contrafacta and bilingual motets, see Anderson, "Notre-Dame Bilingual Motets," "Notre-Dame Latin Double Motets," and "Texts and Music."

6. The hybrid nature of vernacular motets is reflected in the manuscript

tradition: they appear in compilations of Notre Dame sacred polyphony and in trouvère chansonniers. For descriptions of the major manuscripts, see Crocker, "French Polyphony of the Thirteenth Century."

7. For a survey of the phenomenon of lyric insertions in narratives and *dits*, including comments on how poets using this device explored, expanded upon, or subverted lyric conventions, see Boulton, *Song in the Story*. For a discussion of chansonnier organization, see my *From Song to Book*, pp. 46–80.

8. See Everist, "Rondeau Motet" and *French Motets*, pp. 90–108.

9. A motet containing a refrain is known as a *motet enté*. Motets are not strophic compositions, and most do not employ patterns of repetition such as appear in various monophonic lyric forms. A refrain thus is not used in a motet in the same way that it is in a strophic *chanson à refrains*, or in such forms as the ballade, rondeau, and virelai, where the regular recurrence of the refrain is a marker of strophic form. Rather, the refrains are seamlessly embedded in the motet text and can only be recognized as refrains at all from their appearance in other contexts. In this way their use in motets is actually closer to that found in the *fatrasie*, or even in romances and *dits* with lyric insertions, than to that in other lyric genres. For discussion of the *motet enté*, see Evans, "Textual Function of the Refrain Cento"; and Everist, "Refrain Cento" and *French Motets*, pp. 75–89, 109–25.

10. The term *registre* was first introduced into the discussion of medieval literary genres by Zumthor (*Essai de poétique médiévale*, p. 272). Speaking of genres in early troubadour lyric, Bec attributes the establishment of a genre to the combination of a particular register with a particular formal structure; see his "Problème des genres," p. 32. For a concise list of topics found in thirteenth-century French motets, see Tischler, *Style and Evolution*, vol. 1, pp. 204–5.

11. Evans laid the groundwork for the study of motet texts in "Unity of Text and Music." An important overview of the Old French motet as a genre, with analysis of textual and musical structures in many individual motets, is provided by Everist, *French Motets*. See also Evans, "Music, Text, and Social Context" and "Textual Function of the Refrain Cento"; Everist, "Refrain Cento" and "Rondeau Motet"; Brownlee, "Machaut's Motet 15 and the *Roman de la Rose*"; Bent, "Deception, Exegesis, and Sounding Number"; Butterfield, "Language of Medieval Music"; Huot, "Transformations of Lyric Voice" and "Polyphonic Poetry"; Nathan, "Function of Text"; and L. Wright, "Verbal Counterpoint." Reichert examines the interplay of musical structure and verse form, without taking textual content into account, in "Wechselbeziehungen." For a more detailed, if somewhat polemical, discussion of critical views of motet texts and an argument against intellectualized readings, see Page, *Discarding Images*, pp. 43–111.

12. Affinities of the motet with other literary genres are discussed in my "Transformations of Lyric Voice" and "Polyphonic Poetry."

13. In his *De musica* (ca. 1300), for example, Johannes de Grocheio states:

"Tenor autem est illa pars supra quam omnes aliae fundantur quemadmodum partes domus vel aedificii super suum fundamentum et eas regulat et eis dat quantitatem quemadmodum ossa partibus aliis" (The tenor is that part on which all the others are founded, just as the parts of a house or other edifice are [built] on their foundation, and it regulates them and gives them structure just as the bones do for the other body parts [Page, "Johannes de Grocheio," p. 37]). Page provides a corrected edition and an English translation of those passages from Grocheio's treatise that deal with secular music, both monophonic and polyphonic. The fourteenth-century theorist Egidius de Murino stipulates that the process of composing a motet must begin with the selection of a tenor, which is the basis for the other parts; see Leech-Wilkinson, *Compositional Techniques*, vol. 1, pp. 18, 20.

14. For exemplary discussions, see Pesce, "Significance of Text"; and Baltzer, "Aspects of Trope." Egidius de Murino states that the tenor should be taken from a portion of the chant that is textually relevant to the motet's subject matter; see Leech-Wilkinson, *Compositional Techniques*, vol. 1, pp. 18, 20. As time went on, Latin motets became separated from their liturgical origins and developed into chamber music for clerical and aristocratic consumption; the motets of the expanded *Roman de Fauvel* (Paris, Bibl. Nat. fr. 146) are an example. Secular Latin motets sometimes employed nonliturgical tenors; when they did use liturgical tenors, the relationship between tenor and upper voices was analogous to that obtaining in vernacular secular motets.

15. For a list of such instances, see Tischler, *Style and Evolution*, vol. 2, p. 94.

16. For a list of the authors and composers whose names are associated with thirteenth-century French motets, see Tischler, *Style and Evolution*, vol. 1, pp. 205–6. Motets of known or possible attribution represent a small fraction of the corpus.

17. I cite the text from Page, "Johannes de Grocheio," p. 36. The statement appears in Grocheio's *De musica*. For discussion of his use of the terms *vulgares* and *litterati*—which Page interprets as referring to the laity and the clergy, respectively—see Page, *Discarding Images*, pp. 80–84.

18. See Page, *Owl and the Nightingale*, esp. pp. 119, 148–52; and *Discarding Images*, pp. 57–64.

19. Van den Boogaard links the vernacular motet to Parisian university culture—in particular, the milieu of such poets as Rutebeuf—in "Forme des polémiques." Crocker sees the vernacular motet as developing out of the convergence of monastic and courtly musical traditions at Notre Dame of Paris and at the courts of the cathedral nobility; see his "French Polyphony of the Thirteenth Century."

20. Nicole de Margival, *Dit de la panthère d'amours*, ed. Todd, vv. 157–71. On the northern vogue of troubadour lyric—often referred to indiscriminately in Old French texts as *sons poitevins*—see Page, *Voices and Instruments*, pp. 29–

33. It is true that the terms *motet* and *conduis* (Latin *conductus*) could also apply to monophonic compositions, especially in an earlier period. Nicole's emphasis on the profusion of voices, however, strongly implies polyphony.

21. Guillaume de Lorris and Jean de Meun, *Roman de la Rose*, ed. Lecoy, v. 20627.

22. See Page, *Voices and Instruments*, pp. 59–61.

23. See Everist, "Rondeau Motet," for lists of these refrains and conventional phrases and for documentation of their appearance in thirteenth-century motet texts.

24. Jeanroy and Guy, eds., *Chansons et dits artésiens*, no. 1.

25. *Le Roman de Renart*, ed. Mario Roques, branche 9, vv. 9096–99.

26. Tischler, ed., *Montpellier Codex*, motetus of no. 25: *Chançonnete, va t'en tost* (455) / *Ainc voir d'amors n'ai joï* (456) / *A la cheminee* (453) / *Par verité*. For further information about the transmission of this text, see Van der Werf, *Integrated Directory*, p. 68.

27. Auda and Lejeune, eds., *Motets wallons*, vol. 1, pp. 20–21, summarize the range of critical opinion.

28. C. Wright, *Music and Ceremony at Notre Dame of Paris*; Aubry, *Musique et les musiciens*; Hucke, "Dekret 'Docta Sanctorum Patrum.'"

29. *Missa Tornacensis*, ed. Van den Borren. The Tournai Mass evidently includes both thirteenth- and fourteenth-century material. Van den Borren argues that the motet could have been used in the liturgy and notes that Ludwig considered it closer in style to thirteenth-century motets than to fourteenth-century ones (p. ix).

30. Robertson, "Remembering the Annunciation," pp. 295–96.

31. Page has recently taken issue with this characterization of the motet and its "elite" or "sophisticated" audience. His discussion, though useful for a clearer articulation of what concepts such as "cultural elite" and "educated audience" may or may not have meant in the thirteenth century, does not in the end refute the basic idea that motets were primarily aimed at audiences, whether clerical or lay, who had some education and some special aptitude for musical and literary appreciation. See *Discarding Images*, pp. 43–64.

32. Page, "Johannes de Grocheio," p. 36.

33. On the motet's combination of High and Low Style, see Page, *Voices and Instruments*, pp. 74–76.

34. On contrasting lyric types in Renart's *Roman de la Rose*, see Baumgartner, "Citations lyriques."

35. Page comments: "Once a lyric has been written down . . . it ceases to be an event. It becomes an object and can therefore be objectively perceived. Any moorings which may have tied it to a kind of occasion, or a kind of performance, become loosened" (*Voices and Instruments*, p. 52).

36. Page, *Discarding Images*, p. 52; see his discussion, pp. 46–85. Page appar-

ently perceives a conflict between the "festive" and "recreative" qualities of the motet, and critics' claims for its intellectual sophistication and complex play of intertextual meanings. To my mind, there is no conflict here. The motet is indeed a graceful and entertaining art form, pleasing to the ear, whose texts are generally accessible in and of themselves and were no doubt featured in leisure activities. For those so inclined, it offers the added pleasures of intellectual playfulness and the inventive and witty recombination of familiar literary and musical motifs. Page does characterize the thirteenth-century motet as "both playful and learned at the same time," in "Performance of Ars Antiqua Motets," p. 149.

37. Gravdal, *Vilain and Courtois*, p. 10.

38. Zumthor, "Carrefour des rhétoriqueurs," pp. 330–34.

39. Hutcheon, *Theory of Parody*.

40. A similar point is made by Wimsatt, "Chaucer and the Canticle of Canticles"; and Dronke, "Profane Elements in Literature."

41. Bakhtin, *Dialogic Imagination*, pp. 68–82; and *Rabelais and His World*, esp. pp. 83–96. Page notes the relevance of Bakhtinian analysis for the vernacular motet, in *Discarding Images*, pp. 46–52.

42. Jenny, "Stratégie de la forme."

43. I agree with the many scholars who have argued that *courtly love* cannot be reduced to a monolithic system of beliefs and values. As Vinaver stated, however, the term "does represent something for which no more convenient name has been found" ("Landmarks in Arthurian Romance," p. 18), and this is the spirit in which I employ it. For useful discussions of the range of attitudes subsumed under the general heading "courtly love," the psychological and social issues that the poetry of courtly love addresses, and its relationship to devotional literature, see Dronke, *Medieval Latin*; Calin, "Defense and Illustration of *Fin'Amor*"; Singer, *Nature of Love*, vol. 2; and Ferrante and Economou, eds., *In Pursuit of Perfection*. On the relationship of early trouvère lyric to a sacred model, see Ferrand, "*Ut musica poesis*."

44. See Piehler, *Visionary Landscape*, pp. 94–96, on Andreas Cappellanus's fifth dialogue as an extended parody of religious conversion.

45. See my "*Romance of the Rose" and Its Medieval Readers*, p. 120.

46. Dronke, *Medieval Latin*, vol. 1, p. 62, characterizes as parody Gérard's use of profane texts and textual models.

47. Glendinning, "Eros, Agape, and Rhetoric."

48. For comments on the relationship of the *Rose* to its Latin models, see, among many others, Paré, *Scolastique courtoise*; and Wetherbee, *Platonism and Poetry*, pp. 255–66.

49. For elaboration of these points, see Jackson, "Allegory and Allegorization," p. 158; and Quinn, "Beyond Courtly Love."

50. *Aucassin et Nicolette*, ed. Dufournet, p. 58.

51. The parodic aspects of Genius's discourse are discussed by Fleming, *Ro-*

man de la Rose; and Wetherbee, *Platonism and Poetry*, pp. 255–66. I discuss the passage in more detail, including its relevance for a reading of motets, in Chapter 3. For an analogous discussion of the subordination of the sacred to the erotic in the Old Occitan *Flamenca*, and of the ways in which humor defuses the possible dangers of the transgressive text, see Sankovitch, "Religious and Erotic Elements in *Flamenca*."

52. On the *Court de Paradis* and its relevance for vernacular motets, see Chapter 2. For an analogous discussion of Giraut de Bornelh's *Reis glorios*, out-lining the spiritual reading that the first stanza suggests for the erotic *alba* that follows, see Spence, "*Et Ades Sera l'Alba*."

53. Vinaver, "Landmarks in Arthurian Romance," p. 25. This essay offers a concise and illuminating discussion of dilemma and controversy in medieval love poetry: "Ambivalence figures prominently in medieval lyric poetry and fiction as a source of inspiration and of pleasurable emotion" (p. 21).

54. Page, *Owl and the Nightingale*, p. 125. See also Stevens, *Words and Music*, pp. 161–62.

55. Cited by Page, *Owl and the Nightingale*, p. 118.

56. From London, Brit. Libr. MS Harley 3823, fol. 376r, cited by Page, *Voices and Instruments*, p. 79. On the polemics for and against the carol in thirteenth-century Paris, see his *Owl and the Nightingale*, pp. 110–33, 183.

57. Modern scholars also have noted that the rondeau shares certain struc-tural features with chant, and some have posited that the rondeau may in fact have developed through the direct influence of liturgical music and ritual; see Stevens, *Words and Music*, pp. 178–86; and Fernandez, "Notes sur les origines du rondeau."

58. See Page, *Owl and the Nightingale*, pp. 129–33.

59. Diehl makes a similar point in his discussion of pious contrafacta of secular lyric, arguing that the medieval audience would have found a certain excitement in songs that appropriated familiar secular motifs into a religious context, thereby collapsing the normal, careful distinction between sacred and secular spheres; see his *Medieval European Religious Lyric*, pp. 71–74.

Chapter One

1. Speaking of *Pour escouter le chant du roussignol* (779) / *L'autrier joer m'en alai* (780) / *SECULORUM AMEN* (O52), Butterfield states, "Far from obliterating the sense of the words, the music actually creates new semantic possibilities for the texts, by enabling them to make meaning through the timing of their melodic conjunction" ("Language of Medieval Music," p. 15).

2. Tischler, ed., *Montpellier Codex*, no. 87.

3. On the *début printanier*, see Dragonetti, *Technique poétique*, pp. 169–83.

4. Châtelain de Couci, *Chansons attribuées*, ed. Lerond, no. 3.

5. The lyric insertions of Renart's *Roman de la rose* have received con-

siderable study. Of particular relevance to the present context is Baumgartner's "Citations lyriques." See also my *From Song to Book*, pp. 108–16; and Boulton, *Song in the Story*, pp. 26–35, 83–87.

6. Tischler, ed., *Montpellier Codex*, no. 142.

7. For a discussion of the songs in the *Roman du Castelain de Couci*, see my *From Song to Book*, pp. 117–31; and Boulton, *Song in the Story*, pp. 61–66.

8. Tischler, ed., *Montpellier Codex*, no. 133.

9. Tischler, ed., *Montpellier Codex*, no. 129.

10. Anderson, ed., *Bamberg Manuscript*, no. 12.

11. Adam le Bossu, *Jeu de Robin et Marion*, ed. Langlois, vv. 1–8.

12. Tischler, ed., *Montpellier Codex*, no. 258. See my "Transformations of Lyric Voice," pp. 155–56.

13. The only exception is Tr, v. 23 ("et si riant"), which parallels the "Ont" in the motetus (v. 16).

14. Tischler, ed., *Montpellier Codex*, no. 256. I have discussed this piece in "Polyphonic Poetry." Evans, in "Unity of Text and Music" (pp. 111–27), pays particular attention to the interplay of first-person and third-person discourse and to the structure of the motet as determined by its virelai tenor.

15. On the manuscript transmission of the two- and three-part versions of the motet, see Van der Werf, *Integrated Directory*, p. 56. Both versions appear in the Montpellier codex and in additional manuscripts as well.

16. See my "Transformations of Lyric Voice," pp. 156–58. The tenor remains unidentified; it is designated SUPER TE in MS *Mo* and ET SUPER in the manuscript containing Adam's collected works (Bibl. Nat. fr. 25566).

17. Adam de la Hale, *Lyric Works*, ed. Wilkins, rondeau no. 5.

18. See Rokseth, ed., *Polyphonies du XIIIe siècle*, vol. 4, p. 78n6.

19. I refer to Villon's ballade of La Belle Heaulmière, "Ne que monnoye qu'on descrie," in his *Testament*, vv. 533–60.

20. Tischler, ed., *Montpellier Codex*, no. 261.

21. On the motif of rape in the pastourelle and the fantasy that the shepherdess acquiesces, see Gravdal, "Camouflaging Rape."

22. *Missa Tornacensis*, ed. Van den Borren.

23. See Sankovitch, "Religious and Erotic Elements in *Flamenca*," p. 218.

24. This interpretation of the tenor was offered by Professor Wulf Arlt of the University of Basel during a panel discussion at the Congress of the International Musicological Society in Madrid, 1992.

25. Anderson, ed., *Bamberg Manuscript*, no. 41.

26. Both versions of the motet appear in the Montpellier codex, and each is also in one other manuscript; see Van der Werf, *Integrated Directory*, pp. 112–13. I cite Tischler, ed., *Montpellier Codex*, no. 22. The text formerly referred to as triplum is now quadruplum; the new triplum is the text here given.

27. Tischler, ed., *Montpellier Codex*, no. 95. Everist notes the contrasts be-

tween the pastourelle motetus and the courtly triplum, in *French Motets*, pp. 155–58.

28. For a discussion of the pastourelle as a "demystification" of courtly love, see Calin, "Contre la fin'amor?," pp. 66–72.

29. Some bilingual examples are *Salve virgo virginum* (727) / *Est il donc einsi* (728) / APTATUR (O46); *Quant repaire la verdor* (438) / *Flos de spina rumpitur* (437) / REGNAT (M34); *Or voi je bien* (428) / *Eximium decus virginum* (429) / VIRGO (M32). Examples of French motets combining secular and Marian texts include *Celui en qui je me fi* (390) / *La bele estoile de mer* (389) / *La bele en qui je me fi* (388) / JOHANNE (M29); *Plus bele que flor* (652) / *Quant revient fuelle et flor* (650) / *L'autrier joer m'en alai* (651) / FLOS FILIUS EJUS (O16).

30. See Van der Werf, *Integrated Directory*, p. 96. I cite from Tischler, ed., *Montpellier Codex*, no. 264.

31. Anderson and Close, eds., *Motets of the Manuscript La Clayette*, no. 22. The family to which this piece belongs is discussed in Anderson, ed., *Latin Compositions*, vol. 1, pp. 1–14; and Everist, *French Motets*, pp. 135–37.

32. The other one is *Un chant renvoisie et bel* (829b), in honor of Saint Elizabeth of Hungary, which is transmitted with the unidentified tenor DECANTANTUR. See Everist, *French Motets*, pp. 137–38.

33. Meyer, "Henri d'Andeli et le chancelier Philippe," p. 213.

34. See Billy, "Une Imitation indirecte de *L'altrier cuidai aber druda*."

35. Tischler, ed., *Montpellier Codex*, no. 26. The motetus, without the opening word *Viderunt*, also exists as the sole texted voice of a motet on the tenor OMNES (M1); musically, motetus (with *Viderunt*) and tenor are identical to a two-part organum on VIDERUNT OMNES. See Van der Werf, *Integrated Directory*, p. 13.

36. For a similar contrasting of the motifs of amorous separation and the Incarnation, including another motet on the tenor OMNES, see Chapter 2, in the section entitled "Contextualizing Love: The Lyric Insertion and the Motet."

37. Tischler, ed., *Montpellier Codex*, no. 27.

38. Kuhn, *Poétique de François Villon*, pp. 466–69.

Chapter Two

1. See Bec, "L'Accès au lieu érotique"; and Delbouille, "Sur les traces de 'Bele Aëlis.'"

2. Bartsch, ed., *Altfranzösischen Romanzen und Pastourellen*, no. 71.

3. See Pfeffer, *Change of Philomel*.

4. I cite from Paris, Bibl. Nat. fr. 12467, fols. 53v–54r.

5. Cited by Hunt, "De la chanson au sermon," p. 436.

6. I cite from the sermon as published by Hunt, "De la chanson au sermon."

7. Tuve, *Allegorical Imagery*, pp. 219–334.

8. Zink, *Prédication romane*, pp. 146–48, 291.

9. I cite from the sermon as published by Hunt, "De la chanson au sermon."

10. Bec, "Lyrique profane et paraphrase pieuse," pp. 235, 243n21. Bec points out that the word *main* (v. 1), a later addition in the manuscript, violates the meter and can only be a residue of the original formula "Bele Aelis main s'est levee." The complete poem, of which this is the second stanza, is printed by Järnström and Långfors, eds., *Recueil de chansons pieuses*, vol. 2, no. 131.

11. Gautier de Coinci, *Miracles de Nostre Dame*, ed. Koenig, no. 62.

12. I cite *Hyer matin a l'enjornee* (764) / DOMINO (BD VI), from Tischler, ed., *Earliest Motets*, no. 57-3. Two Latin motets use the same melody, originally the duplum part of an organum for three voices. The family of pieces is discussed in Anderson, ed., *Latin Compositions*, vol. 1, pp. 299–307. For a brief account of the background of Gautier's piece—from organum to Latin motet, French contrafactum, and finally chanson—see Chailley's introduction to his edition of Gautier's *Chansons à la Vierge*, pp. 54–55. Chailley provides a musical edition of Gautier's song, the French motet, and the source organum, pp. 138–42.

13. On Old French summaries, paraphrases, and amplifications of the Lord's Prayer, see Långfors, "Traductions et paraphrases."

14. Ilvonen, ed., *Parodies de thèmes pieux*, pp. 134–42. The poem appears in the late-thirteenth-century MS Paris, Bibl. Nat. fr. 837, a large and diverse anthology.

15. Machaut used the phrase *Fiat voluntas tua* from the Pater noster as the tenor in a vernacular motet about the travails of love, *Aucune gent m'ont demandé que j'ay / Qui plus aimme plus endure / FIAT VOLUNTAS TUA*. Here the tenor refers simultaneously to the suffering lover's submission to the lady's will, and to the acceptance of God's will by all those who are victims of worldly injustice and adversity.

16. See Lehmann, *Parodie im Mittelalter*; and Ferrante, "Bible as Thesaurus." For the texts, see Lehmann, ed., *Parodistische Texte*.

17. *Sequencia leti evangelii secundum Lucium*, in Lehmann, ed., *Parodistische Texte*, p. 70. The biblical passages parodied here are Christ's cursing of the barren fig tree (Matt. 21:19), John the Baptist's metaphor of the barren tree (Matt. 3:10), and Christ's rejection of temptation in the wilderness (Matt. 4:4).

18. Boncompagno da Signa, *Rhetorica novissima*, ed. Gaudenzi, p. 284. See Vulgate Ps. 88:25 and 22:4. Many similar examples appear in Boncompagno's treatise on the writing of love letters, *Rota Veneris*. On his parodic appropriation of biblical passages into the discourse of erotic love, see Purkart, "Boncompagno of Signa."

19. Gerson, "Talia de me," in Hicks, ed., *Débat sur le Roman de la Rose*, p. 166.

20. Cited by Purkart, "Boncompagno of Signa," p. 331.

21. Dronke, *Medieval Latin*, vol. 1, pp. 318–30; Robertson, "Two Poems from the *Carmina Burana*." See also the brief discussion by Brückmann and Couch-

man, "Du 'Cantique des cantiques' aux 'Carmina Burana,'" pp. 44–46; and the insightful comments by Wimsatt, "Chaucer and the Canticle of Canticles."

22. I cite the text as edited by Dronke, *Medieval Latin*, vol. 1, pp. 319–22. References are to strophe number and to line number within each strophe.

23. Tischler, ed., *Montpellier Codex*, no. 32.

24. See my "Polyphonic Poetry," pp. 271–72.

25. "Ero quasi ros: Israel germinabit sicut lilium, et erumpet radix eius ut Libani" (I will be like the dew: Israel will sprout like the lily, and its root will grow like the cedar of Lebanon [Hosea 14:6]).

26. For an overview of the Song of Songs in medieval culture, see Matter, *Voice of My Beloved*. For further discussions of erotic and nuptial motifs in medieval mysticism, including the role of the Song of Songs in the development of that imagery, see Hamburger, *Rothschild Canticles*.

27. Gerson, "Traité contre le Roman de la Rose," in Hicks, ed., *Débat sur le Roman de la Rose*, p. 74; Saint Bernard, *Sermones in Cantica Canticorum*, ed. Migne, 1.12.

28. *Song of Songs*, ed. Pickford, vv. 3505–6.

29. Gerson, "Talia de me," in Hicks, ed., *Débat sur le Roman de la Rose*, p. 168.

30. Gérard's use of vernacular love lyrics is discussed briefly by Dronke, *Medieval Latin*, vol. 1, pp. 59–62. For a complete list of Gérard's lyric insertions and their identification in other medieval texts, see Van den Boogaard, "Insertions en français."

31. Gérard de Liège, *Qinque incitamenta*, ed. Wilmart, 3.1.2. I have added punctuation to Wilmart's transcription of the Old French song and have arranged it in a line-by-line format.

32. Saint Bernard, *Sermones in Cantica Canticorum*, ed. Migne, 1.9, 1.11.

33. For this motet and the Latin motet that shares its melody, see Anderson, ed., *Latin Compositions*, vol. 1, pp. 357–59.

34. The text appears in Paris, Bibl. Nat. fr. 14966. Tony Hunt describes the text in "*Song of Songs* and Courtly Literature," to which he appends an edition of one of the lyric insertions.

35. *Art d'amours*, ed. Roy, p. 149.

36. *Court de Paradis*, ed. Vilamo-Pentti, vv. 427–29.

37. *Art d'amours*, ed. Roy. The refrains in question are "Tout le cuer me rit de joye / Quant je la voy" (p. 170), an adapted version of which is sung in the *Court de Paradis* by all the souls in Heaven with regard to God; and "Je tien par la main m'amie / Si en vois plus mignotement" (p. 161), sung in the *Court de Paradis* by Christ as he ushers in Mary Magdalene and the Virgin. In the *Art d'amours*, the latter refrain is sung by "li sage jouvencel es karoles" (prudent young men at carols [p. 161]).

38. See Hamburger, *Rothschild Canticles*, pp. 57–59 and fig. 21, for a minia-

ture from a devotional manuscript representing the Five Wise Virgins being admitted to a carol in Heaven while the Foolish Virgins are captured outside the locked door by the devil's grappling hook. Hamburger cites other examples of the "dance in Heaven" as a motif in mystical writings. Gérard de Liège expresses the soul's exclusive love for God in terms of an amorous maiden who wishes to dance only with her beloved, citing a vernacular dance refrain: "Felix anima, cui dulcis Ihesus tam dulciter sapit . . . Talis anima bene potest dicere: *Ceste danse ne me plaist nient, puis ke mes amis ne tient*" (Happy soul, savoring sweet Jesus so sweetly. . . . Such a soul can well say: *This dance does not please me, since my beloved is not in it* [*Quinque incitamenta*, ed. Wilmart, 3.3.3]).

39. *Eructavit*, ed. Jenkins. The poem is discussed briefly by Jung, *Etudes sur le poème allégorique*, pp. 229–31. Jung accepts the attribution to Adam de Perseigne.

40. Jung, *Etudes sur le poème allégorique*, p. 230.

41. Boulton comments on the use of courtly refrains in a noncourtly context in the *Court de Paradis*, observing the humor generated by the incongruity of popular refrains in a celestial setting and noting that the refrains have the effect of reinterpreting heavenly joy in terms of earthly joy, in *Song in the Story*, pp. 103–5, 111.

42. The *Court de Paradis* also appears in MS Paris, Bibl. Nat. fr. 837, which includes religious and secular poetry. In MS Paris, Bibl. Nat. fr. 1802, it follows the *Mireour de l'ame*, a text describing the soul's love of Christ and the amorous union in Heaven, drawing heavily on the Song of Songs. The arrangement of the anthology as a whole thus provides a context for the spiritual appropriation of the language of erotic love.

43. Another motet using this refrain employs a tenor derived from the same gradual: *Se j'ai amé folement* (123) / *HEC DIES* (M13).

44. In MS Paris, Bibl. Nat. fr. 1802, in fact, the refrain is in this (presumably original) form: "Tout le cuer me rit de ioie quant la voi" (fol. 104r).

45. Tischler, ed., *Montpellier Codex*, no. 115.

46. An answering refrain, *G'en main par la main m'amie, s'en vois plus mignotement* (I lead my beloved by the hand, thus I go more gaily [v. 470]), is sung by Jesus as he joins the dance. The motet in which this refrain is used, *Sans orgeuil et sans envie* (387) / *JOHAN[NE]* (M29), is less relevant to the *Court de Paradis*, since the tenor—an alleluia for the feast of Saint John the Baptist—does not contribute a biblical or ritual context appropriate to the motetus. John the Baptist prepared the way for the arrival of the Bridegroom, but this motif is not exploited in the motet, in which the relationship between the texts of the tenor and motetus is not as tightly constructed as it is in the previous examples.

47. On this group of motets, see Everist, *French Motets*, pp. 121–25.

48. I cite from Tischler, ed., *Earliest Motets*, nos. 169, 309, and 314.

49. Everist notes the specifically Artesian character of this group of motets,

which is apparently unrelated to the Parisian repertoire, in *French Motets*, pp. 124–25.

50. For discussion, texts, and translations of Latin motets on the tenor REGNAT, see Baltzer, "Aspects of Trope," pp. 13, 21–22, 39–42.

Chapter Three

1. For an overview of the language and imagery used in trouvère lyric in praise of the lady, see Dragonetti, *Technique poétique*, pp. 248–72.

2. For a survey of chant texts figuring in the liturgy of Assumption and a discussion of the Latin motets composed for tenors from the Marian liturgy, see Baltzer, "Aspects of Trope." Ecclesiasticus 24 provides the Epistle for Assumption.

3. *CAO*, no. 5162, antiphon for Assumption and Nativity of the Virgin; see Song 2:10–13, 4:7–8, 10–11.

4. *CAO*, no. 2887, antiphon for Assumption and Nativity of the Virgin; Song 4:15.

5. *CAO*, no. 4929, antiphon for Assumption; see Ecclus. 24:20.

6. *CAO*, no. 7461, responsory for the Common of Virgins; Song 4:1, 6:3.

7. *CAO*, no. 7826, responsory for Assumption, also used in the consecration of nuns; Ps. 44:11, 12. See also, with virtually the same text, the antiphon for the Common of Virgins, no. 5323; and the gradual *Propter veritatem. Audi filia* (M37) and the alleluia *Veni electa mea* (M54), used in the Mass for Assumption and the Common of Virgins. The *CAO* actually gives the wording "ponam in te thronum meum" (I will place my throne in you); I have emended to the more logical reading found in a variety of other sources.

8. *CAO*, no. 6436. For the motif of dressing the bride in finery, see Song 1:9–10; Ps. 44:14–15; Isa. 61:10; and Ez. 16:10–13. The text of the responsory is taken from the pseudo-Ambrosian *Gesta Sanctae Agnes*; see Denomy, ed., *Old French Lives of Saint Agnes*, p. 68.

9. *CAO*, no. 6992. For the source text in the *Gesta Sanctae Agnes*, see Denomy, ed., *Old French Lives of Saint Agnes*, p. 69.

10. Wimsatt comments on the dramatic quality of the Assumption liturgy, in "Chaucer and the Canticle of Canticles," pp. 70–71.

11. *CAO*, no. 7878, responsory for Assumption; see Song 2:1, 12–14; 3:6, 4:11, 8:5.

12. *CAO*, no. 6806, responsory for the Common of Virgins, Saint Agnes, and Saint Cecilia; see Matt. 25:6, 10. The parable of the Wise and Foolish Virgins also supplies the text for numerous antiphons of the Common of Virgins, as well as contributing to other responsories for that feast, for Assumption, and for various individual saints.

13. This text is also an antiphon for various Marian feasts (*CAO*, no. 4332).

14. I cite from Baltzer, "Aspects of Trope," p. 27. Baltzer identifies these

alleluias as having been used for Assumption Mass in thirteenth-century Paris.

15. See Leclercq, *Monks and Love*, pp. 37–40; and Matter, *Voice of My Beloved*, pp. 153–58.

16. Portions of the following discussion appear in my essay, "Languages of Love." See also Baltzer, "Aspects of Trope," pp. 16–17.

17. For example, in both *Bele Aelis par matin se leva* (678) / *Haro, haro! Je la voi la* (679) / FLOS FILIUS EJUS and *Par un matinet l'autrier* (658) / *Hé sire, que voz vantés* (659) / *Hé berchier, si grant envie* (657) / EJUS, the intertextual dialogue generated by the upper voices is of greater importance than the interplay between those texted voices and the tenor.

18. Tischler, ed., *Montpellier Codex*, no. III.

19. See Baltzer, "Aspects of Trope," pp. 16–17, 23.

20. Tischler, ed., *Montpellier Codex*, no. 239.

21. Tischler, ed., *Montpellier Codex*, no. 21. I have, however, amended the text of Q, v. 10 in accordance with the text as printed by Anderson and Close, eds., *Motets of the Manuscript La Clayette*, no. 23. Tischler's reading is "qui si voz, amis"; Stakel and Relihan's translation of verses 9–12 in that edition reads: "she is the mother of our Lord who wants forever to possess you, friend, and the two of us together." For a discussion of this piece and its relationship to the *Flos filius ejus* clausula and the Latin contrafactum motet *Stirps Jesse* (647) / *Virga cultus* (648) / FLOS FILIUS EJUS, see Everist, *French Motets*, pp. 43–51.

22. *CAO*, no. 5325, antiphon for Assumption or Nativity of the Virgin; Song 5:1.

23. *CAO*, no. 5329, antiphon for Assumption or Nativity of the Virgin; Song 5:1.

24. See, e.g., "Dilectus meus descendit in hortum suum ad areolam aromatum, / Ut pascatur in hortis, et lilia colligat. / Ego dilecto meo, et dilectus meus mihi" (My beloved went down to his garden to the spice beds, to graze in the gardens, and to gather lilies. I belong to my beloved, and my beloved to me [Song 6:1–2]).

25. *CAO*, no. 3137, antiphon for Assumption; see Song 4:12, 2:10.

26. For a discussion of analogous patterns in the bilingual motets of the Montpellier codex, see Evans, "Music, Text, and Social Context."

27. The motet family can be traced to a clausula (MS *F*, fol. 11, no. 2). The Latin motets are *Stirps Iesse progreditur* (647) / *Virga cultus nescia* (648) / FLOS FILIUS EJUS and *Castrum pudicicie* (653) / *Virgo viget melius* (654) / FLOS FILIUS. In addition, the motetus music is transmitted in a two-part Latin motet, *Candida virginitas ut lilium* (649) / FLOS FILIUS EJUS. I cite the various Latin texts for this family from Anderson, ed., *Latin Compositions*, vol. 1, pp. 97–98. On the manuscript dissemination of the various members of the family, see Van der Werf, *Integrated Directory*, p. 112.

28. The other Latin motet using this music, the two-part *Candida virgini-*

tas / FLOS FILIUS EJUS, combines in its single texted voice the motifs of Incarnation and Redemption.

29. Anderson and Close, eds., *Motets of the Manuscript La Clayette*, no. 7.

30. For a discussion of a similar phenomenon in one of Machaut's motets, in which the seeming opposition set up between the motetus and the triplum is countered by that operating between the two upper voices and the tenor, see Brownlee, "Machaut's Motet 15 and the *Roman de la Rose.*"

31. The gradual is constructed from Ps. 44:5, 11, 12.

32. Tischler, ed., *Earliest Motets*, no. 311.

33. See Picot, "Monologue dramatique," pp. 411–14. For a complete text of the sermon, see "Sermon pour une nopce," in Koopmans, ed., *Recueil de sermons joyeux*, pp. 409–42.

34. Tischler, ed., *Earliest Motets*, no. 308.

35. Hugh of St. Victor, *Sermones centum*, ed. Migne, no. 47. Honorius of Autun also glosses the olive as a figure for the Virgin; he arrives at this reading through an understanding of the olive as a symbol for mercy and an association of the fields, as uncultivated land, with virginity. The waters, however, represent for him secular people living in the state of marriage, above whom the Virgin is exalted. See the *Sigillum Beatae Mariae*, PL 172:499.

36. Hugh of St. Victor, *Sermones centum*, ed. Migne, nos. 12, 43.

37. Everist, "Rondeau Motet," lists the formulae and identifies various refrains, rondeaux, and rondeau-motets using them.

38. Medieval readers perceived the spiritual significance in Genius's Heavenly Park, as rubrics and miniatures in numerous manuscripts show. In certain other manuscripts, however, textual variants or miniatures indicate a reading of the discourse of Genius as parody. On the various medieval readings and reactions to this passage, see my *"Romance of the Rose" and Its Medieval Readers*.

39. In the literary *querelle* of 1401–2, both Christine de Pizan and Jean Gerson criticized this blend of sacred and profane elements in Genius's discourse. Christine stated that Jean "mixes filth with the joys of paradise," and Gerson commented that the blasphemy of the text was comparable to throwing the Eucharistic Host into a pigsty or burying the Crucifix in a dung heap. Readers willing to enter into the humor of Jean's parody include the illuminator of MS Douce 195 (Bodleian Library, Oxford), who portrayed the triune fountain as a woman with streams emanating from her breasts and genitals; and the artists of Paris, Bibl. Nat. fr. 25526, who portrayed in the margins their own version of the fruit-bearing tree of life: a tree laden with phalluses. On the latter manuscript, see my *"Romance of the Rose" and Its Medieval Readers*, pp. 273–322; on the vernacular motet as a literary analogue for this manuscript's illustrative program, see pp. 317–18.

40. There is ample evidence that the *Rose* circulated among university and

clerical readers. See Badel, *Roman de la Rose au XIVe siècle*; and my *"Romance of the Rose" and Its Medieval Readers.*

41. This motet is discussed by Everist, "Rondeau Motet" and *French Motets*, p. 106; and by Frank, " 'Tuit cil qui sunt enamourat.' " Frank concludes that the motet is not based on a preexistent rondeau, but is an original composition. He also feels that it is the work of a French poet imitating Occitan forms in order to create an artificial connection with the folklore of that region. I cite from Tischler, ed., *Montpellier Codex*, no. 169.

42. Frank notes this refrain in the *Court de Paradis* and its association with the Virgin; he hesitates as to whether the *Court de Paradis* and the motet represent independent uses of a preexisting refrain, or whether the motet might have been the original source.

43. Hunt, "De la chanson au sermon," p. 447; see Matt. 25:41.

44. C. Wright, *Music and Ceremony at Notre Dame of Paris*, p. 254; Baltzer, "Aspects of Trope," pp. 15, 24. *Veni electa mea* also draws on Psalm 44: "Veni electa mea et ponam te in thronum meum: quia concupivit rex decorem tuum, quoniam ipse est dominus tuus" (Come my chosen one and I will place you on my throne: for the king has desired your beauty, for he is your lord).

45. The fourteenth-century *Ovide moralisé* glosses Cupid as a figure for the Christian God, explaining that his arrows are the divine commandments that enter the hearts of the faithful and turn them to the love of God (ed. de Boer, 1: 3320–27). In *Etudes sur le poème allégorique*, Jung comments on the allegory of bow and arrow in the vernacular *Eructavit*, suggesting that the original audience at the court of Champagne would have been amused at the parallels with the image of love's arrow in *Cligés* (p. 231).

46. Järnström and Långfors, eds., *Recueil de chansons pieuses*, vol. 2, no. 134.

47. Tischler, ed., *Earliest Motets*, no. 310. This tenor and others included in this section—*PORTARE* and *DOCEBIT*—are discussed in more detail in Chapter 4.

48. Jeanroy and Långfors, eds., *Chansons satiriques*, no. 29. The piece is attributed to Perrin d'Angecourt in three manuscripts and to Jaquemin de La Vente in one; it is anonymous in two others. The refrain "Ja ne mi marierai, / Mès par amors amerai" appears in stanza 4 (vv. 36–37).

49. Järnström and Långfors, eds., *Recueil de chansons pieuses*, vol. 2, pp. 33–34.

50. Dreves and Blume, eds., *Lateinischer Hymnendichtung*, vol. 1, p. 80. Since the editors do not number lines, here and elsewhere I identify citations by stanza number and by line number within the stanza.

51. Published by Järnström and Långfors, eds., *Recueil de chansons pieuses*, vol. 2, no. 127. The piece is discussed in vol. 2, pp. 31–36.

52. Van den Boogaard, *Rondeaux et refrains*, nos. 263, 895.

53. Tischler, ed., *Montpellier Codex*, no. 243.

54. Second alleluia of the Mass for Pentecost. The text is adapted from John 14:26.

55. Saint Jerome, *Select Letters*, no. 22, p. 94.

56. Examples of this motif abound, and several can be found in Cazelles, *Lady as Saint*. See her translations of the lives of Saint Catherine of Alexandria (p. 130), Saint Christina (p. 147), Saint Faith (pp. 195–96), Saint Juliana (p. 208), and Saint Margaret of Antioch (pp. 225, 227).

57. For an example of Christ as cuckold, betrayed by an ungrateful humanity, see Wenzel, *Poets, Preachers*, pp. 219–20. Wenzel cites a sermon on *Luna mutatur* (Ecclus. 27:12) in which Christ is likened to a *cokewold* and assigned the lyric "Ich aue a loue vntrewe" (I have an unfaithful beloved).

58. This text appears in several motets with the tenor DOMINO (of unidentified origin): in one it is the sole texted voice; in another it is accompanied by a French triplum; and in two others it is accompanied by a Latin triplum. All three of the double motets are musically identical. See Van der Werf, *Integrated Directory*, p. 134. I cite Tischler, ed., *Montpellier Codex*, no. 40.

59. *Ovide moralisé*, ed. de Boer, 10: 3678–953.

60. Lines 475–80 appear only in one of the two manuscripts that transmit the poem; see the discussion in *Oeuvres complètes de Rutebeuf*, ed. Faral and Bastin, vol. 2, p. 66.

61. For example, see Reinsch, ed., "Dichtungen," vv. 425–746. For an insightful analysis of the Joseph's Troubles with Mary motif in English mystery plays, see Coletti, "Purity and Danger."

62. Anderson and Close, eds., *Motets of the Manuscript La Clayette*, no. 25. The motetus has been attributed to Guillaume d'Auvergne, bishop of Paris (ca. 1180–1249). More recently, however, Dronke has attributed it to Chancellor Philip of Paris (d. 1236), author of the three-part conductus motet *Agmina milicie celestis* (532) / AGMINA (M65) in honor of Saint Catherine (see Chapter 1); see Dronke, "Lyrical Compositions."

63. The motetus figures in a three-part conductus motet in three sources and as a two-part motet in two more; three other sources transmit the piece as a Latin double motet. Anderson discusses these various versions, in *Latin Compositions*, vol. 1, pp. 118–27. He points out that the bilingual form, Latin/French/Latin, is extremely rare.

64. I cite text and translation from the Loeb Classical Library. To avoid confusion in the ensuing discussion of the three-part Latin motet and the four-part bilingual one, I will refer to *In salvatoris nomine* (452) as the quadruplum at all times, even though it is actually the triplum of the Latin double motet.

65. "Dum medium silentium tenerent omnia, et nox in suo cursu iter perageret, omnipotens Sermo tuus, Domine, a regalibus sedibus venit, alleluia" (*CAO*, no. 2461).

66. See Pfeffer, *Change of Philomel*, pp. 25–51.

67. Järnström and Långfors, eds., *Recueil de chansons pieuses*, vol. 2, no. 132.

68. The device is a favorite of Boncompagno, as was mentioned briefly in Chapter 2. Another passage in the *Rota Veneris*, for example, suggests that a married woman wishing to summon her lover during her husband's absence might also creatively adapt the Song of Songs: "Recessit enim aquilo; veniat igitur auster, intret ortum meum et faciat illius aromata suis flatibus redolere" (The north wind has departed; so let the south wind come, let it enter my garden and scatter the scents with its breezes [p. 23; see Song 4:16]).

69. The story of Tamar and Judah appears in Genesis 38:11–26. Tamar was Judah's widowed daughter-in-law. As was his obligation under Jewish law, he promised to marry her to one of his younger sons when the boy became old enough, but failed to do so. Determined to bear the children—Judah's descendants—to which she was entitled, Tamar disguised herself as a prostitute and seduced Judah. Upon hearing of her pregnancy, Judah at first intended to burn her for adultery, but relented and acknowledged the justice of her acts when he learned the truth of the matter.

70. *Glossa Ordinaria, PL* 113. For an overview of Jewish and Christian commentaries on the story of Judah and Tamar, see Barney, "*Ordo paginis*."

Chapter Four

1. For discussion of the pain of absence from one's beloved as a motif common to the discourse of both spiritual and erotic love, see Wack, *Lovesickness in the Middle Ages*.

2. Bec, ed., *Lyrique française*, vol. 2, pp. 66–67. The piece is also in Järnström and Långfors, eds., *Recueil de chansons pieuses*, vol. 2, no. 137.

3. Gérard de Liège, *Quinque incitamenta*, ed. Wilmart, 3.3.4 (Wilmart's emphasis and capitalizations).

4. Tischler, ed., *Montpellier Codex*, no. 41. The motet is also transmitted in two contrafactual versions entirely in Latin, briefly considered by Pesce, "Significance of Text." The Latin texts all treat the Cross and thus relate in a straightforward way to the tenor. Here I discuss only the bilingual version.

5. I quote from Dreves and Blume, eds., *Lateinischer Hymnendichtung*, vol. 1, pp. 303–4.

6. Dreves and Blume, eds., *Lateinischer Hymnendichtung*, vol. 1, p. 392.

7. Published by Acher, "Essai." Acher's addition of the Ave Maria is not justified by anything in the manuscript; there is no evidence that *Quant li solleiz* ever figured in the liturgy. See Dronke, "Song of Songs and Medieval Love Lyric."

8. The alleluia for Assumption appears in a Rouen missal and is not documented for Parisian usage. See Bukofzer, "Unidentified Tenors." The tenors PORTARE and SUSTINERE are not clearly distinguished by many editors and catalogers of motets; they identify both as M22. Tischler, however, assigns the designation M34a to PORTARE, in his *Style and Evolution*, vol. 2, p. 49.

9. For an overview of the liturgy of Pentecost Mass, see Yudkin, *Music in Medieval Europe*, pp. 87–134.

10. Gregory the Great, *In Evangelia*, ed. Migne, no. 30.

11. Hugh of St. Victor, *Sermones centum*, ed. Migne, no. 70.

12. Ribard, in the note to vv. 345–47 of his edition of Jean de Condé's *Messe des oisiaus*, draws this conclusion and cites a passage of the hymn *Lauda, Sion, Salvatorem*—sung at Pentecost—celebrating Christ's unbroken and indivisible body.

13. See Ribard's note to *Messe des oisiaus*, v. 118.

14. In this regard it is interesting to consider Winn's contention, in *Unsuspected Eloquence*, that polyphony began as an effort to recreate the mystic simultaneity of Old and New Testament events or, as he says, "in an attempt to imitate a literary technique, the idea of polysemous writing elaborately developed in the medieval theory of fourfold allegory" (p. 89).

15. Second alleluia for the Sunday after Ascension. The text is adapted from John 14:18 and 16:22.

16. Second alleluia of the Mass for Pentecost. The text is adapted from John 14:26.

17. Alleluia for Pentecost week.

18. Tischler, ed., *Earliest Motets*, no. 290.

19. For a discussion of feudal vocabulary and related imagery in trouvère lyric, see Dragonetti, *Technique poétique*, pp. 61–113.

20. Tischler, ed., *Montpellier Codex*, no. 245.

21. Tischler, ed., *Earliest Motets*, no. 202.

22. Tischler, ed., *Montpellier Codex*, no. 201.

23. Tischler, ed., *Earliest Motets*, no. 198.

24. Adam de la Hale, *Lyric Works*, ed. Wilkins, chanson no. 14.

25. Adam de la Hale, *Lyric Works*, ed. Wilkins, chanson no. 33.

26. Tischler, ed., *Earliest Motets*, no. 313.

27. Tischler, ed., *Earliest Motets*, no. 325.

28. Tischler, ed., *Montpellier Codex*, no. 241.

29. Mass and Vespers responsory for Tuesday of Easter week; it was also used for the feast of Mary Magdalene. The text is from Matthew 28:9.

30. Tischler, ed., *Montpellier Codex*, no. 184.

Chapter Five

1. This is also one of several refrains that appear in a collection of vernacular proverbs with biblical glosses in the MS Hereford Cathedral, Close P. 3.3. In "Recueils d'anciens proverbes français," Morawski describes numerous collections of French proverbs with Latin glosses, which he categorizes as scholastic, biblical, allegorical, juridical, and profane. Such collections are further evidence for the ways vernacular material was appropriated into learned Latin discourse.

2. *CAO*, no. 4006.

3. Cassiodorus, *Expositio Psalmorum*, p. 171.

4. *Si vis vera frui luce*, a sequence for the Finding of the Cross; quoted from Dreves and Blume, eds., *Lateinischer Hymnendichtung*, vol. 1, p. 302.

5. The *Fasciculus morum*, a fourteenth-century Franciscan preaching manual, also identifies the Cross with the midday refuge of Song 1:6; see Wenzel, *Poets, Preachers*, pp. 232–33.

6. Dreves and Blume, eds., *Lateinischer Hymnendichtung*, vol. 2, pp. 282–83. The editors note the similarities between this piece and Chancellor Philip's *Crux, de te volo conqueri*.

7. *Estas in exilium* (Carmina Burana 69), as cited by Dronke, *Medieval Latin*, vol. 1, p. 298.

8. Honorius of Autun, *Expositio in Cantica Canticorum*, PL, 172, col. 419.

9. For general discussion of this motif, see Wenzel, *Poets, Preachers*, pp. 233–37. See the exemplary sermon for Good Friday on *Amore langueo*, which includes the tale of the unfaithful wife who repents and returns to her husband, as well as a description of Christ's Passion in terms of the seven signs of a languishing lover; published by Wenzel, *Macaronic Sermons*, pp. 212–67.

10. On the use in trouvère lyric of language and imagery drawn from devotional discourse, with particular reference to the motifs of suffering, martyrdom, and penance, see Dragonetti, *Technique poétique*, pp. 113–22.

11. Châtelain de Couci, *Chansons attribuées*, ed. Lerond, no. 7.

12. Thibaut de Champagne, *Chansons*, ed. Wallensköld, no. 34 [R2075]. In "Présentation des chansons de Thibaut de Champagne," Baumgartner characterizes the image of the unicorn slain in the maiden's lap as "la 'scène primitive' du lyrisme courtois . . . le moment primordial où l'amant, séduit par la dame, succombe à la blessure infligée par cet impitoyable chasseur qu'est Amour" (p. 43).

13. The tenor SUSTINERE is in MS *Cl*, PORTARE in MSS *Mo* and *Ba*.

14. Anderson and Close, eds., *Motets of the Manuscript La Clayette*, no. 16.

15. It is not clear whether the subject of the verb *tiegne*—"ele"—refers to the lady or to love itself. In both the Montpellier and the Bamberg codices, the subject is the plural "eles," which must refer to the sentiments of love. In either case, however, the reference to erotic dreams or fantasies is clear.

16. The fourteenth-century poet-composer Guillaume de Machaut, using a tenor unrepresented in the thirteenth-century repertoire, also drew the analogy of the suffering courtly lover and the Man of Sorrows in his motet *Hareu! hareu! le feu, le feu / Helas! où sera pris confors / OBEDIENS USQUE AD MORTEM*. The upper voices are both laments for unrequited love in which the unhappy lover proclaims himself ready to die; the tenor is from the Good Friday gradual *Christus factus est pro nobis*, which draws on Philippians 2:8.

17. Tischler, ed., *Montpellier Codex*, no. 183.

18. Cf. the statement in *Si linguis angelicis* (discussed in Chapter 2), "Omnium amantium pondera portavi" (I carried the burdens of all lovers [19:4]), which also contributes to the association of erotic passion with the Passion of Christ.

19. Tischler, ed., *Montpellier Codex*, no. 163.

20. See Stevens, *Words and Music*, pp. 318–19. The biblical source is Micah 6:3–4. On this liturgical dialogue and Middle English devotional poetry, see Wenzel, *Poets, Preachers*, p. 153.

21. The interplay of textual and musical echoes is noted by Everist, *French Motets*, p. 171.

22. Tischler, ed., *Earliest Motets*, no. 16–1.

23. Tischler, ed., *Earliest Motets*, no. 16–2.

24. I cite all texts from Anderson and Close, eds., *Motets of the Manuscript La Clayette*, no. 9, with the following exceptions: *Deboinerement atendrai merci* (638), from Tischler, ed., *Montpellier Codex*, no. 31; and the piece *Tamquam agnus / Tamquam suscipit / TAMQUAM*, from Anderson, ed., *Bamberg Manuscript*, no. 88. For discussion of the piece and its versions, see Anderson, ed., *Latin Compositions*, vol. 1, pp. 147–53.

25. The contrafactual relations are *Tanquam suscipit vellus* (636) = *Deboinerement atendari merci* (638); *Tamquam agnus ductus ad victimam* (640) = *Quant naist la flor en la pree* (637). Only one text survives for the quadruplum melody. A clausula has been identified as the source of the Latin motetus *Tanquam suscipit vellus*. See Van der Werf, *Integrated Directory*, p. 103.

26. The birth of Christ is allegorically figured as the flowering of the branch of Jesse in the famous prophecy of Isaiah 11:1–2, an image used in the Assumption responsory *Stirps Jesse*. *Virgo dei genetrix* (O16) and incorporated into the motet repertoire through the tenor FLOS FILIUS EJUS (THE FLOWER [IS] HER SON), discussed in Chapter 3.

27. The strophe is as follows: "Quant li tens comence a doucir / et li douz venz a venter / et li arbres a florir / et li oisel a chanter / et l'erbe a verdir" (When the weather begins to grow soft and the trees to blossom and the birds to sing and the grass to grow green), quoted in Zink, *Prédication romane*, p. 274.

Conclusion

1. Origen, *Hom.* 1, 2, cited by Purkart, "Boncompagno of Signa," p. 323.

2. Hunt, "De la chanson au sermon," p. 442.

3. I cite Machaut's motets from his *Poésies lyriques*, ed. Chichmaref, vol. 2. For analysis of the interplay of sacred and profane elements in Machaut's motets, see Brownlee, "Machaut's Motet 15 and the *Roman de la Rose*"; Bent, "Deception, Exegesis, and Sounding Number"; and Huot, "Patience in Adversity." On the political and spiritual content of motet 21, *Christe, qui lux est et dies / Veni,*

creator spiritus | *TRIBULATIO PROXIMA EST ET NON EST QUI ADJUVAT*, see Yudkin, *Music in Medieval Europe*, pp. 476–82.

4. Brownlee alludes to this piece in "Machaut's Motet 15 and the *Roman de la Rose*," pp. 13–14.

5. Cerquiglini, for example, compares the coexistence of different voices and discourses in the *Voir Dit* to the construction of the motet: "Guillaume de Machaut crée la polyphonie littéraire, forme subtile sur laquelle s'ente une ambiguïté fondamentale" (*"Un Engin si soutil,"* p. 103). Boulton stresses the diversity and effect of "discontinuity" in the fourteenth-century *dit amoureux* with lyric insertions, noting that the component parts "are not always in accord and create an effect reminiscent of the layered voices in a polyphonic chanson" (*Song in the Story*, p. 182); she also stresses the dialogism of the *Voir Dit*, with its multiple voices and genres (p. 202). Maurice discusses the dialogue of *auctoritas* and popular beliefs in the bestiary section of Brunetto Latini's *Trésor* as a type of polyphony, in " 'Croyances populaires' et 'histoire,' " pp. 164–72.

6. Page broaches this question in *Discarding Images*, pp. 44–49. Although Page understandably (and wisely) refrains from offering a definitive response, he implies that the parodic impulse was an important factor in the rise of the genre.

7. In *Song in the Story*, Boulton lists 70 texts with lyric insertions (pp. 295–97), to my knowledge the most complete listing to date. Aside from the *Fauvel*, motets appear only in the *Meliacin* (*Conte du cheval de fust*) of Girart d'Amiens. These, however, are monophonic motets—lyric compositions of a single stanza transmitted without tenor or other accompanying voice. For the texts of these pieces, see Stengel, "Altfranzösischen Liedercitate." One of the lyric insertions in *Meliacin*, *Quant la saisons desiree* (Stengel, no. 21), is transmitted as the motetus of a polyphonic motet with fully texted French tenor, *Sens penser folur ai servi* (890) | *Quant la saisons desiree* (891) | *QUI BIEN AIME A TART OUBLIE*. This motet appears only in MS *Tu*. *Quant la saisons desiree* is monophonic in all manuscripts of *Meliacin*, and it is the first stanza of an anonymous monophonic song in several trouvère chansonniers.

Works Cited

~~~~~

Motet Manuscripts

Ba   Bamberg, Staatsbibliothek, Lit. 115 (olim Ed.IV.6)

Cl   Paris, Bibliothèque Nationale, nouv. ac. f. fr. 13521 (*chansonnier de La Clayette*)

Mo   Montpellier, Bibliothèque Interuniversitaire, Section Médecine, H 196

N   Paris, Bibliothèque Nationale, fr. 12615 (*chansonnier de Noailles*; trouvère chansonnier *T*)

R   Paris, Bibliothèque Nationale, fr. 844 (*chansonnier du Roi*; trouvère chansonnier *M*)

Tu   Turin, Biblioteca Reale, MSS vari 42

W₂   Wolfenbüttel, Herzog August Bibliothek, 1099 (olim Helmst. 1206)

Motet Anthologies

Anderson, Gordon Athol, ed. *Compositions of the Bamberg Manuscript: Bamberg, Staatsbibliothek, Lit. 115 (olim Ed.IV.6)*. Translations by Robyn E. Smith. Corpus Mensurabilis Musicae, 75. Neuhausen-Stuttgart: Hänssler Verlag; American Institute of Musicology, 1977.

———. *The Latin Compositions in Fascicules VII and VIII of the Notre Dame Manuscript Wolfenbüttel Helmstadt 1099 (1206)*. 2 vols. Musicological Studies, 24/1. Brooklyn: Institute of Mediaeval Music, 1968.

Anderson, Gordon A., and Elizabeth A. Close, eds. *Motets of the Manuscript La Clayette: Paris, Bibliothèque Nationale, nouv. ac. f. fr. 13521*. Corpus Mensurabilis Musicae, 68. N.p.: American Institute of Musicology, 1975.

Auda, Antoine, and Rita Lejeune, eds. *Les "Motets wallons" du manuscrit de Turin: Vari 42*. 2 vols. Brussels: [by Antoine Auda], 1953.

Rokseth, Yvonne, ed. *Polyphonies du XIII ᵉ siècle: Le Manuscrit H196 de la Faculté de Médecine de Montpellier*. 4 vols. Paris: Oiseau-Lyre, 1935–39.

Tischler, Hans, ed. *The Earliest Motets (to circa 1270): A Complete Comparative Edition.* 3 vols. New Haven: Yale University Press, 1982.

——. *Motets of the Montpellier Codex.* Translations by Susan Stakel and Joel C. Relihan. Recent Researches in the Music of the Middle Ages and Early Renaissance, 2–8. Madison: A-R Editions, 1978–85.

Other Primary Sources

Adam de la Hale. *Lyric Works.* Ed. Nigel Wilkins. Corpus Mensurabilis Musicae, 44. New York: American Institute of Musicology, 1967.

Adam le Bossu [Adam de la Halle]. *Le Jeu de Robin et Marion, suivi du Jeu du pèlerin.* Ed. Ernest Langlois. Classiques Français du Moyen Age. Paris: Champion, 1924.

Art d'amours. Traduction et commentaire de l'Ars amatoria d'Ovide. Ed. Bruno Roy. Leyden: Brill, 1974.

Aucassin et Nicolette. Ed. Jean Dufournet. Paris: Garnier-Flammarion, 1973.

Augustine, Saint. *Confessionum libri XIII.* Ed. Joseph Capello. Turin: Marietti, 1948.

Bartsch, Karl, ed. *Altfranzösischen Romanzen und Pastourellen.* Leipzig: Vogel, 1870.

Bernard, Saint. *Sermones in Cantica Canticorum. Patrologiae cursus completus: Series latina,* 183: 785–1198. Ed. J.-P. Migne. Paris: Migne, 1879.

Biblia Sacra iuxta vulgatam clementiam. Ed. Alberto Colunga, O.P., and Laurentio Turrado. 4th ed. Madrid: Biblioteca de Autores Cristianos, 1965.

Boncompagno da Signa. *Rhetorica novissima.* Ed. A. Gaudenzi. Bologna, 1892. Repr. Turin, 1962.

——. *Rota Veneris.* Ed. Friedrich Bäthgen. Texte zur Kulturgeschichte des Mittelalters 2. Rome: Regenberg, 1927.

Cassiodorus, Aurelius. *Expositio Psalmorum.* 2 vols. Corpus Christianorum, Series Latina, 97–98. Turnhout: Brepols, 1958.

Cazelles, Brigitte. *The Lady as Saint: A Collection of French Hagiographic Romances of the Thirteenth Century.* Philadelphia: University of Pennsylvania Press, 1991.

Châtelain de Couci. *Chansons attribuées au Chastelain de Couci.* Ed. Alain Lerond. Publications de la Faculté des Lettres et Sciences Humaines de Rennes, 7. Paris: Presses Universitaires de France, 1964.

Corpus Antiphonalium Officii. Ed. Renato-Joanne Hesbert. 4 vols. Rerum Ecclesiasticarum Documenta, Series Major: Fontes, 7–10. Rome: Herder, 1963–70.

La Court de Paradis. Ed. Eva Vilamo-Pentti. Annales Academiae Scientiarum Fennicae, Ser. B, 79. Helsinki: Suomalainen Tiedeakatemia, 1953.

Denomy, Alexander Joseph, ed. *The Old French Lives of Saint Agnes and Other*

Vernacular Versions of the Middle Ages. Harvard Studies in the Romance Languages, 13. Cambridge, Mass.: Harvard University Press, 1938.

Dreves, Guido Maria, and Clemens Blume, S.J., eds. *Ein Jahrtausend Lateinischer Hymnendichtung.* 2 vols. Leipzig: Reisland, 1909.

Eructavit: An Old French Metrical Paraphrase of Psalm XLIV. Ed. T. Atkinson Jenkins. Gesellschaft der Romanischen Literatur 20. Dresden: GRL; Halle: Max Niemeyer, 1909.

Gautier de Coinci. *Les Chansons à la Vierge.* Ed. Jacques Chailley. Publications de la Société Française de Musicologie. Paris: Heugel, 1959.

————. *Les Miracles de Nostre Dame.* Ed. V. Frederic Koenig. 3 vols. Textes Littéraires Français. Geneva: Droz, 1966.

Gérard de Liège. *Quinque incitamenta ad deum amandum ardenter.* In Dom André Wilmart, "Les Traités de Gérard de Liège sur l'amour illicite et sur l'amour de Dieu." *Analecta Reginensia,* Studi e Testi 59, pp. 181–247. Vatican City: Biblioteca Apostolica Vaticana, 1933.

Glossa Ordinaria. Patrologiae cursus completus: Series latina, 113. Ed. J.-P. Migne. Paris: Migne, 1852.

Gregory the Great. *XL Homiliarum in Evangelia libri duo. Patrologiae cursus completus: Series latina,* 76: 1075–1314. Ed. J.-P. Migne. Paris: Migne, 1865.

Guillaume de Lorris and Jean de Meun. *Roman de la Rose.* Ed. Félix Lecoy. 3 vols. Classiques Français du Moyen Age. Paris: Champion, 1973–75.

Hicks, Eric, ed. *Le Débat sur le Roman de la Rose.* Bibliothèque du XVe Siècle, 43. Paris: Champion, 1977.

Honorius of Autun. *Expositio in Cantica Canticorum. Patrologiae cursus completus: Series latina,* 172: 347–496. Ed. J.-P. Migne. Paris: Migne, 1854.

————. *Sigillum Beatae Mariae. Patrologiae cursus completus: Series latina,* 172: 495–518. Ed. J.-P. Migne. Paris: Migne, 1854.

Hugh of St. Victor. *Sermones centum. Patrologiae cursus completus: Series latina,* 177: 899–1210. Ed. J.-P. Migne. Paris: Migne, 1879.

Ilvonen, Eero, ed. *Parodies de thèmes pieux dans la poésie française du moyen âge: Pater-Credo-Ave Maria-Laetabundus.* Helsingfors: Société de Littérature Finnoise, 1914.

Järnström, Edward, and Arthur Långfors, eds. *Recueil de chansons pieuses du XIIIe siècle.* 2 vols. Annales Academiae Scientiarum Fennicae, Ser. B, 3: 1. Helsinki: Suomalaisen Tiedeakatemian Toimituksia, 1910–27.

Jean de Condé. *La Messe des oiseaux.* Ed. Jacques Ribard. Textes Littéraires Français. Geneva: Droz, 1970.

Jeanroy, Alfred, and Henry Guy, eds. *Chansons et dits artésiens du XIIIe siècle.* Bibliothèque des Universités du Midi, 2. Bordeaux: Feret, 1898.

Jeanroy, Alfred, and Arthur Långfors, eds. *Chansons satiriques et bachiques du XIIIe siècle.* Classiques français du Moyen Age. Paris: Champion, 1921.

Jerome, Saint. *Select Letters*. With a translation by F. A. Wright. Loeb Classical Library. Cambridge, Mass.: Harvard University Press; London: William Heinemann, 1963.

Koopmans, Jelle, ed. *Recueil de sermons joyeux*. Textes Littéraires Français. Geneva: Droz, 1988.

Lehmann, Paul, ed. *Parodistische Texte: Beispiele zur lateinischen Parodie im Mittelalter*. Munich: Drei Masken, 1923.

Machaut, Guillaume de. *Poésies lyriques*. Ed. Vladimir Chichmaref. 2 vols. Paris: Champion, 1909.

Missa Tornacensis. Ed. Charles Van den Borren. Corpus Mensurabilis Musicae, 13. New York: American Institute of Musicology, 1957.

Nicole de Margival. *Le Dit de la panthère d'amours*. Ed. Henry A. Todd. Société des Anciens Textes Français. Paris: Firmin Didot, 1883.

Ovid. *Metamorphoses*. Trans. Frank Justus Miller. Loeb Classical Library. 2 vols. Cambridge, Mass.: Harvard University Press; London: William Heinemann, 1968.

Ovide moralisé. Ed. Cornelis de Boer. 5 vols. Verhandelingen der Koninklijke Akademie van Wetenschappen te Amsterdam. Afdeeling Letterkunde. N.S. 15, 21, 30, 37, 43. Amsterdam: Müller, 1915–38.

Page, Christopher. "Johannes de Grocheio on Secular Music: A Corrected Text and a New Translation." *Plainsong and Medieval Music* 2 (1993): 17–41.

Reinsch, Robert, ed. "Dichtungen Gautiers von Coinsy, II. Die Geburt und Kindheit Jesu." *Archiv für das Studium der Neueren Sprachen und Literaturen* 67 (1882): 233–68.

Renart, Jean. *Roman de la Rose ou de Guillaume de Dole*. Ed. Félix Lecoy. Classiques Français du Moyen Age. Paris: Champion, 1970.

Richard de Fournival. *Li Bestiaires d'amours di Maistre Richart de Fornival e li Response du Bestiaire*. Ed. Cesare Segre. Documenti di Filologia, 2. Milan and Naples: Riccardo Riccardi, 1957.

Le Roman de Renart. Ed. Mario Roques. 6 vols. Classiques Français du Moyen Age. Paris: Champion, 1948–63.

Rutebeuf. *Oeuvres complètes de Rutebeuf*. Ed. Edmond Faral and Julia Bastin. 2 vols. Paris: Picard, 1969.

The Song of Songs: A Twelfth-Century French Version. Ed. Cedric Edward Pickford. Oxford: Oxford University Press, 1974.

Thibaut de Champagne. *Les Chansons de Thibaut de Champagne, roi de Navarre*. Ed. Axel Wallensköld. Société des Anciens Textes Français. Paris: Champion, 1925.

Van den Boogaard, Nico H. J. *Rondeaux et refrains du XIIe siècle au début du XIVe*. Bibliothèque Française et Romane. Paris: Klincksieck, 1969.

Virgil. *Eclogues*. With a translation by H. Rushton Fairclough. Loeb Classical Library. Cambridge, Mass.: Harvard University Press; London: William Heinemann, 1974.

Secondary Sources

Acher, J. "Essai sur le poème *Quant li solleiz converset en Leon.*" *Zeitschrift für Französische Sprache und Literatur* 38 (1911): 47–94.

Anderson, Gordon. "Notre-Dame Bilingual Motets: A Study in the History of Music, 1215–1245." *Miscellanea Musicologia* 3 (1968): 50–144.

———. "Notre-Dame Latin Double Motets, ca. 1215–1250." *Musica Disciplina* 25 (1971): 35–92.

———. "Texts and Music in 13th-Century Sacred Song." *Miscellanea Musicologica* 10 (1979): 1–27.

Aubry, Pierre. *La musique et les musiciens d'église en Normandie au XIIIe siècle d'après le "Journal des visites pastorales" d'Odon Rigaud.* Paris: Champion, 1906.

Badel, Pierre-Yves. *Le Roman de la Rose au XIVe siècle: Etude de la réception de l'oeuvre.* Publications Françaises et Romanes, 153. Geneva: Droz, 1980.

Bakhtin, Mikhail M. *The Dialogic Imagination: Four Essays.* Trans. Caryl Emerson and Michael Holquist. Austin: University of Texas Press, 1981.

———. *Rabelais and His World.* Trans. Hélène Iswolsky. Bloomington: Indiana University Press, 1984.

Baltzer, Rebecca. "Aspects of Trope in the Earliest Motets for the Assumption of the Virgin." In *Studies in Medieval Music: Festschrift for Ernest H. Sanders,* ed. Brian Seirup and Peter M. Lefferts, pp. 5–42. New York: Trustees of Columbia University, 1991.

Barney, Stephen A. "*Ordo paginis*: The *Gloss* on Genesis 38." *South Atlantic Quarterly* 91 (1992): 929–43.

Baumgartner, Emmanuèle. "Les Citations lyriques dans le *Roman de la Rose* de Jean Renart." *Romance Philology* 35 (1981–82): 260–66.

———. "Présentation des chansons de Thibaut de Champagne dans les manuscrits de Paris." In *Thibaut de Champagne, prince et poète au XIIIe siècle: Actes du colloque organisé par le Centre de Recherche sur la littérature du Moyen Age et de la Renaissance de l'Université de Reims (janvier 1986),* ed. Yvonne Bellenger and Danielle Quérule, pp. 35–44. Archives de Champagne. Lyon: La Manufacture, 1987.

Bec, Pierre. "L'Accès au lieu érotique: Motifs et exorde dans la lyrique popularisante du moyen âge à nos jours." In *Love and Marriage in the Twelfth Century,* ed. Willy van Hoecke and Andries Welkenhuysen, pp. 250–97. Médiévalia Lovanensia, 1: 8. Louvain: Louvain University Press, 1981.

———. *La Lyrique française au moyen âge (XIIe–XIIIe ss.): Contribution à une typologie des genres poétiques médiévales, études et textes.* 2 vols. Publications du Centre d'Etudes Supérieures de Civilisation Médiévale de l'Université de Poitiers, 6–7. Paris: Picard, 1977–78.

———. "Lyrique profane et paraphrase pieuse dans la poésie médiévale (XIIᵉ–XIIIᵉ s.)." In *Jean Misrahi Memorial Volume: Studies in Medieval Literature*, ed. Hans R. Runte, Henri Niedzielski, and William L. Hendrickson, pp. 229–46. Columbia, S.C.: French Literature Publications, 1977.

———. "Le Problème des genres chez les premiers troubadours." *Cahiers de Civilisation Médiévale* 25 (1982): 31–47.

Bent, Margaret. "Deception, Exegesis, and Sounding Number in Machaut's Motet 15." *Early Music History* 10 (1991): 15–27.

Billy, Dominique. "Une Imitation indirecte de *L'altrier cuidai aber druda*: Le Motet *Quant froidure trait a fin / Encontre la saison d'esté*." *Neophilologus* 74 (1990): 536–44.

Boulton, Maureen Barry McCann. *The Song in the Story: Lyric Insertions in French Narrative Fiction, 1200–1400*. Philadelphia: University of Pennsylvania Press, 1993.

Brownlee, Kevin. "Machaut's Motet 15 and the *Roman de la Rose*: The Literary Context of *Amours qui a le pouoir / Faus Samblant m'a deceü / Vidi Dominum*." *Early Music History* 10 (1991): 1–14.

Brückmann, John, and Jane Couchman. "Du 'Cantique des cantiques' aux 'Carmina Burana': Amour sacré et amour érotique." In *L'Erotisme au moyen âge*, ed. Bruno Roy, pp. 35–50. Montreal: Aurore, 1977.

Bukofzer, Manfred. "Unidentified Tenors in the Manuscript La Clayette." *Annales Musicologues* 4 (1956): 255–58.

Butterfield, Ardis. "The Language of Medieval Music: Two Thirteenth-Century Motets." *Plainsong and Medieval Music* 2 (1993): 1–16.

Calin, William. "Contre la *fin'amor*? Contre la femme? Une relecture de textes du Moyen Age." In *Courtly Literature: Culture and Context*, ed. Keith Busby and Erik Kooper, pp. 61–82. Amsterdam and Philadelphia: John Benjamins, 1990.

———. "Defense and Illustration of *Fin'Amor*: Some Polemical Comments on the Robertsonian Approach." In *The Expansion and Transformation of Courtly Literature*, ed. Nathaniel B. Smith and Joseph T. Snow, pp. 32–48. Athens: University of Georgia Press, 1980.

Cerquiglini, Jacqueline. *"Un Engin si soutil": Guillaume de Machaut et l'écriture au XIVᵉ siècle*. Bibliothèque du XVᵉ Siècle, 47. Paris: Champion, 1985.

Coletti, Theresa. "Purity and Danger: The Paradox of Mary's Body and the En-gendering of the Infancy Narrative in the English Mystery Cycles." In *Feminist Approaches to the Body in Medieval Literature*, ed. Linda Lomperis and Sarah Stanbury, pp. 65–95. Philadelphia: University of Pennsylvania Press, 1993.

Crocker, Richard. "French Polyphony of the Thirteenth Century." In *New*

Oxford History of Music, vol. 2: *The Early Middle Ages to 1300*, ed. Richard Crocker and David Hiley, pp. 636–78. Oxford: Oxford University Press, 1990.

Delbouille, Maurice. "Sur les traces de 'Bele Aëlis.'" In *Mélanges de philologie romane dédiés à la mémoire de Jean Boutière*, ed. Irénée Cluzel and François Pirot, vol. 1, pp. 199–218. Liège: Soledi, 1971.

Diehl, Patrick S. *The Medieval European Religious Lyric: An Ars Poetica*. Berkeley: University of California Press, 1985.

Dragonetti, Roger. *La Technique poétique des trouvères dans la chanson courtoise: Contribution à l'étude de la rhétorique médiévale*. Bruges: De Tempel, 1960. Repr. Geneva: Slatkine, 1979.

Dronke, Peter. "The Lyrical Compositions of Philip the Chancellor." *Studi Medievali*, 3d ser., 28 (1987): 563–92.

———. *Medieval Latin and the Rise of the European Love Lyric*. 2 vols. 2d ed. Oxford: Clarendon Press, 1968.

———. "Profane Elements in Literature." In *Renaissance and Renewal in the Twelfth Century*, ed. Robert L. Benson and Giles Constable, with Carol D. Lanham, pp. 569–92. Cambridge, Mass.: Harvard University Press, 1982.

———. "The Song of Songs and Medieval Love Lyric." In *The Bible and Medieval Culture*, ed. W. Lourdaux and D. Verhelst, pp. 237–62. Louvain: Louvain University Press, 1979.

Evans, Beverly J. "Music, Text, and Social Context: Reexamining Thirteenth-Century Styles." *Yale French Studies*, special issue (1991): 183–95.

———. "The Textual Function of the Refrain Cento in a Thirteenth-Century French Motet." *Music and Letters* 71 (1990): 187–97.

———. "The Unity of Text and Music in the Late Thirteenth-Century French Motet: A Study of Selected Works from the Montpellier Manuscript, Fascicle VII." Ph.D. diss., University of Pennsylvania, 1983.

Everist, Mark. *French Motets in the Thirteenth Century: Music, Poetry, and Genre*. Cambridge Studies in Medieval and Renaissance Music. Cambridge: Cambridge University Press, 1994.

———. "The Refrain Cento: Myth or Motet?" *Journal of the Royal Musical Association* 114 (1989): 164–88.

———. "The Rondeau Motet: Paris and Artois in the Thirteenth Century." *Music and Letters* 69 (1988): 1–22.

Fernandez, Marie-Henriette. "Notes sur les origines du rondeau: Le 'Répons bref'—les 'preces' du Graduel de Saint-Yrieix." *Cahiers de Civilisation Médiévale* 19 (1976): 265–75.

Ferrand, Françoise. "*Ut musica poesis*: La Relation de la lyrique profane des XIIᵉ–XIIIᵉ siècles à un modèle sacré." In *L'Imitation: Aliénation ou source de liberté?*, pp. 107–28. Rencontres de l'Ecole du Louvre. Paris: Documentation Française, 1985.

Ferrante, Joan M. "The Bible as Thesaurus for Secular Literature." In *The Bible in the Middle Ages: Its Influence on Literature and Art*, ed. Bernard S. Levy, pp. 23–49. Binghamton, N.Y.: Medieval and Renaissance Texts and Studies, 1992.

Ferrante, Joan M., and George D. Economou, eds. *In Pursuit of Perfection: Courtly Love in Medieval Literature*. Port Washington, N.Y.: Kennikat Press, 1975.

Fleming, John V. *The Roman de la Rose: A Study in Allegory and Iconography*. Princeton: Princeton University Press, 1969.

Frank, István. " 'Tuit cil qui sunt enamourat' (Notes de philologie pour l'étude des origines lyriques, II)." *Romania* 75 (1954): 98–108.

Glendinning, Robert. "Eros, Agape, and Rhetoric Around 1200: Gervase of Melkley's *Ars poetica* and Gottfried von Strassburg's *Tristan*." *Speculum* 67 (1992): 892–925.

Gravdal, Kathryn. "Camouflaging Rape: The Rhetoric of Sexual Violence in the Medieval Pastourelle." *Romanic Review* 76 (1985): 361–73.

———. *Vilain and Courtois: Transgressive Parody in French Literature of the Twelfth and Thirteenth Centuries*. Regents Studies in Medieval Culture. Lincoln: University of Nebraska Press, 1989.

Hamburger, Jeffrey F. *The Rothschild Canticles: Art and Mysticism in Flanders and the Rhineland circa 1300*. New Haven: Yale University Press, 1990.

Hucke, Helmut. "Das Dekret 'Docta Sanctorum Patrum' Papst Johannes' XXII." *Musica Disciplina* 38 (1984): 119–31.

Hunt, Tony. "De la chanson au sermon: *Bele Aalis* et *Sur la rive de la mer*." *Romania* 104 (1983): 433–56.

———. "The *Song of Songs* and Courtly Literature." In *Court and Poet*, ed. Glyn S. Burgess, pp. 189–96. Liverpool: Francis Cairns, 1981.

Huot, Sylvia. *From Song to Book: The Poetics of Writing in Old French Lyric and Lyrical Narrative Poetry*. Ithaca: Cornell University Press, 1987.

———. "Languages of Love: Vernacular Motets on the Tenor FLOS FILIUS EJUS." In *Conjunctures: Medieval Studies in Honor of Douglas Kelly*, ed. Keith Busby and Norris J. Lacy, pp. 169–80. Amsterdam: Rodopi, 1994.

———. "Patience in Adversity: Job and the Courtly Lover in Machaut's Motets 2 and 3." *Medium Aevum* 63 (1994): 218–34.

———. "Polyphonic Poetry: The Old French Motet and Its Literary Context." *French Forum* 14 (1989): 261–78.

———. *The "Romance of the Rose" and Its Medieval Readers: Interpretation, Reception, Manuscript Transmission*. Cambridge Studies in Medieval Literature, 16. Cambridge: Cambridge University Press, 1993.

———. "Transformations of Lyric Voice in the Songs, Motets, and Plays of Adam de la Halle." *Romanic Review* 78 (1987): 148–64.

Hutcheon, Linda. *A Theory of Parody: The Teachings of Twentieth-Century Art Forms*. New York: Methuen, 1985.

Jackson, W. T. H. "Allegory and Allegorization." In *The Challenge of the Medieval Text: Studies in Genre and Interpretation*, ed. Joan M. Ferrante and Robert W. Hanning, pp. 157–71. New York: Columbia University Press, 1985.

Jenny, Laurent. "La Stratégie de la forme." *Poétique* 27 (1976): 257–81.

Jung, Marc-René. *Etudes sur le poème allégorique en France au moyen âge*. Romanica Helvetica 82. Bern: Editions Francke, 1971.

Kuhn, David. *La Poétique de François Villon*. Paris: Armand Colin, 1967.

Långfors, Arthur. "Traductions et paraphrases du *Pater* en vers français du moyen âge." *Neuphilologische Mitteilungen* 14 (1912): 35–45.

Leclercq, Jean, O.S.B. *Monks and Love in Twelfth-Century France: Psycho-Historical Essays*. Oxford: Clarendon Press, 1979.

Leech-Wilkinson, Daniel. *Compositional Techniques in the Four-Part Isorhythmic Motets of Philippe de Vitry and His Contemporaries*. 2 vols. New York: Garland, 1989.

Lehmann, Paul. *Die Parodie im Mittelalter*. 2d ed. Stuttgart: Hiersemann, 1963.

Ludwig, Friedrich. *Repertorium organorum recentioris et motetorum vetustissimi stili*. 2 vols. Vol. 1: *Catalogue raisonné der Quellen*, pt. 1, *Handschriften in Quadrat-Notation*. Halle: Max Niemeyer, 1910. Vol. 1, pt. 2: *Handschriften in Mensural-Notation*. Ed. Friedrich Gennrich. Summa Musicae Medii Aevi, 7. Langen bei Frankfurt, 1961. Vol. 2: *Musikalisches Anfangs-Verzeichnis des nach Tenores Geordneten Repertorium*. Ed. Friedrich Gennrich. Summa Musicae Medii Aevi, 8. Langen bei Frankfurt, 1962.

Martin, June Hall. *Love's Fools: Aucassin, Troilus, Calisto and the Parody of the Courtly Lover*. London: Tamesis Books, 1972.

Matter, E. Ann. *The Voice of My Beloved: The Song of Songs in Western Medieval Christianity*. Philadelphia: University of Pennsylvania Press, 1990.

Maurice, Jean. " 'Croyances populaires' et 'histoire' dans le *Livre des animaux*: Jeux de polyphonie dans un bestiaire de la seconde moitié du XIIIe siècle." *Romania* 111 (1990): 153–78.

Meyer, Paul. "Henri d'Andeli et le chancelier Philippe." *Romania* 1 (1872): 190–215.

Morawski, Joseph. "Les Recueils d'anciens proverbes français analysés et classés." *Romania* 48 (1922): 481–558.

Nathan, Hans. "The Function of Text in French Thirteenth-Century Motets." *Musical Quarterly* 28 (1942): 445–62.

Page, Christopher. *Discarding Images: Reflections on Music and Culture in Medieval France*. Oxford: Clarendon Press, 1993.

———. *The Owl and the Nightingale: Musical Life and Ideas in France, 1100–1300*. Berkeley: University of California Press, 1989.

————. "The Performance of Ars Antiqua Motets." *Early Music* 16 (1988): 147–64.

————. *Voices and Instruments of the Middle Ages: Instrumental Practice and Songs in France, 1100–1300.* London: J. M. Dent, 1987.

Paré, Gaston, O.P. *Le Roman de la Rose et la scolastique courtoise.* Publications de l'Institut d'Etudes Médiévales d'Ottawa, 10. Paris: Vrin; Ottawa: Institut d'Etudes Médiévales, 1941.

Pesce, Dolores. "The Significance of Text in Thirteenth-Century Latin Motets." *Acta Musicologica* 58 (1986): 91–117.

Pfeffer, Wendy. *The Change of Philomel: The Nightingale in Medieval Literature.* American University Studies, Ser. 3: Comparative Literature, 14. New York: Peter Lang, 1985.

Picot, Émile. "Le Monologue dramatique dans l'ancien théâtre français." *Romania* 15 (1886): 358–422.

Piehler, Paul. *The Visionary Landscape: A Study in Medieval Allegory.* London: Edward Arnold, 1971.

Purkart, Josef. "Rhetoric in Later Latin: Boncompagno of Signa and the Rhetoric of Love." In *Medieval Eloquence: Studies in the Theory and Practice of Medieval Rhetoric*, ed. James J. Murphy, pp. 319–31. Berkeley: University of California Press, 1978.

Quinn, Esther C. "Beyond Courtly Love: Religious Elements in *Tristan* and *La Queste del Saint Graal.*" In *In Pursuit of Perfection: Courtly Love in Medieval Literature*, ed. Joan M. Ferrante and George D. Economou, pp. 179–219. Port Washington, N.Y.: Kennikat Press, 1975.

Reichert, Georg. "Wechselbeziehungen zwischen musikalischer und textlicher Struktur in der Motette des 13. Jahrhunderts." In *In Memoriam Jacques Handschin*, ed. Higinio Anglès et al., pp. 151–69. Strasbourg: Heitz, 1962.

Robertson, Anne Walters. "Remembering the Annunciation in Medieval Polyphony." *Speculum* 70 (1995): 275–304.

Robertson, D. W., Jr. "Two Poems from the *Carmina Burana.*" In *Essays in Medieval Culture*, pp. 131–50. Princeton: Princeton University Press, 1980.

Sanders, Ernest. "The Medieval Motet." In *Gattungen der Musik in Einzeldarstellungen: Gedenkschrift Leo Schrade*, ed. Wulf Arlt et al., vol. 1, pp. 497–573. Bern: Francke, 1973.

Sankovitch, Tilde. "Religious and Erotic Elements in *Flamenca*: The Uneasy Alliance." *Romance Philology* 35 (1981): 217–23.

Sargent, Barbara N. "Parody in *Aucassin et Nicolette.*" *French Review* 43 (1970): 597–605.

Singer, Irving. *The Nature of Love.* Vol. 2: *Courtly and Romantic.* Chicago: University of Chicago Press, 1984.

Smith, Norman. "The Earliest Motets: Music and Words." *Journal of the Royal Musical Association* 114 (1989): 141–63.

————. "From Clausula to Motet: Material for Further Studies in the Origin and Early History of the Motet." *Musica Disciplina* 34 (1980): 29–65.

Smith, Robyn. "Music or Literary Text? Two Ways of Looking at the Thirteenth-Century French Motet." *Parergon* 4 (1986): 35–47.

Spanke, Hans. *G. Raynauds Bibliographie des altfranzösischen Liedes, neu bearbeitet und ergänzt.* Leiden: E. J. Brill, 1955.

Spence, Sarah. "*Et Ades Sera l'Alba*: 'Revelations' as Intertext for the Provençal *Alba.*" *Romance Philology* 35 (1981): 212–17.

Stengel, E. "Die altfranzösischen Liedercitate aus Girardin's d'Amiens Conte du cheval de fust." *Zeitschrift für Romanische Philologie* 10 (1886): 460–76.

Stevens, John. *Words and Music in the Middle Ages: Song, Narrative, Dance and Drama, 1050–1350.* Cambridge: Cambridge University Press, 1986.

Tischler, Hans. *The Style and Evolution of the Earliest Motets (to circa 1270).* 4 vols. Musicological Studies, 40. Ottawa: Institute of Mediaeval Music, 1985.

Tuve, Rosemond. *Allegorical Imagery: Some Mediaeval Books and Their Posterity.* Princeton: Princeton University Press, 1966.

Van den Boogaard, Nico H. J. "La Forme des polémiques et les formes poétiques: Dits et motets du XIIIe siècle." *Miscellanea Mediaevalia* 10 (1976): 220–39.

————. "Les Insertions en français dans un traité de Gérard de Liège." In *Mélanges de philologie et de littératures romanes offertes à Jeanne Wathelet-Willem,* ed. Jacques de Caluwé, pp. 679–97. Liège: Marche Romane, 1978.

Van der Werf, Hendrik. *Integrated Directory of Organa, Clausulae, and Motets.* Rochester, N.Y.: [by the author], 1989.

Vinaver, Eugène. "Landmarks in Arthurian Romance." In *The Expansion and Transformation of Courtly Literature,* ed. Nathaniel B. Smith and Joseph T. Snow, pp. 17–31. Athens: University of Georgia Press, 1980.

Wack, Mary Frances. *Lovesickness in the Middle Ages: The Viaticum and Its Commentaries.* Philadelphia: University of Pennsylvania Press, 1990.

Wenzel, Siegfried. *Macaronic Sermons: Bilingualism and Preaching in Late Medieval England.* Recentiores: Later Latin Texts and Their Contexts. Ann Arbor: University of Michigan Press, 1994.

————. *Poets, Preachers, and the Early English Lyric.* Princeton: Princeton University Press, 1986.

Wetherbee, Winthrop. *Platonism and Poetry in the Twelfth Century: The Literary Influence of the School of Chartres.* Princeton: Princeton University Press, 1972.

Wimsatt, James. "Chaucer and the Canticle of Canticles." In *Chaucer the Love Poet,* ed. Jerome Mitchell and William Provost, pp. 66–90. Athens: University of Georgia Press, 1973.

Winn, James Anderson. *Unsuspected Eloquence: A History of the Relationship Between Poetry and Music.* New Haven: Yale University Press, 1981.

Wright, Craig. *Music and Ceremony at Notre Dame of Paris, 500–1500.* Cambridge Studies in Music. Cambridge: Cambridge University Press, 1989.

Wright, Laurence. "Verbal Counterpoint in Machaut's Motet *Trop plus est belle - Biauté paree de valour - Je ne sui mie.*" *Romance Studies* 7 (1985–86): 1–11.

Yudkin, Jeremy. *Music in Medieval Europe.* Englewood Cliffs, N.J.: Prentice-Hall, 1989.

Zink, Michel. *La Prédication romane avant 1300.* Nouvelle Bibliothèque du Moyen Age, 4. Paris: Champion, 1976.

Zumthor, Paul. "Le Carrefour des rhétoriqueurs: Intertextualité et rhétorique." *Poétique* 27 (1976): 317–37.

———. *Essai de poétique médiévale.* Paris: Seuil, 1972.

Index

In this index an "f" after a number indicates a separate reference on the next page, and an "ff" indicates separate references on the next two pages. A continuous discussion over two or more pages is indicated by a span of page numbers, e.g., "57–59." *Passim* is used for a cluster of references in close but not consecutive sequence.

Library of Congress Cataloging-in-Publication Data

Huot, Sylvia.
  Allegorical play in the Old French motet : The sacred and the
profane in thirteenth-century polyphony / Sylvia Huot.
     p. cm. — (Figurae)
  Includes bibliographical references and index.
  ISBN 0-8047-2717-1 (cloth)
  1. Motet — France — 500–1400.   2. Part-songs, Old French — 500–1400 —
History and criticism.   3. Part-songs, Latin — 500–1400 — History and
criticism.   4. Allegory.   5. Music and literature.   6. Music and
language.   I. Title.   II. Series: Figurae (Stanford, Calif.)
ML2627.2.H86   1997
782.2'6'094409022 — dc20

96-13240
CIP

Original printing 1996
Last figure below indicates year of this printing:
05 04 03 02 01 00 99 98 97 96